21st-Century Japanese Management

21st-Century Japanese Management

New Systems, Lasting Values

James C. Abegglen

First published 2006 by
PALGRAVE MACMILLAN
Houndmills, Basingstoke, Hampshire RG21 6XS and
175 Fifth Avenue, New York, N.Y. 10010
Companies and representatives throughout the world

PALGRAVE MACMILLAN is the global academic imprint of the Palgrave Macmillan division of St. Martin's Press, LLC and of Palgrave Macmillan Ltd. Macmillan® is a registered trademark in the United States, United Kingdom and other countries. Palgrave is a registered trademark in the European Union and other countries.

ISBN-13: 978–1–4039–9876–7 hardback
ISBN-10: 1–4039–9876–0 hardback

This book is printed on paper suitable for recycling and made from fully managed and sustained forest sources.

A catalogue record for this book is available from the British Library.

Library of Congress Cataloging-in-Publication Data
Abegglen, James C.
   21st century Japanese management : new systems, lasting
   values / by James C. Abegglen.
      p.   cm.
   Includes bibliographical references and index.
   ISBN 1–4039–9876–0
   1. Industrial management—Japan.   I. Title: 21st-century Japanese
   management.   II. Title.
   HD70.J3A259 2006
   658.00952—dc22   2005056579

10   9   8   7   6   5
15   14   13   12   11   10   09

Printed and bound in Great Britain by
Antony Rowe, Chippenham and Eastbourne

Contents

List of Tables

Preface

This book is written as Japan's economy and businesses emerge from a long and hard decade of transition to economic and demographic maturity. Business policies and strategies that were effective in the environment of historically rapid growth from the mid-1950s became suddenly counterproductive in the mid-1990s. Making the needed changes in industrial structures, company financial structures, and business strategies, the task compounded by continued deflation, has taken a full decade.

In an era of high growth, financing through bank debt, measuring success by market share, investing very heavily in plant and equipment, hiring a surplus of workers in anticipation of growth – all these and more were the right policies as high growth continued, and indeed they made high growth possible. All these key elements of corporate strategy required basic change as growth stopped.

The redesign of Japan's companies and industries has now been largely accomplished. The economy is recovered as deflation ends and growth resumes. Japan's companies are again the dynamic organizations that have made the economy great and the country rich. No less important, these necessary changes have been made while the basic values that shape Japan's companies – the company as a social organization – have continued in place as well. This book is an effort to analyze and understand both the financial and industrial changes that have taken place along with the underlying social continuity, and to indicate the future directions of Japan's companies in this new era.

The perspective from which this book is written is that of a full half-century. While I first learned about Japan as a US marine in the Central Pacific campaigns in 1943–45 and as a member of the US Strategic Bombing Survey in Tokyo and Hiroshima in 1945–46, my research into and work with Japanese companies began in 1955–56, some 50 years ago, when as a Ford Foundation Fellow I came to Japan to conduct a study of Japanese industrial organizations. That was the pioneering research into the organization and management systems of large Japanese companies that led to the publication of my first book on Japanese management, *The Japanese Factory*.

It is curious that like this present book, written as a new era dawns for Japan's economy, the first book of mine on Japan was prepared at the beginning of another era, that of the several decades of high growth. The Economy White Paper of 1956 stated, "Japan is no longer a postwar country." Recovery from the wartime disasters was largely completed by 1955 and full-fledged high growth got underway. I had the great good fortune to be studying Japan's companies precisely as that new era began.

While this and the earlier book each deal with the beginning of a new era for Japanese companies, it is also the case that both in the earlier research and in the current research the same companies have played an important role in instructing me about management in Japan. In 1955–56 among the many companies visited, five were at the center of study, and it was the management of those companies that were so very generous in hospitality and time, instructing me into the mysteries of their businesses. This time, the same five companies were again the source of much of my learning – NEC (then Nippon Electric Company), Sumitomo Electric Industries, Sumitomo Chemical Co., Toray (then Toyo Rayon), and Fuji Seitetsu, now Nippon Steel after its re-merger with Yawata Steel in 1970.

By another stroke of fortune, these companies represent a range of technologies, from textiles and steel to chemicals and electronics. They are on the whole rather well placed to serve as case studies. Their growth from the mid-1950s was phenomenal – NEC grew 1400 times in 45 years. And then from 1998 NEC underwent a degree of reorganization and reshaping the likes of which I at least had never seen, much less seen done successfully. These companies all went through the storm of the past decade of redesign and reshaping, and have emerged again as strong industry leaders. This book aims to analyze their success in redesign and the successes of Japan's companies overall.

After 50 years, not surprisingly the men I knew earlier in the top management of these companies were no longer there. In consequence, meeting with top management in the key companies studied depended very much on the gracious support and personal involvement of Mr Tetsuro Kawakami, former President and Chairman, now Senior Advisor of Sumitomo Electric Industries, a long-time acquaintance and one of Japan's most respected business leaders.

It is simply not possible to trace out and list all those who over a half-century have helped me understand better the intricacies of Japanese society and business. Without even attempting any of that, let me note that in the research for this book the following businessmen were especially helpful:

NEC: Shigeo Matsumoto, Executive Vice President; Hiroshi Sato, Chief Financial Officer at NEC Electronics; Hajime Matsukura, Manager, Corporate Planning Office; Sumio Imaizumi, Human Resources Department.

Nippon Steel: Akira Chihaya, Chairman; Yasushi Aoki, Senior Manager; Makoto Haya, Managing Director.

Sumitomo Electric Industries, Ltd: Norio Okayama, President; Yoshiaki Nishimura, Director.

Sumitomo Chemical Co., Ltd: Akio Kosai, Chairman; Mitsuhiro Moroishi, Senior Managing Director; Hideaki Watanabe, Managing Director; Susumu Yoshida, General Manager, Planning; Tomiya Atsumi, Manager, Planning; Hisashi Shimoda, Manager, Finance and Accounting.

Toray: Sadayuki Sakakibara, President; Yoshiyuki Inamoto, General Manager, Finance.

Toray Business Research Center: Koishi Fuchino, Director; Masatoshi Kitahara, Special Researcher.

Mitsubishi Chemical Corp.: Yosuke Yamada, Managing Director.

MNET Corporation: Tetsuho Yajima, President.

Fuji Electric: Takeo Kato, Chairman.

Toyobo: The late Chairman Saburo Takizawa.

In the research and other support needed in preparing this book, Hideya Takahashi has been a very valuable assistant and I am most grateful for his support and for his companionship in our small office.

Key to making this book possible has been Yoichi Yamaoka, considered by a great many to be Japan's outstanding translator. He is both a highly valued friend and a demanding critic, and has done much to ensure accuracy while making the book accessible to its key audience, the Japanese business community.

All of these men, and many others, have helped greatly in making research in Japan – and indeed, living in Japan – most pleasant and rewarding. My deepest appreciation, however, is not for any of these fine men, but for a marvelous woman, my beloved wife Hiroko, who has made it all possible and all worthwhile. Her intelligence matches her great charm; I dedicate the book to her – and prayerfully hope she finds it a good one.

James C. Abegglen
Tokyo, October 2004

1
Perspective on a Half-Century

Japan enters the 21st century in a paradoxical position. It is a nation of great wealth and of exceptional social health. It is civilized to a rare degree, a society in which people are by choice civil with each other. It aspires to change no governments, supplying aid and humanitarian support rather than arms, threats of wars, or wars to the world. But Japan is at the same time a nation prone to self-deprecation, seemingly with little national pride, unsure of its place in world affairs, self-described in humble terms and described in largely negative terms abroad.

Rich country; healthy society

The wealth of Japan is real. Japan holds net foreign assets totaling some $1.5 trillion and has been the largest supplier of capital to the world for more than 15 years. In contrast, the United States has net foreign liabilities of more than $2.5 trillion, increasing by more than a billion US dollars each day. Japan's foreign reserves increased to over $800 billion by mid-2004, much the largest reserve position of any nation. Its current account surplus, the measure of net savings in the economy, has for some years been the world's largest, totaling in early 2004 more than $150 billion on the year (the United States minus $550 billion). Per-capita gross national income was about equal to that of the United States at $35,000 in 2003 even before yen revaluation and dollar devaluation.

Much is made of high government debt in Japan, a result of government spending in the post-bubble years and a result too of a low level of taxation, tax levels about the same as the United States as a percent of scarcely necessary to remark that a stationary condition of capital and production implies no stationary state of human improvement. There would be as much scope as ever for all kinds of mental culture, and more and social progress; as much room for improving the Art of Living, and much more likelihood of its being improved, when minds ceased to be engrossed in the art of getting on."[2]

Might Japan over the next century focus on enhancing the quality of life rather than on expanding the quantity of production? Or is the preoccupation with growth so entire that the alternative cannot be even envisioned, much less pursued? Japan's leadership and people have a rare opportunity now to look away from growth as the objective and to improve still further their already healthy society.

Whatever the shape of future ambitions, the key to the nation's future success is achievement in research and development. Japanese R&D expenditure as a percent of GDP has for some years been the world's highest. Japanese companies are among the world's leaders in patents obtained at home and abroad as one indicator of effective research output. Creativity levels in Japan are high – more than a millennium of superb literature output, unique theatre forms, current leadership in fields from architecture and fashion design to anime.

Lack of creativity is not the problem. However, success in basic research is needed and will require increased government investments in graduate programs at universities and in scientific facilities nationwide. The rapid increase in cooperative programs between companies and universities in the early 2000s is a very positive sign, as is the increase in venture capital companies established by university staff. These emerging cooperative academic-business links need further strengthening.

Moreover, Japan remains relatively isolated in the world of R&D, the result of history, geography, and language, with few resident scientists from abroad, with Japanese scientific papers seldom cited abroad, and with foreign recognition of Japanese science achievements at a low level. Scientists from abroad must be attracted to work in Japan for more than brief stays and foreign student programs must be greatly encouraged. The future of Japan's companies and economy depends on high levels of R&D productivity as low level domestic operations move abroad in search of less costly labor, and domestic operations move toward higher levels of value added. More effective R&D must be international, not simply local.

A major technological weakness is the fact that the kaisha have so far largely failed to vigorously defend and to profit from their intellectual properties. Especially with respect to China, Japanese companies risk repeating the mistake made by Western companies in postwar Japan of failing to defend intellectual properties or of selling the technology at cheap price to potential competitors. For example, while NEC is second only to IBM in US patent approvals, NEC's income from patent licensing is negligible while this is a major source of income for IBM. The great numbers and high level of patents held by Japan's Canons, NECs, and Hitachis have great unrealized values and their careless handling greatly weakens their competitive positions.

A probable future pattern for Japan's companies can be sketched out. The labor market in Japan will be more flexible, while employees remain the main stakeholders in the companies. The company will remain a complex socio-economic entity, not a simple economic machine, with the values on which the company is based those special to Japanese culture. The needs for labor will be filled by a shift of labor intensive work abroad, by more effective utilization of women and older persons in the labor force, and by massive use of automation and robotics. The labor union will remain in place, a cooperative agency in company management. Compensation in the company will be relatively equal, in sharp contrast to the exploitative compensation of the Anglo-American companies. Training of employees will represent major investments, and extended job tenure will continue to be the rule for regular, full-time employees.

The center of domestic business will shift toward services, software, and finance with standardized hardware imported rather than made at home, with Japan being the source of the key, high-value components for the hardware. Exports as a percent of output will decline steadily – as was the case historically in turn with Britain and the United States. However, income from investment abroad will support a still healthy current account surplus for a great many years. Company management will be focused on cash flow and technology advance, rather than on growth. The kaisha will have major manufacturing and marketing positions abroad with the focus overwhelmingly on East and Southeast Asia. The kaisha will be drawing managers and scientists, but not simple laborers, to Japan in increasing numbers. Through all this, the kaisha will determine the shape of the Japan of the future – a rich, stable, socially healthy center of world research and high technology, leader of an integrated East Asia.

While the economics of the future can be sketched with some confidence, the question of Japan's role in the world remains a conundrum. We can see now an emerging quandary for the nation. Economic forces are moving Japan more and more into close ties with and even dependency on East and Southeast Asia. Trade with Europe and the United States lessens while trade with East Asia and with China in particular increases rapidly. Free Trade Agreements will be reached with Northeast Asia – China, Korea, and Japan, as well as with members of ASEAN, with the Singapore agreement the initial example. Company investments from Japan into East Asia and especially into China will continue to grow rapidly.

Japan and China are complementary in economic terms, with Chinese labor and markets in need of Japanese capital and technology. As with France and Germany, Japan and China can build close economic relations without their peoples being terribly fond of each other. And on that relationship can be built an East and Southeast Asia trading area, leading in time to a common Asian currency. With an increasingly integrated Europe, and with the US-controlled NAFTA region, the need for an integrated East Asia will become more and more intense – "hang together or we shall hang separately."

Against these forces pulling Japan more deeply into East Asia is the strategic need for close alliance with the United States, at least as the current Japanese government sees its policy imperatives. The Japanese government is very far indeed from deciding to build the needed domestic missile defense and establish defense autonomy. Some part of the Japanese leadership elite, notably in such sectors as the Foreign Ministry, is tied tightly to the United States. And Japan has a history of alliance with the strongest, going back to the Meiji period alliance with the then dominant Britain. With this, there is no fondness to spare between the Chinese, Koreans, and Japanese. It will take that rare Japanese commodity, strong and committed political leadership, to overcome these obstacles and make the necessary changes. Yet a successful future for Japan both economically and politically depends critically on distancing from the United States and committing the nation in all respects to East Asia, clearly the dominant region of the world in the next era and key to a prosperous and peaceful Japan.

The US connection is of lessening economic importance and is being rapidly replaced by East Asia even though the US strategic connection is seen as having no substitute now. The US strategic alliance will diminish in importance as Japan improves its defenses and as US credibility depreciates from unilateral policy decisions in the fashion of the Iraq invasion. It will be a major task of Japan's political leadership to keep a balance between East and West for a time, as has been done – but it takes no great imagination to see near ahead a time when the United States is the isolate in policy as East Asia moves to quite different and even opposing policies from those of the United States. This shift is in fact in process politically. And in any case, as Marx well noted, economics will determine. Japan must in its own long-term interests join in and help lead the integration of East Asia, an absolute necessity to ensure the security of Japan's economic and political future.

Kaisha redesign

Japan has moved from total defeat and utter poverty to great economic power and wealth in little more than 50 years. This success is without precedent in world history, worth closest study as other peoples seek to escape from economic duress. The causes of so great an achievement are of course many. Much has been made by academics of Japan's "industrial policy." The real driving force however has been Japan's private companies and Japan's business leaders. Japan was the first non-Western society to fully industrialize, to build a Western industrial system on a distinctly non-Western social base. The private companies of Japan, the kaisha, made this historic feat possible by their brilliance in adopting Western technology and putting that technology to use in organizations based entirely on Japanese cultural values. Japanese methods of recruiting, training, and rewarding staff were developed; Japanese systems of union membership and relations came into practice; Japanese systems of relating to government, financial institutions, and share-holders were put in place. All of these were based on and derived from the values and beliefs dominant in Japanese society. "If we learn anything from the history of economic development, it is that culture makes all the difference.... Culture, in the sense of the inner values and attitudes that guide a population."[3]

Japanese companies are social organizations, communities of workers seeking to secure the future well-being of members of the community while meeting the requirements of effective economic performance. Thus there came into practice in Japan in the 1950s "Japanese style management," with consensual decision-making, career employment security, and an emphasis on length of service in deciding pay and promotion, with union membership taking in all employees of the company in a single negotiating unit. Japanese companies are not simple economic machines with the purpose of rewarding shareholders and executives. The curious Anglo-American notion that all is owed to the shareholder has no currency in Japan. The primary stakeholders in the kaisha are its members, the employees.

Not all of the Japanese pattern is unique. Many of the features of Japanese management can be found as well in companies in Western Europe, notably in German companies. Nor is the system of management in Japan an unchanging one. The overall pattern of "Japanese style management" came into place largely in the postwar era. As social and economic change occurs, the system adapts to the changes.

However, Japan's economic success is owed to the genius of building a management system based on Japan's own culture. Any moves away from that base can be taken only at very great risk. Note that the very best of Japan's companies – companies like Toyota, Canon, Nippon Steel – are precisely the companies that adhere most closely to the full application of "Japanese style management." Japan's economy and companies must not ape the systems and values of the Anglo-American world if they are to continue in good health. And the Japanese habit of self-denigration and self-deprecation must not undermine the continued strength of the Japanese systems of corporate management. They are vital to the nation's future well-being.

The underlying values in Japanese society instilled over 2000 years have not greatly changed, nor yet have the bases of the systems of human management of the kaisha changed. Financial systems and mechanical systems must adapt to changing times and technology. But in all that deals with people, continuity must be and is the rule.

A decade of company redesign

The economic environment for the kaisha changed greatly and suddenly in the early 1990s after more than 40 years of extraordinary economic success. From 1992–93, land and share price values collapsed. Increased asset values were the collateral making increased debt and thus high investment and rapid growth possible. The sudden loss of asset values put the kaisha into effective bankruptcy. With this, the banking system too went into crisis as the companies' inability to handle the debt created a mountain of non-performing loans.

The initial reaction to the sudden collapse of the "bubble" of the late 1980s was to conclude that this was simply another of the periodic cyclic recessions that hit all economies. Therefore the usual remedies of lowered interest rates and increased government spending would fix the problem, it was assumed. The usual remedies did not work, and by around 1995 there was a general understanding that more basic and far-reaching changes needed to be put into effect to deal with the situation. Japan had quite abruptly moved from high growth – an economic teenager – to full economic and demographic maturity. The policies and methods of the high growth era were now, quite suddenly, counter-productive. To restore health and move forward in the 21st century, redesign of companies and of industries was now urgently necessary.

This difficult, often painful, task of redesign was carried out, not by crude and savage slashing and cutting as nicely distant US commentators proposed. Much time has been required to make the necessary changes while avoiding massive company and human write-offs, and while leaving the strengths of the system in place. The period from 1995 to 2004 was not a "lost decade" as it is often described, all too carelessly. The term is nonsense. This has been a decade not "lost" but used vigorously and effectively. Nor has it been a decade of "stagnation" as many like to phrase it. It has been a decade of critical reshaping of the strategies and structures of the kaisha. It has been a decade of vitally needed redesign, and far from being stagnant, has been a decade filled with putting in place urgently needed new programs.

The beginning of the redesign at a government level might be dated from the financial deregulations measures – the "big bang" – of the Hashimoto government. At the corporate level too, realization of the need for redesign began to be general around that time, with, for example, Sumitomo Chemical introducing an entirely new corporate plan, and Toshiba as another example beginning a considerable restructuring of its non-core businesses. Some companies, like Sony, came late to the realization of the need for redesign and are only now getting programs underway. Almost no companies however have escaped the need for change.

And culture still controls. It is fascinating to see that the major changes in kaisha have been in the finance area, the least personal, least "human" part of the total company complex. Where people matter, adaptive change has occurred but within very clear cultural constraints.

The finance area has changed, substantially. One needs first to recall the special requirements for companies to be successful under conditions of very high growth. Success with high growth means a focus on market share as corporate objective. Holding share with high growth means high investment – if the market doubles in a year, so must capacity. For high investment to be feasible, high levels of bank debt, the least expensive form of capital, are required. Thus strategies of successful companies were formed around growth/market share, high bank borrowing levels, and high investments. And with the run-up in asset values during the bubble period, banks increased loans to companies as company collateral for the loans – land and shares – increased. And companies expanded nearly at will.

And then the party ended. Fearful of massive asset inflation, the Bank of Japan stopped increasing money supply and raised interest rates sharply. Asset values collapsed. Demand for product dried up. Overcapacity forced cost and margin cuts, which further reduced demand, and so into deflation. While inflation helps pay off debt, deflation increases the debt burden. With asset values collapsed, companies were in fact bankrupt. The focus of management changed from market share to cash flow, with the cash flow used to pay off debt. Capital investment stopped for a full ten years, further reducing the growth rate, but easing cash flow needs.

Debt levels for Japan's manufacturing companies, once at towering levels, are now at new lows. The main bank pattern is very much weakened as the bank's role in company financing has shrunk greatly. With this, banks and companies have sold off shareholdings, again to raise cash, and thus the keiretsu ties, once critical, are very much weakened.

No doubt with renewed investment and growth there will be some returning to the banks for borrowings, and some increases in cross shareholdings. But a return to main bank and keiretsu controls is not at all likely. Kaisha are and will be using bonds and the equity market – direct financing. Nor is a return to a focus on growth and market share going to happen. Cash flow is and will be the measure of financial success, since it allows the kaisha, the community, to secure its future.

It is when we look to the people side of the kaisha that we see continuity as the main theme rather than change. And so we should expect, because it is the systems of dealing with people that distinguish the kaisha from other systems, and on which the culture of the kaisha is based. These are above all social organizations. The people that made them up are the center of the system. The people in the kaisha are the main stakeholders. It is they that make up the community that is the kaisha.

It should come as no surprise therefore to find that the commitment of the kaisha to its members is unchanged. There has been and continues to be a constant yelping that the system of "lifetime employment has ended." It has not. Its end has been announced each year since I first used the term in 1958, when I analyzed the "lifetime commitment" which became distorted in popular parlance as "lifetime employment." Then, and no less now, this is the measure of the degree to which the kaisha as social organization is meeting its obligations to its members. Job tenure has not decreased under recent economic stress. Rather, the length of job tenure has steadily increased, and continues to do so. The kaisha continue to honor their promises to their people.

This is the basic continuity in the system. There are of course adaptive changes, as the society and economy change. Living in an economy with considerable real wealth, Japan's youngsters can defer job-taking, and indeed can choose not to enter full employment, giving rise to a group of under-35s, generally lesser educated, unmarried, mostly women – but including as well those who are trying out various career approaches to avoid full-time employment. Changes in regulations mean that companies can employ part-timers in place of earlier contract or seasonal workers, and can order short-term staff from agencies as required, especially in IT-related work.

In terms of compensation and promotion, the earlier nenko joretsu approach of seniority-determined pay and promotion is being experimented with. There has been a certain fashion for discussing seika shugi, "resultism," with efforts to tie compensation and promotion to productivity and measures of merit. Certainly the preponderant role of seniority in pay and promotion is in process of some change. Still, however, promotion is within fairly clear age brackets – and seniority-based pay is still an important part of the total pay package. Change here is rather experimental still, with some efforts at moving toward annual pay and setting pay by type of job. Also it looks as though there will be more weight to bonus payments with reductions in the types of other fringe benefits provided. Here too, as in other personnel-related matters, some change is occurring but continuity continues as the dominant theme.

Perhaps more significant in this area of pay and promotion is the continuing relative equality of compensation in the kaisha. Various sources over recent years have provided data indicating that the Japanese corporate chief executive receives in total compensation about ten times as much as the average employee. For large companies, the spread between executives and salary workers in cash compensation – salary plus bonus – is 10 times and has been at that difference since the mid-1970s with almost no change in degree of difference.

This can be measured against a recent report that in 2000, "the annual income of US CEOs peaked at a multiple of 531 times the average production worker's wage; in short, the combination of cash, bonuses, stock grants, benefits and options has decoupled CEO compensation from performance."[4] This degree of crude exploitation of the mass of employees is quite simply inconceivable in the kaisha. Indeed no self-respecting community of any sort should tolerate this kind of inequality in reward under any conditions. It might be noted that the Japanese spread in compensation is similar to that in German companies. It is the Anglo-American companies in which exploitation of the workers is rampant now; it could not take place in the companies of most societies, least of all in Japan.

Another recent fashion in management discussions was around the term, "corporate governance." The apparent success of US and British companies during 1990s when Japanese companies were struggling with redesign made for a preoccupation with the issues of corporate governance – for example, the makeup of the board of directors from within or from outside the company; focus on share price through granting of stock options to executives; optimal transparency in corporate accounts; board committees making key decisions; separation of the offices of Chairman and President, and so on.

Share price as the critical measure of performance, and use of stock options as incentive for management to boost share prices, has not been accepted by the kaisha as the purpose of corporate governance. The shareholder is entitled to a fair return on investment, but has no further claim, in the view of the kaisha. Further benefits should accrue instead to employees and such other stakeholders as customers and suppliers. The shareholder is only one of a group of entitled stakeholders, in this view. Moreover, the collapse of the credibility of the US governance system was signaled by such appalling cases as Tyco, Enron, Adelphi, World Com, and Global Crossing, along with the scandals in the investment banking communities. US governance built in a system for full realization of the greed of the top few.

Instead of outside directors in the Anglo-American fashion, governance in many of the kaisha now includes a group of outside experts who make up an advisory committee, bringing the benefits of third-party views and experience without preempting the Director's title that an employee might otherwise enjoy, and without presuming to be able to share in running a company that they only occasional visit. There are outside directors in some kaisha – indeed, there always have been – but they are few and occasional. Many larger companies now are separating board members, responsible for policy, from executives (shikkoin) responsible for operations, to speed decision-making in operating divisions.

So again the people aspect is one of continuity – inside directors for the most part, no stock options generally. However, again there is change in the non-human aspect. The laws requiring transparency have been greatly changed – and improved. Consolidated returns are required – mistakes cannot be hidden now in unconsolidated subsidiaries. Assets must be marked to market value – the balance sheet must be clean. Pension liabilities must be recognized. The change here is real, and positive, and again is in an area that does not touch on human relations.

So, the basic values that control the community of the kaisha continue very much as before. Around these, adaptations are being made in such matters as pay systems and non-core employment. Substantial change has been made in the area of finance, and the closely related area of transparency. The redesign of the kaisha for the next stage of their lives is largely completed.

We might note there that unlike the case in many other economies, the kaisha have rather long lives.

The average life expectancy of a multinational corporation – Fortune 500 or its equivalent – is between 40 and 50 years. This figure is based on most surveys of corporate births and deaths. A full one-third of the companies listed in the 1970 Fortune 500, for instance, had vanished by 1983 – acquired, merged, or broken to pieces. Human beings have learned to survive, on average, for 75 years or more, but there are very few companies that are that old and flourishing.[5]

Kaisha seem to be exceptions to this rule. The oldest kaisha, and indeed probably the oldest company in the world, is Kongo Gumi, founded in 578 and run by the 40th generation of the Kongo family, Osaka based, specializing in temple construction and general contracting. The second oldest is probably Hoshi, managing a hotel founded in 718, run by the 46th generation. Among listed companies, Kongo Gumi and Hoshi being family owned, the oldest is Surugaya, founded in 1461, before Columbus set off for America, still a favored producer of Japanese sweets. Sumitomo Metal Mining, founded in 1590, is still a major company with ¥360 billion in sales. Matsui Kensetsu, a listed construction firm specializing in shrines and temples, was founded in 1586, with current sales of ¥85 billion. Of surviving listed Japanese companies, 11 were founded in the 17th century, 9 in the 18th century, and 75 in the 19th century.

Apart from the inherent interest in companies so long-lived, we can take all these time-tested survivors to be testimony to the fact that the kaisha, and not simply family-owned ones, are communities with the objective of perpetuating themselves. These are not simple collections of physical assets to be bargained over, bought and sold. These are social organizations that seek a long life on behalf of the well-being of all of their members.

Redesigning industries

The decade of redesign was used by the kaisha to make changes in financial policies and practices and to make adjustments in employment, compensation, and governance practices. The kaisha as organizations have adapted to changed conditions while keeping basic people-related systems intact. However, just as the kaisha needed to make changes as the economy reached maturity, so Japan's industries have used the "lost" decade to restructure and redesign to deal with the requirements of a changed economic world.

Too many producers

Long-sustained high growth resulted in a large number of companies in each of Japan's major industries. High growth provides an umbrella under which less competitive companies can continue in business, while the more successful companies focus on taking the growth. When the growth stops, the companies with high market shares and thus low costs turn on the weaker competitors, making industry consolidation inevitable either through mergers of stronger with weaker, or through bankruptcies of the weaker.

Another driver of industry consolidation is the fact that many important basic industries are scale driven – costs depending on total output size, with competition global and the winners the world's largest firms in each industry. The materials-based industries of Japan, like cement, pulp and paper, and oil, started when the economy was small. Many companies got underway then, domestic focused and not of world scale, before global competition was a reality. Small scale and high cost among massive, low-cost world competitors, with domestic demand flat, resulted in the requirement that these industries consolidate rapidly or disappear rapidly. The years since the mid-1990s saw quite exceptional consolidation.

The numbers are impressive – 14 oil companies now 4; 7 cement majors now 3; 14 pulp and paper companies now 3 majors; industrial gas from 7 to 3; steel from 5 majors to 4 and still combining. Some of this consolidation was by product rather than company – polystyrene, for example, from 8 producers to 4, even though the parent chemical companies did not combine. All of this massive consolidation took place in only a few years, and all through mergers – none through acquisitions. Much was done following the ending of the law against holding companies. A holding structure merging two or more companies can work to achieve economies of scale over time, not requiring the drastic actions of factory closings, mass dismissals, and the like all too frequent with acquisition.

Note that most of these industries and companies have for some time been slow-growing. In consequence, given Japanese employment practices, very few younger staff was hired. Thus the average age of employees goes up nearly a year with each passing year. And as a result, retirements, encouraged by early retirement incentives, can go far to bring labor force size into line with cost requirements – without the damage to families and careers that goes with slashing labor forces through firings. There is of course no assurance that all of these combinations will be successful in world competition. But the consolidation was a requirement for staying in the game at all.

Industry restructuring will continue, as competitive pressures continue. The steel industry process began, but is not complete with four integrated producers still. The chemical industry of Japan is by world standards made up of relatively small companies. The planned merger of Sumitomo Chemical and Mitsui Chemical failed to come off – but consolidation in the industry is needed. The pharmaceutical industry finally saw a major merger when Yamanouchi and Fujisawa came together – but it is another industry in which nearly all companies are well below the scale needed for major research and product development, with consolidation much needed.

Note that in all of these industry changes in the 1990s and after, the role of the Japanese government has been confined almost entirely to the easing of regulations that made consolidation difficult. The repeal of the anti-holding company act has been noted, but in addition a series of new laws and changes in laws made possible share-for-share exchange, introduced a company split system and generally opened the paths to restructuring of companies. The industry changes have been driven by the decisions of company managements and have been done without government instruction or aid.

Historically, the Japanese economy has been a highly dynamic one. The changes of the redesign decade are only one more phase in a continuing process. Coal mining in the early 1950s employed more than 350,000 workers in more than 800 mines. There are no active coal mines or coal miners in Japan today, as world economics made the domestic industry ineffective. Japan once was site for nearly 15 percent of world bauxite smelting capacity. There is one very small smelter left now, as Japan's major chemical companies found themselves unable to compete in a world business. Textiles were a third of

Japan's exports as recently as 1960 – and are less than 1 percent of exports now. So too for steel exports, as the economy has moved rapidly up the value-added ladder – as it must if growth and wealth appreciation are to continue. In these past cases of industrial restructuring and company redesign, the government of Japan played a large, often central, role. However, the era of central government programming of industrial change ended more than 20 years ago. For Japan now, as for other of the advanced economies, the market place and market players are the key decision-makers. The economy continues to be a dynamic one, but now without government as a central player in shaping the process.

Too many businesses

Long continued high growth made for large numbers of competitors in nearly all of Japan's industries, and consolidation has been required. But long continued high growth also made for a high degree of diversification of companies. With high growth, entry to a new business can be rather easy – new games are fun in any case, and sales come readily in a high growth environment. The result has been a massive strategic failure on the part of all too many of Japan's largest companies. Successful strategy requires focus. Resources of money and people are limited. They must be concentrated in a particular business until market leadership in that business has been clearly established. And only then is entry into still another business warranted – and again, a drive for dominance – and so on.

This basic strategic commandment was popularized as Jack Welch of GE fame insisted that all of GE's businesses be first, second, or third in market share or else be disposed of. Not at all a new idea with Welch, but quite correct, a rule largely forgotten in the flush days of Japan's high growth. Everything was up, seemingly forever. But in fact not forever, and as the growth stopped, the hazards of over-diversification became all too clear.

The over-diversification was most extreme and costly for the large electronics companies – Hitachi, Mitsubishi Electric, Toshiba, NEC, Fujitsu, Sanyo, Sharp, Matsushita, and Sony. The growth of these companies was spectacular, and for a long time. Sony increased its sales from 1955 to 2003 by 8350 times, with nearly 1200 subsidiaries in 2003. Fujitsu and NEC in telecomm and industrial electronics grew 1400 times over that period. The nine had by 2004 average sales of ¥5 trillion, but had operating losses steadily from 1997 to 2003, with essentially no growth, deeply in debt, taking massive financial losses through asset write-down in addition to operating red ink.

These companies each went into everything, or so it seemed. NEC was leader in the world in semi-conductors in 1990. But NEC was in all categories of semiconductors – and had company in all product categories from the other eight diversified Japanese companies.[6] As the semiconductor industry grew, specialist makers like Intel and Samsung picked particular semiconductor products to focus on. NEC lost position in all categories as did the other Japanese competitors. NEC went from first to sixth in share in ten years – and has since spun out its semiconductor business. This disastrous lack of focus was not only in sophisticated electronic products but was the case as well in domestic appliances – everyone made refrigerators and washing machines.

Yet in their defense, let it be said that these companies without exception have moved hard and fast to correct their competitive positions, to rebuild their balance sheets, and to return to effective strategies. The extent of the design can be appreciated from the table showing the redesign efforts of NEC, leader in industrial electronics, and Matsushita Electric, leader in consumer electronics. As is implicit in these data, NEC had its main problem that of being in too many businesses; Matsushita had its greater problem in the need to integrate its subsidiaries. Given that these companies had for many years done little or nothing by way of disinvestments or consolidation, the few years following recognition of near-disaster in 2000 have witnessed exceptional redesign (Table 1.1). Will it all succeed? It seems likely. These are basically very strong companies, and sales and profits recovered well following all this redesign.

The fault here was not that of the industry. A good number of the most successful of Japanese companies over the redesign decade have

Table 1.1 Business redesign from 2000 through 2003

	NEC	Matsushita
Acquisitions	5	5
Sale of businesses and facilities	18	2
Spin off of businesses	11	3
New joint ventures	11	7
New Minority investments	22	22
Mergers of divisions and subsidiaries	18	15

Source: Company announcements, Recof *Marr*, Nikkei Telecom 21.

been electronics companies. Firms like Mabuchi Motors, Keyence, Kyocera, Murata Manufacturing, Rohm, Nidec, Fanuc, and Hirose Electric have been fast growing and highly profitable with very strong balance sheets. They are highly focused companies, dominating the world market in their specialized products. They are each first-rate examples of what can be accomplished by following a sound product strategy. This is not an electronics phenomenon, nor yet one of smaller companies. Toyota has stayed in autos; Honda has stayed in motors; Canon has moved to new products only after dominating its current product markets; Hoya is in optical glass; Shin-Etsu is world leader in PVC and one of the leaders in silicone wafers; Nippon Steel disengaged from its diversification efforts and is back as a world leader in steel. The issue here is focus. The lesson has been an expensive one, hopefully well-learned.

Redesign of industries and companies has not been limited by any means to the manufacturing sector. There have been massive mergers in the banking industry, most notably the combination of the banks of Japan's two oldest financial groups, Sumitomo and Mitsui, a truly historic merger with direct impact on insurance and construction firms in the two groups as well. In banking restructuring, inevitably, the role of government, in the person of the central bank and the Finance Ministry, has been of central importance. The long continued practice of loaning against collateral led to near-on disaster as the value of collateralized assets collapsed and as companies focused on reducing bank borrowings as rapidly as possible. Inevitably in so deep a financial crisis, the central bank and treasury must play a major part, and did. The banking crisis looked by 2004 to have been largely dealt with.

Airlines merged, retailers were bankrupted or bought up, life insurance companies were much reduced in numbers by mergers and bankruptcy buy-outs – there are really no sectors of Japan's enormous economy that have not to greater or lesser degree been redesigned. Both at the level of industry structure and at the level of company redesign there have been massive changes. It is a tribute to the competence of staff at all levels of the kaisha that the changes have been carried out so thoroughly and with such success. The process has required a full decade, and has been done without the companies or the economy losing the strengths that had made for earlier success and that are required for the future.

Foreign factors in the redesign

Foreign capital and foreign companies have been factors in the redesign, with special impact in the auto manufacturing industry and in the life insurance business. Before looking at these however the issues of Japan as a closed economy and as a closed market need brief review.

Is the Japanese market closed?

Japan is the country with the largest trade and current account surpluses in the world. This has led some observers to charge that Japan's markets are closed to imports and that only by applying consistent pressure will openness increase and the surpluses subside. But the evidence regarding overtly protectionist government policies is scarce: for example, Japan's average tariff rates and recourse to non-tariff barriers have been lower than in other major trading zones for the past decade at least.[7]

In fact, the charge of closed borders is made by inefficient exporters as an excuse for poor performance. Thus the US Trade Representative writes in the Economist about "Japan's mercantilist, zero-sum approach to trade."[8] A more inaccurate and irresponsible remark from a senior officer of an allied country is hard to imagine.

Agriculture is usually the lead topic as a trade issue for Japan and its trading partners. Is Japan closed to agricultural products? Certainly not. Japan imports 60 percent of its caloric requirement, including half of its fruit needs, two-thirds of its beef, and nearly half of its fish. Total Japanese food and drink imports are larger in value than those of the United States with less than half of the US population. Given the current openness of Japan's market for agricultural goods, the strategic danger of further increasing import dependence for food supply is a very real one that must be and will be guarded against. This does not denote a closed market; it defines the limits of what is already a very considerable openness and the risks of depending for supply on countries that may use food supply as a weapon.

As with trade, so with investment – there is a widespread mistaken view that the economy is closed, and sadly, stupidly, the Japanese government and such ministries as METI do nothing to correct this view. First, portfolio investment has no barriers of any sort. Foreigners now own nearly 20 percent of corporate shares, with holdings of 30 and 40 percent in interesting companies not unusual.

The issue is foreign direct investment. The usual estimate is that foreign direct investment accounts for 1 or 2 percent of Japan's GDP. However, in fact there are more than 3000 foreign capital-related firms in Japan the majority foreign owned. In manufacturing, foreign firms account for no less than 10 percent of Japan's total sales revenues and in finance and services certainly now are at an additional 5 percent of economic activities. Given Japan's historic, geographic, and cultural distance from the other advanced economies, this seems a very high share position by foreign direct investors by any standard. And it makes nonsense of the often-repeated 1 or 2 percent estimate often used to minimize the position of foreign firms.

The real problem quite evidently lies in the fact that successful Japanese businesses and companies are not for sale. They are not for sale to Japanese companies nor foreign companies. This is not an entry barrier; rather it is local business practice. Japan's is a highly competitive economy, with high land and personnel costs. Distribution systems are complex. Staffing can be difficult. How much better it might be if the foreign company could enter by buying a sound company than by slowly and at great expense putting together the land, facilities, staff, and distribution of a newly established company. Moreover, the capital costs incurred by acquisition do not impact the profit statement; on the other hand, long drawn-out expense investment in building a new business could cost executives their jobs. "Let's do an acquisition," so the thinking of the foreign manager goes.

But the kaisha is a social organization, as we have seen, a community. It is not simply a collection of physical and financial assets. It can be purchased, but only when the company is in such serious difficulties that its future and its people's futures are better served by sale of the company than by the alternative, bankruptcy. And so the foreign company can make acquisitions – but with very rare exceptions can acquire only troubled companies. And it does not follow that the foreign owner can fix a troubled Japanese company – witness General Motors' problems with Isuzu, Merrill Lynch tripping over its Yamaichi purchase, and Daimler with Mitsubishi Motors as examples of foreign fumbling with badly run Japanese companies.

The auto industry has been a special arena for foreign takeovers. That industry as so many others has had too many producers – there were 11 car, truck, and bus producers in Japan, slightly fewer now, but 3 is surely ample. General Motors bought into Isuzu in the early 1970s, to save that truck producer's passenger car business. GM failed, lost a bundle of money, and Isuzu is out of the passenger car business after all, now doing very well in trucks with GM holdings marginal. Ford bought into Toyo Kogyo, now Mazda, which has lost market share and lost money very consistently, not much helped by annual changes in the Ford-appointed president of the company. Daimler Chrysler for reasons hard to understand bought into Mitsubishi Motors. The purchase price for the shares turned out to be a fraction of cost as losses mounted; heavy recapitalization was required with Daimler Chrysler finally retreating. Renault bought into Nissan, and the takeover is considered a success as Renault copied the strategy Lee Iacocca used when he took over Chrysler in the 1980s: massive initial write-offs, quick sales of attractive non-core businesses, drastic reduction in platforms, brutal price pressure on suppliers. Iacocca had great early success, but longterm was a disaster. The Nissan case is early still, too early to judge its long-term outcome.

Barring foreign investment, Japan's auto industry would have gone to two or three producers in the natural course of affairs, with Toyota and Honda dominating the industry and pushing the weaklings out. Foreign capital has kept the losers alive – but can hardly be reckoned successful investments. A good deal of problem here is caused by the risks involved in cross-cultural acquisitions. Foreign acquisitions in Japan have generally done poorly – GE and Toho Seimei, Merrill Lynch and Yamaichi Securities, the auto cases of GM, Ford, and Daimler Chrysler. But Japanese acquisitions abroad have similarly been unsuccessful – Bridgestone with Firestone, NEC with Packard Bell, Furukawa with the optic fiber business of Lucent, Matsushita with Universal. Acquisitions of all kinds everywhere fail to return profits in more than half the cases, according to various studies. Cross-cultural acquisitions do even less well, and should be avoided in favor of the kinds of green-field successes of Toyota, Honda, Kyocera, and the like.

Life insurance too has had heavy foreign investment, again by foreign purchase of failed or failing Japanese insurance firms. Foreign firms now hold nearly one-fifth of Japan's very large life insurance business, a good part through the purchase of failed local companies. AIG and AFLAC are exceptions, both startup companies in Japan, and very successful. GE failed in its purchase of a bankrupted Toho. The outcome of the others remains to be seen.

Conclusions: Japan's economy is as open to imports and to investment as any other, and has been for several decades now. Foreign companies have enjoyed very considerable success by keeping control of their technology and their investments and establishing themselves in the market. Japan's economy has been protected at least as much by foreign ignorance and incompetence as it has been protected by Japanese laws and habits. The accusations of Japan's being a closed market and economy are entirely unjustified.

Redesign of labor supply?

The graying of Japan, the aging of the population, impacts all discussions of the nation's future. The aging of the population has many implications. At the simplest level is the issue of labor supply. The size of Japan's labor force, commonly defined as persons 15–65 years of age, peaked several years ago and will decline steadily over the coming decades. Mass immigration is proposed as a solution. In terms of labor supply, for at least the next generation mass immigration is not at all needed, leaving aside the terrible hazards for Japan of mass immigration.

The factors at work to deal with the anticipated "labor shortage" include the following: (1) Heavy use of automation and robotics. Each robot is equivalent to two laborers and Japan has now half of the world's robot population installed, nearly 400,000. They are low-cost workers with no tea breaks, unions, sick leaves, or holidays. (2) The current retirement age of 60 years is nonsense in a country with the longest life expectancies in the world. Continue current plans to extend the working age – and defer pension startups. (3) Women can be the ready source of well over an additional million workers simply by providing adequate child-care facilities, maternity leaves, and the like. (4) China and the rest of East Asia have masses of inexpensive workers now unemployed. Take the low skill, labor intensive jobs to them, rather than importing the laborers. This is not hollowing out; it is economic development as those economies benefit and Japan's labor force is moved up to higher value-added work.

True, an aging population poses problems – loss of vigor as younger people are fewer; costs of medical and pension care for the elderly; and lowered economic growth because of a shrinking population. However, and it seems often overlooked, mass immigration poses problems of even greater magnitude. Few countries can handle mass immigration – the United States, Canada, and Australia as exceptions perhaps. But these three have no common domestic culture and only a low level of social integration. They offer both physical and social space in large measure, and can absorb large numbers of immigrants. A well-integrated society like Japan's would take very great social risks with mass immigration, and incur all manner of costs as a result. Conclusion: Labor shortage is not an imminent problem, and mass immigration is in any case not an appropriate solution.

Looked at more broadly, the demographic transition, the graying of Japan, and its impact on labor force size, on consumption patterns, and on social welfare costs are all part of the shift to maturity that is occurring as well in the world's other advanced economies. The demographic transition is not unique to Japan – much of Western Europe shows very similar patterns – but it is happening exceptionally rapidly in Japan, making adjustment more difficult. After a careful review of the issues in a recent study, "the final policy implication is that Japan's demographic transition is going to be manageable."[9]

Japan's is now a mature society and mature economy. The past half-century has seen truly extraordinary change in the economy, from poverty to wealth with all manner of crises periodically through the decades – currency crises, oil crises, explosive inflation, asset bubble and asset collapse, sustained deflation, Red Army incidents, student uprisings – the list is a long one. Yet the exceptional health and civility of Japanese society continues. The marvelous attention in businesses to the well-being and future security of employees continues. Japan has been a constructive and peace-abiding world citizen. It warrants admiration abroad, and pride at home, for the achievements of the past half-century and for the promise it holds for the next century for its own well-being and as a model for the world.

Notes

1. *The Economist*, 26 June 2004, p. 78.
2. Shigeto Tsuru, *Japan's Capitalism: Creative Defeat and Beyond*, Cambridge: Cambridge University Press, 1993, p. 146.
3. David Landes, *The Wealth and Poverty of Nations*, New York: Norton, 1998, p. 516.
4. Robert Felton, "Overhaul", *McKinsey Quarterly*, 2004, No. 2, p. 37.
5. Arie de Geus, *The Living Company*, Boston: Harvard Business School Press, 1997, p. 1.
6. For a useful analysis of this issue, see Development Bank of Japan Research Report, No. 34, "Prospects and Challenges Surrounding Japan's Electrical Equipment Industry", November 2002, especially pp. 13–17.
7. OECD Economic Surveys: Japan. Paris: OECD, 1999, p. 220.
8. Robert Zoellick, "Unleashing the Trade Winds", *The Economist*, 7 December 2002, p. 28.
9. Christian Broda and David E. Weinstein, "Happy News from the Dismal Science: Reassessing Japanese Fiscal Policy and Sustainability", www.ny.frb.org/research/economists/broda/pub.

2
Redesign for a Competitive Future

Japan's decade of economic problems and the massive redesign of Japan's businesses are a direct result of Japan's amazing economic success since the mid-1950s. In 1955 Japan's economy was half the size of the economies of France and Britain with per capita output well under that even of Italy. Over the next 40 years the economy grew in US dollar terms by 230 times, becoming by 1995 more than three times the size of the French economy and more than four times the size of the British economy, second in the world to the United States. On a per capita basis Japanese output in 1995 was half again as great as that of the United States. The advance from the poverty of the immediate postwar years to real wealth in so short a time by a major nation has no precedent in world history.

And then the growth stopped. The early 1990s saw two years of growth barely over zero. Asset values – land and share prices especially – virtually collapsed from the highs of the "bubble" of the late 1980s. It took some time before there was full realization, both in the public and private sectors, that this was not simply another brief recession, but was rather a basic shift to an industrially and demographically mature economy, requiring drastic structural change to regain growth and competitiveness. Generally this realization began around 1995–96, signaled in the public sector by the Hashimoto government's program to deregulate the financial sector, the "big bang," and in the private sector by the restructuring of companies and whole industries. Japan's economic apparatus, both public and private, had to be redesigned in order to regain competitive strength.

Managing when growth is high

The approaches to corporate strategy of Japanese management had inevitably been shaped by the requirements of dealing with and competing in high-growth environments. There were of course dying industries, labor intensive with low technology levels, coal mining and cotton spinning the prototypes. But in the higher value-added sectors where the growth was taking place the requirements for success were clear. First, market share is the critical measure of success; loss of share to a competitor gives him immediate advantage; profits are a later result of successful high growth.

In a high-growth economy, where demand may well be doubling annually and therefore capacity needs be doubled annually, very high rates of capital investment are required. For this investment to be cost effective it must depend on the heavy use of bank debt for funding; equity is more expensive than debt, and financing from earnings requires growth-destroying high prices. Banks throughout the decades of growth lent based on collateral, and as the value of collateral increased, so then did the scale of bank borrowing and of investment. These patterns reached levels of high hazard during the "bubble" period when land and share prices tripled and made possible explosive levels of debt and of investment – much of the investment indiscriminate in nature.

Success has a price, and the bill for Japan's economic success came due in the early 1990s. Capacity continued to increase – but demand flattened in what had become rather suddenly a rich and mature economy. With over-capacity, companies cut overtime and bonuses and cut back on employment, all this further reducing demand – the beginning of a classic deflationary downward spiral – less demand still, more cuts still, and so on. Asset values plummeted with the end to growth, but liabilities did not. The result was effective balance sheet bankruptcies, and an end to investment as cash flows went to pay off debt and restore balance sheet strength. Real business investment, which grew an annual average of 8.4 percent from 1980 to 1990, averaged an extraordinary 0.0 percent from 1991 to 2002!

Too many companies; too many businesses

The redesign of Japanese business that has taken place since the mid-1990s has required a focus on two sets of industry structure problems, both the consequence of high growth and the behaviors that go with high growth. The first of the problems to be dealt with has been the very large numbers of competitors in most Japanese industries. High growth provides an umbrella against the competitive storm for weaker companies. The marginal competitor can exist while growth is high since the industry leaders are focused on capturing growth. As growth slows however, the high-share low-cost leaders begin to take market share from the weaker. Consolidation must take place as the economy matures. The number of competitors must, one way or another, be greatly reduced.

The second of the structural problems inherited from the era of high growth is over-diversification. In a high-growth economy, with cash flow and bank debt amply available, it is all too tempting to diversify. With ample funds and ample staff, the temptation to enter new businesses can become nearly irresistible – and all too many Japanese managements yielded to the temptation.

It is virtually a truism of business strategy that success in any given business sector requires concentration of resources in that particular business until a commanding market share is achieved. The requirement is focus. This strategic thinking has a long history, but achieved a particular vogue when Jack Welch was CEO of General Electric and ordered that each of GE's many businesses should be first or second in market share, or have a clear plan to achieve first or second place – or be terminated as a GE business.

Such outstanding Japanese managements as the top executives of Canon, Toyota, Shin-Etsu Chemical, and the like understand this very well. Management of a great many other companies failed to meet the test, notably the managements of Japan's very large electronic companies.

Redesign of the economy to achieve new strength has required that these two massive structural problems – too many producers and over-diversification – be dealt with. As we will see, the redesign has been taking place. Certainly not all companies are not in perfect shape; all companies will never be in perfect shape in any economy in the world. And it has been a long decade. However, the reshaping of Japan's business for the needs and demands of the 21st century has largely been completed, and in fine fashion.

There has been a fashion to refer to recent years as Japan's "lost decade," and the economy as in a state of "stagnation." This is utter nonsense. The economy, far from stagnant, has been in sustained period of high activity as the industrial system has been restructured and redesigned. Economic growth has been cyclic with two major highs but longer sustained lows, the average at the level of Germany's over the decade, a bit over 1 percent. However, the decade has not been "lost." Instead it has witnessed a very difficult, very far reaching and very necessary process of change.

It is curious to observe how inaccurate the reporting about Japan's economy can be, especially in the Western press. Reference to stagnation is only one example. Very recently a large headline in one of the world's leading financial newspapers read "Restructuring only skin-deep in Japan," and went on in the text to refer to "the unreconstructed state of much of corporate Japan."[1] This kind of stupid reporting about Japan is all too common. Some of this is ignorance – few Western reporters on Japan even have a command of the language. Some is prejudice – Japan's successes have damaged badly the Western assumption of Western world supremacy. Some is arrogance toward the unenlightened heathen of Asia. Whatever the causes, and they are no doubt many, inaccurate and misleading reporting serves Japan and those of us concerned with Japan very badly.

Redesign I: Fixing the strategic disasters of Japan's electronics companies

The most complex restructuring and redesign process has been taking place in the electronics industry. The Bank of Japan remarked, "Reorganization under enhanced concentration policies is typified by the electronics industry.... There has been a growing awareness within the industry of the necessity of focusing on strategically important sectors, allocating business resources selectively and intensively."[2] The electronics industry is the extreme case of over-diversification; the large companies in the industry all grew in total abandon of the basic requirements of strategic success, and faced total collapse by the late 1990s.

The nine diversified electronic firms include Hitachi, Toshiba, Mitsubishi Electric, NEC, Fujitsu, Sony, Matsushita, Sanyo, and Sharp. They are large, with average sales in 2002 of over ¥5 trillion. From 1997 to 2002, they as a group experienced less than 1 percent sales growth, with annual losses over the five years of a half-percent on sales, and financial losses in 2002 averaging over ¥200 billion. They were in deep trouble.

The problems of these companies resulted from an utter failure in strategy, a failure to follow the most basic rules of the game – focus in a business until dominance is achieved, and only then move on to the next business, and again focus and dominate. Instead, flush with the specious successes of the bubble years, these companies went into the widest possible range of businesses in their industry, competing with each other – and with foreign companies – with little regard for dominant share. All of the nine were in MOS semiconductors. All had share positions of fourth or lower; none were in the world's top three. So too with other semiconductor products. And so too with consumer electronics and with communications equipment. These companies diversified across entire fields of products, with no regard to holding leading share positions – and thereby lost position in all their businesses.

> The ROA figure for 25 American manufacturers was roughly steady through out the 1980s and rose slightly in the mid 1990s, whereas that for 17 Japanese manufacturers dropped between the late 1980s and early 1990s and remained low at about 4% for the remainder of the 1990s. (The Japanese company ROA for 2001 was below zero.)

> The profitability gap...is partly due to the differences in business model. The top Japanese manufacturers by sales are general manufacturers, whereas the top American ones are specialized manufacturers. There are also differences in business policies. American manufacturers have been radically restructuring their businesses, eliminating unprofitable divisions and concentrating resources in core businesses, such as General Electric in the 1980s and IBM in the early 1990s, while Japanese manufacturers have been expanding.[3]

This analysis was entirely accurate as a description of the large and diversified electronics companies as of the late 1990s. The boom in IT in the late 1990s provided growth and facing the problems was briefly postponed. However, as the magnitude of the problems became evident and losses continued and increased, these companies finally began aggressively to restructure. The change was greatly aided by a series of legal changes, with rules on mergers deregulated, tax exemption for the spinning out of unprofitable operations, easing of rules on stock swaps and on parent takeovers of subsidiaries – a broad range of measures designed to facilitate implementation of the needed corporate changes.

Redesigning product lines

In semiconductors, Toshiba and Mitsubishi Electric got out of the DRAM business, while NEC and Hitachi got together in a new joint company, Elpida. Hitachi and Mitsubishi Electric combined their flash memory businesses into a new company, Renesas. In large LCDs, Fujitsu and NEC got out of the businesses, while Sharp focused on it as a core business, with Toshiba and Matsushita combining in a new company. In plasma display, Pioneer focused on it as core, while Fujitsu and Hitachi combined their plasma business and NEC sold its plasma business to Pioneer, noting that it was a non-core business for NEC, core for Pioneer. In hard disk drives, Hitachi increased its position by acquiring IBM's hard disk drive business, with Fujitsu and NEC withdrawing from hard disk drives.

Matsushita and Minebea combined their small precision motors businesses to become number two in the sector, while Matsushita and Toshiba merged their cathode ray tube businesses to become third largest producer in the world. Toshiba has announced that it will spin off its ¥700 billion white goods business into a new company that will include as well an air conditioning venture with US Carrier Corp. and Toshiba Lighting. Hitachi had earlier spun out its white good business and tied up with Matsushita to develop new Internet-accessible home appliances. NEC had earlier written off and abandoned its consumer appliance business.

Redesigning the organization of these companies was a major factor in the overall changes. Toshiba had led the way in 1998 and 1999 under the then President Nishimuro Taizo, selling its glass subsidiary and its ATM business, joint venturing with competitors in nuclear energy, small and large motors, turbine blades, and switchboards, among a range of moves to focus. Despite all that, its problems remained major and Toshiba hit bottom in fiscal 2001 with a consolidated loss of ¥250 billion. Toshiba then spun off its home appliance manufacturing division and its information processing service division, while selling its US DRAM division to Micron Technology of the United States. The parent Toshiba has three businesses – sophisticated chips, digital equipment, and heavy electrical/social infrastructure equipment. Others of the diversified nine have similarly redesigned their organizations.

These companies had in common an extraordinary proliferation of subsidiaries, led by Sony with 1174 and Hitachi with 1111. Talk about diversification! Even remembering the names of all these subsidiaries would be an achievement, much less presuming to control and supervise them to any degree. Matsushita, the great pioneer in consumer electronics in Japan, lost its way through excessive use of subsidiaries, and has moved hard to change. "Our biggest purpose is to eliminate overlap and dispersal of operations within the group and concentrate on strategic businesses. Overlapping operations…total nearly ¥1 trillion. This indicates that we used to compete internally, rather than with other firms, to attract customers," said CEO Kunio Nakamura, who has designed and led the reorganization of the company's worldwide operations.

Matsushita's great rival, Sony, however came relatively late to the restructuring process, its underlying problems in the electronics business hidden from view for some time perhaps by the high earlier profitability of its home entertainment business, the Play Station. And not all firms have gone full course in restructuring. For example, Hitachi looked to be hedging its bets. The largest in sales of the electronic nine, Hitachi first announced that it planned to withdraw from a full 20 percent or ¥1.6 trillion of its businesses. With some improvement in operating income, the withdrawal target was reduced to 10 percent of total businesses. Sharp, however, focused early on display technology, investing aggressively in a clearly defined core business and realizing solid growth and profits as a result.

Improvement of the results of these companies was not only by correcting strategic errors. Operational improvements have been substantial as well. By using cash flow to pay off debt, the payments burden is lightened, and low interest rates help ease the payments problem as well. Procurement costs were reduced by dramatic cuts in the number of suppliers, consolidating orders to obtain reduced prices and lower handling costs. Sony aimed to cut the number of its suppliers from 4700 to 1000, for example. Labor costs were reduced, by ¥100 billion in the case of Toshiba. All of this began showing results, finally. Free cash flows, negative in 2001, turned positive as early as 2002. Sales for the electronic nine increased by only a very small amount in 2003 over 2002, but operating income increased by nearly 20 percent and net income went from red to black.

A full listing of all the disinvestments, combinations, and other changes leading to focus on the core businesses of these companies would be encyclopedic, but the above examples will serve to indicate the kinds of changes management put in place in redesigning these companies. No major mergers; no major acquisitions; no mass dismissals; rather, a wide range of moves to reach a proper degree of concentration.

Now with restructuring largely completed, future profit and future growth of these companies rests on increases in the total economy of Japan, on successes in off-shore ventures, and on the ability of these companies – all spending heavily on R&D – to develop winning new technologies and products over the coming decades.

Tight focus equals real success

The fault in the case of the nine major electronics companies has not been the industry they are in. Among the most successful of Japan's companies since the mid-1990s have been electronics producers. However, the successful firms are highly focused, concentrating on specific product segments, producing high value-added products, and holding comm-anding world market share positions in their chosen product areas. They are substantial in size but are smaller in scale than the nine diversified companies described earlier, and are little known outside Japan. This group of nine focused companies includes Hirose Electric, Mabuchi Motors, Murata Manufacturing, Rohm, Keyence, Fanuc, Kyocera, TDK, and Nidec Corporation.

To appreciate the differences, note that the nine diversified electronics companies produced ¥45 trillion in sales in fiscal 2002 but grew only 0.8 percent, with an average loss on sales of 0.1 percent. In fact, their ten-year average profit margin on sales was only 0.1 percent – nothing. The focused nine electronics companies on the other hand grew 4.7 percent with a net income of 7.6 percent and a ten-year average profit of 7.7 percent. In financial strength, the diversified nine have a debt to equity ratio of 1.9 to 1.0, heavily in debt, while the focused nine have a debt to equity ratio of 0.1 to 1.0 – a very healthy balance sheet. In sum, the focused nine are financially very much stronger, growing faster, with much greater profit margins than the diversified nine – and this has been a case for a full decade.

Mabuchi Motor holds over half of the world market for DC small motors – with its production in China. Murata has an 80 percent world share in capacitors. Keyence dominates Japan's motor sensor market – and subcontracts all its manufacturing, a "fab-less" company. TDK specializes in tape. Fanuc is world leader in numerical controls and in robot manufacture. Kyocera focused on chip packaging. Hirose leads in connectors. Rohm makes very specialized semiconductors. Nidec is leader in small motors. In terms of rate of return on shares since the early 1980s, Hirose ranks first among all Japanese companies with a rate of return of 5300 percent, Murata is fifth with 3250 percent, and Fanuc tenth with a rate of return of 2250 percent. All these companies are top-ranked in the annual Nihon Keizai Shimbun analysis of Japan's excellent companies. There are winners as well as losers in Japan's electronics industry. The winners are focused. Strategy, intelligently and steadily applied, does pay.

Nippon Electric Company: Paragon of redesign

The redesign of the very large, very diversified electronics companies has been a complex process, made much more difficult by acute financial problems and by the low-growth, deflationary economic environment in which the redesign had to take place. No company went through a more difficult period, and no company moved so drastically in redesign, than did NEC. NEC has long enjoyed a special position as main supplier to Japan's telecommunications utilities. From the early 1920s, it was a central company in the Sumitomo group of companies, technology leader in the group. It has been the pioneering company in Japan's computer industry. Like Toshiba and Fuji Electric, it was founded by a major foreign company, in NEC's case by International Western Electric, its long-time headquarters and Tokyo factory building a copy of Western Electric's Hawthorne plant.

More perhaps than any of the others of the nine diversified electronics companies, NEC became a deeply troubled company in serious danger by the late 1990s. A series of calamities struck the company. First was a scandal that broke in 1998, regarding knowingly overcharging the Japan Defense Agency for equipment supply. The long-time top executive of the company, Tadahiro Sekimoto, resigned as a result of the scandal. At the same time, a major US acquisition in Sekimoto's field of special interest, personal computers, began to fail. A $1 billion cash injection from NEC to keep the acquired Packard Bell going failed to fix the problems, a write-off of Packard Bell was necessary and due in part to this situation, NEC took a ¥224 billion pre-tax loss in fiscal 1999.

With only brief respite, NEC was hit next by the collapse of the world telecommunications equipment market following the massive excess investments in capacity during the IT bubble, joining Nortel, Lucent, and Alcatel in deep trouble in this business. At the same time, and related, the semiconductor business turned bleak. Thus, the two main sectors of NEC's total business suffered seriously. In fiscal 2002, NEC reported a pre-tax loss of ¥461 billion. Moreover, earnings through the period beginning in fiscal 1999 through fiscal 2003 were battered by massive restructuring charges and losses stemming from the new rule requiring that assets be marked to market. Extraordinary losses were ¥206 billion, ¥216 billion, ¥265 billion, ¥361 billion, and ¥137 billion, a total of about ¥1.1 trillion over the five years. That the company survived and is recovering is a tribute to a deep and brilliant redesign effort.

Nippon Electric Company has a long history. It was founded in 1899, the first US–Japan joint venture, with International Western Electric holding 54 percent of equity, Kunihiko Iwadare, who had been Western's Japan sales agent, holding most of the balance. The need for telecom equipment in Japan was considerable and Western Electric was holder of much of the key technology. Thus the venture was a welcome one, with early success. Western Electric increased its share to 64 percent in 1906. A real change in ownership took place in 1925 when, under orders from the US Supreme Court to withdraw from international investment, Western Electric sold its interest to International Telephone and Telegraph, a venture put together by Sosthenes Behn, which had major positions in Britain, Belgium, France, and Germany as well as Japan. The Western Electric patents could be obtained through purchase from IT&T so NEC, as it was then, continued to have access to Western Electric's technology.

By 1932, as Japan's military era began, Sumitomo increased its holding to 14 percent and took over direct management of Nippon Electric, moving its shareholding up as war with the United States neared to 46 percent in 1941. IT&T's shares were sequestered during the war, but in 1951 IT&T through its subsidiary International Standard Electric recovered 33 percent of Nippon Electric shares, along with a 15 percent position in Sumitomo Electric Industries, a producer of cable and wiring for telecom. Then in an excess of narrow-minded and short-term profit seeking, ISE sold off shares. As IT&T sold off its telecom business, NEC grew its sales from the mid-1950s to the turn of the century by 1400 times. Holding those shares would have made IT&T a world power in telecom – and the chance was lost for a quick gain on share sales around 1960!

Nippon Electric Company is for me a special case in a very personal sense. As I came to Japan in 1955 as a Ford Foundation Fellow to undertake a comparative study of industrial organization, I found Japanese university professors not at all welcoming. I had however by good chance a letter of introduction from the president of International Standard Electric, the father of a friend, to the then Nippon Electric President Toshihide Watanabe. He in turn arranged meetings, interviews, and factory visits, and most fortunately put me under the guidance of Koji Kobayashi, a marvelous man to whom I am obliged for the best teaching a young researcher might hope for. It was the first Japanese company that I studied, and the one I most admired and still feel most close to. It was then a company with sales of only $25 million, compared to the $40 billion of recent years, then of a size that made deep research – factory visits, questionnaires, extensive interviews – all not only possible but encouraged and aided by company management.

Dr Kobayashi had been wartime manager of the Kawasaki works of Nippon Electric and was made Director of the company as I began my studies. In 1964 he succeeded Mr Watanabe as President of the company, gaining special fame as author of the phrase "C and C," computers and communication, used first in a speech at MIT. Dr Kobayashi, a dedicated engineer, avoided political circles with some care and devoted his entire energies to building NEC to a great company. He was rated in surveys as the most admired of Japanese businessmen of his time, and deserved the rating.

His successor, Sekimoto, was a very different person. His career success had been in sales of the personal computer, in which NEC achieved dominant domestic market share. It was he who arranged the Packard Bell acquisition and in general drove for growth with little regard for focus or share dominance. Typical of the strategies of his era of leadership, NEC held largest world share of semiconductors in 1991, and was second only to Intel in 1995. By 2001 NEC was sixth in world share position, its semiconductor sales less than half the 1995 total. The cause is revealing. As the semiconductor business exploded in size and became in fact an agglomeration of different products and technologies, NEC chose to compete in all sectors of the industry, with a significant share position in none. Intel took aim at one segment of the total. Samsung took aim at still another segment. NEC specialized in none, and failed in all.

Following the resignation of Sekimoto, there was a brief interregnum, with an emerging consensus that drastic reorganization and redirection was required. To that end Koji Nishigaki, an economics major who was managing the systems-based solutions business, became president in 1999. The redesign of NEC began with a vengeance. The goals of the company were defined as that of becoming an IT-driven solutions provider, with broadband and mobile Internet operations the core strategic business areas. Internet-related fields were stated to be the key to NEC's sustained growth. The shift is similar to that of IBM, from a focus on hardware to a focus on software.

As Nishigaki took command, changes were rapid. The Packard Bell investment was written off, and the home appliance business of NEC, an inappropriate non-core by any measure, was closed down. The DRAM business was spun off into a joint venture with Hitachi. The number of Directors was halved, with three from outside the company. An in-house company system was set up with three autonomous businesses, NEC Solutions, NEC Networks, and NEC Electron Devices, one basic aim being to provide for faster decision-making. A management advisory committee of outside specialists was introduced. The headquarters building, an overdone monument to past glories, was sold.

The interest of NEC in Ando Electric was sold, as was its interest in Thomson SA of France, along with a refusal to participate in a refunding of the ailing Bull SA of France where NEC was a 17 percent shareholder. NEC sold factories in Oregon, Brazil, and Scotland along with three factories in Japan. It sold its laser printer business to Fuji Xerox, and its electronic control units operations to Honda. Its plasma display business went to Pioneer, and its printed circuit board business went to a joint venture with Toppan. It sold its stake in Samsung NEC Mobile Display Co., an organic electro-luminescence business, to its partner Samsung.

Internally, seven communications subsidiaries were consolidated into one company. Five computer-related subsidiaries were combined. It acquired four software companies in Japan and four in the United States – all small but specialized in the area that NEC is concentrating its efforts in. The shift in business mix was evident early, as software and services grew 13 percent annually from 1999 to 2001 while hardware revenues declined by 8 percent per year.

The move out of hardware manufacturing is reinforced by comparative costs. President Nishigaki said,

> Since labor costs in China are one-thirtieth those in Japan, we aim to use China for production and parts procurement. We transferred our entire PC motherboard production to China last year. We will continue to develop and produce cutting edge products in Japan, but we have no choice but to consign mass production to other countries.

Now in addition to its own production in China, NEC has begun sourcing products made by Chinese companies and is now selling routers and other devices for Internet access made by Huawei Technologies, China's largest communications device maker into the Japanese and other Asian markets.

The financial position of NEC, battered by massive losses from operations and from restructuring costs, has been undergoing emergency repairs and is still in hazard despite major efforts at strengthening the financial base. NEC's total assets under the expansive policies of the Sekimoto era nearly tripled from 1986 to 1996, investments greatly exceeding cash flow. NEC's debt-to-equity ratio, earlier just under 1 to 1, increased to 2.56:1.00 by the end of 1998, the increase in debt financing growth and covering losses as well. With the write-offs from the mark-to-market requirement in addition to restructuring costs causing huge losses in the 1999–2002 period, NEC's debt level exploded to a debt to equity ratio of over 4:1, with shareholder equity as a percent of total assets dropping below 10 percent, near enough to bankruptcy.

Efforts to counter the financial crisis were considerable. Fixed assets peaked in March, 1998, and were reduced by more than 40 percent as of March 2003. Total debt was reduced from the March 1998 peak by 37 percent, with bank borrowings down nearly 60 percent and commercial bonds down only 15 percent. In order to stem the drain on equity, and in an effort to rebuild the equity position, NEC took five of its fast growth businesses out in IPOs, retaining full control but cashing in just under a third of the shares. And in its largest effort, what had been the in-house company, NEC Electron Devices, was taken public with great success – and again NEC retained a controlling share position while realizing a gain of ¥155 billion. By issuing new shares in 2003, debt was further reduced as the sale of shares totaled ¥249 billion. In a further effort to strengthen the balance sheet, NEC passed its 2003 dividend payment although the dividend payment resumed in fiscal 2004.

Has all this worked? Certainly there has been a strengthening. The debt to equity ratio, still very high at 3.5 to 1.0 was down from its peak. Shareholder equity as a percent of assets was still low, but rising. Operating income more than doubled and net profit was up 15 times on the year. The balance sheet remained weak but all the signs and trends were up. Assume a reasonably positive economic environment and continued strategic focus, and it appears that NEC is in fact recovering from its self-inflicted and near-fatal financial illness and regaining the strength that has characterized its century-long history.

Personnel management inevitably was caught up in the need to tighten and rationalize. NEC had in 1946 established a system to encourage and reward long service. After 20 and 30 years of continuous service, the employee received special holiday time and a gift of money. This system was ended and instead, on reaching 30, 40, and 50 years of age, the company will provide five to ten days for "career support" studies, and at age 50, providing as well financing for post-retirement career planning. Nishigaki stated, "Employees must hone their skills in preparation for any number of job changes in the course of their careers. We have implemented an in-house personnel placement system designed to shift resources to growth areas. Employees must study on their own and acquire skills needed to change positions." In addition, overtime payments were reduced from 150 percent of regular pay to the legal minimum of 125 percent, and the company contribution for stock purchases was reduced.

On the whole, however, NEC has not attempted to solve its financial problems at the expense of employees in the Western manner. Total staff peaked in the mid-1990s and is down 7 percent since 1995, a rather small change in numbers of staff given all the changes in the company structure. There has been a sharp increase in the number of staff shukkoed – transferred – to subsidiaries, now nearly a quarter of total staff. The number of new hires continues to decline, while part time and temporary staff numbers have increased. Average age of both male and female workers has increased, most sharply among the 20 percent of staff who are female. Of special interest given the "life time employment" concept is the fact that average job tenure continues to increase, from 8 to 15 years for men and from 5 to 11 for women over the period from 1975 to the present.

The employment system that I was encouraged to study around the mid-1950s has changed rather little. The deep commitment to those who make up the company remains intact.

With the present under control, what of the future? The future for NEC as for the economy as a whole depends in large part on successes in research and development. NEC's commitment to R&D is great, with 6–7 percent of sales devoted to research and development annually. Despite what must have been a real temptation, the research budget was not cut even during the most severe period of financial problems. The company holds more than 68,000 patents, the largest number of any Japanese company. The NEC-developed supercomputer remains first in the world, still beyond the capacity of US makers to build.

Nippon Electric Company is considered the leader in the hot research field of nanotechnology and has been the pioneer in research into carbon nanotubes – discovered by Sumio Iijima of NEC – with more than 100 related patents. The company has announced that researchers in their 30s will be appointed as chief researchers in a bid to further activate research operations. Interestingly, the first employee to be so promoted while before reaching 40 years is Ms Kazue Sako – another indication of the increased role of women in NEC affairs.

However, NEC has been slow to realize income from its intellectual property. It has now established a department to oversee intellectual assets, planning to sell unused patents, to pursue firms that are violating its patents, and maximize royalty income from the licensing of its technology. Although NEC has the second-largest number of registered patents in the United States, following IBM, it obtained licensing income of only ¥10 billion in 2002 compared with IBM's $1 billion. NEC aims to increase that cash flow to ¥50 billion by 2006.

So the redesign of NEC has largely been completed, a company with a long and distinguished history, a rare background of foreign ownership, long the leader in telecommunications and computers. It will be leader again, this time in new technologies and in Internet-related software and services. The past few years have been dangerously difficult, but NEC has weathered the storm, an excellent example of how the electronic companies of Japan have faced up to and largely solved their problems of the late 1990s.

Redesign II: Making too many a competitive few

High growth rates make room for many competitors in a business. Japan's long sustained high growth left a great many industries with a very large number of companies, many in fact low share and high cost, marginal in the business. As growth slows and demand drops, investment tends to continue with resulting overcapacity. Consolidation is required. It can be done through bankruptcy. It also can be done by constructive combinations of firms.

In the words of the Bank of Japan,

> The industry that stands out most vividly in terms of consolidation of its excess capital is the materials industry. With domestic demand trending down and the pressures from international competition ever mounting, (companies) have been facing an inevitable deterioration in profitability and a chronically low capacity utilization rate... Over the course of the last few years, however, there has been an increasing degree of consolidation, with a substantial rise in the market share of the largest two or three firms in each industry.[4]

The problem was clear enough: too many producers in scale-driven businesses with major global competitors. Solution to the problem: mergers to achieve greater scale and efficiency. The process began in the mid-1990s – more evidence that the realization of the restructuring requirement began at that time. Much of the consolidation has now been completed.

The *oil* industry has gone from a total of 14 companies in petroleum refining and distribution to the current total of 4 – and Idemitsu, the fourth in the industry has serious problems. Nippon Oil after the merger with Mitsubishi Oil has a dominant 36 percent market share.

The *cement* industry has gone from seven major producers to three with a few small companies still independent. The three majors have a total share position of 82 percent, with the leader, Taiheiyo, holding a 38 percent share. Note too that the cement majors all have substantial production and trading position in East Asia, including China, Taiwan, Hong Kong, Indonesia, and Malaysia.

The *pulp and paper* industry, like oil, had a grand total of 14 companies, with consolidation beginning in 1993 and accelerating greatly in 1999, combining into three companies after all the mergers. While there are small producers still, the top two companies in pulp and paper, Oji and Unipac, together hold half the market.

The *industrial gas* industry, more supplier to the materials industries than a materials industry itself, went from a total of seven companies to three today. In industrial gases as in petroleum, a foreign-owned company is a survivor of all the merger activities – Air Liquide and British Oxygen-owned Osaka Sanso merged and are one of the three industrial gas competitors just as Shell and ExxonMobil remain majors in the petroleum industry.

The *steel* industry had five basic steel producers and was on its way to two. Kawasaki Steel and NKK merged through a holding company system into JFE, and Nippon Steel looked like combining with Kobe Steel and Sumitomo Metals. But pride and improved prosperity intervened and while there has been some combining – Nippon Steel and Sumitomo Metals in stainless steel for example – the industry still has four main producers.

Even the *sugar* industry is combining, as Mitsui interests put together three sugar producers with a combined share of 23 percent. We can assume more combines will be arranged in this industry too.

Merging as a way of dealing with too many producers has not been confined to the combinations of entire companies. The chemical industry no doubt would benefit from corporate mergers, and there have been a few, but the long-planned combination of Sumitomo Chemical and Mitsui Chemical into a world-scale company broke down at the last moment in a dispute over share values. Japan still has no really large-scale chemical company although in its core businesses Shin-etsu Chemical has major world market share. What has happened in the chemical industry however is the combining of product divisions rather than the merging of entire companies. The case of polystyrene is notable; there were eight producers until 1997 and now there are only four, a notable success in achieving greater scale of production in a specific product category.

Restructuring a mature industry: The case of steel

The steel industry of Japan is undergoing a major restructuring to improve profitability while holding position as world leader. It is an outstanding example of the degree to which Japanese companies are reorganizing and preparing for a more competitive future, even in what is often considered an industry doomed to decline as the economy matures.

The steel industry has been the prototype of Japan's industrialization. Its successes – and subsequent problems – display many of the special features of Japanese industrial structure. Government played a major role in much of the industry's history. Foreign technology was eagerly sought and very rapidly introduced. Postwar growth of the industry took output from virtually nothing to world leadership. Market share patterns and pricing practices invited accusations of cartel arrangements. And US complaints of unfair trade practices by Japan's steel producers have, for well over 30 years, been a standard feature of the steel industry landscape, from "export restraints" of the late 1960s to the punitive Bush tariffs on steel imports of the past few years.

The growth of the steel industry following World War II was spectacular. The wartime submarine blockade – not bombing – had turned the industry off by war's end. In 1946 steel output was only a half-million tons, down from 7 million tons in 1940. Prewar output levels were regained by 1952, thanks in good part to steel being designated a priority production industry with special access to capital and to raw material imports, and to Korean War related orders as well. In the 20 years from 1952 to peak production in 1972–73, crude steel output increased 17 times to nearly 120 million tons. Steel output in the ensuing 30 years has declined hardly at all. Annual output of 100 million tons has been maintained, with production in 2003 around 110 million tons. Japan's steel output is about 12 percent of the world total, second in volume only to China's fragmented and largely unsophisticated industry.

The continued high level of steel production is the more surprising since in a highly developed economy like Japan's material industries are expected to be in decline. Witness the collapse of British steel companies and the general bankruptcy of players in the US industry. Japan's industry has invested heavily in research, and moved its output steadily up the value-added chain to ever more specialized grades of steel for the electronics and auto industries. Total output has been steadily constant at a high level; the quality of the output has steadily advanced.

Much is made abroad of the importance to Japan of steel exports. Not the case. The continued high level of crude steel production is not due to increases in exports. On the contrary, steel exports as a percent of total production peaked in the mid-1970s, and have been about 30 percent of output in recent years. Loud and continuing US complaints not withstanding, East Asia is very much the most important market for Japanese steel exports. For some years now, more than three-quarters of exports are to Asia, and only about 10 percent of total exports go to the United States and Europe combined.

China is not the critical market for steel exports, over-excited news reports to the contrary not withstanding. By a good margin, the industry's largest export market is South Korea, itself the site of what may well be the world's low-cost steel producer, Posco. And Korea is in turn the largest exporter of steel to Japan. Japan's industry is no longer competitive in some standard grades of carbon steel, much coming now from Korea, but Japanese producers are unmatchable in steel at the highest levels of value-added products. Thus the electronics and auto industries of East Asia depend on Japan's producers for sophisticated grades of steel. As a footnote to the export issue, Japan makers export about three times more steel to Taiwan than to the United States, while Taiwan is the second largest source of Japanese steel imports. (US makers seem not to export steel to Japan.)

However, from the early 1970s, the industry has been under pressure, met first by cost and capacity reductions, next by diversification adventures, and finally from the mid-1990s by thoroughgoing restructuring. Domestic demand for steel has been slowly declining as Japanese companies invest in offshore production. Pressures on export sales increase as tariffs in the United States increase and China periodically places "safeguard" limits on imports. Key customers like autos are consolidating and look to low-cost competitors like Posco for low-priced supply. Effective capacity in the Japanese industry is rated at 125 million tons indicating a need to reduce capacity. The merged European steel company, Arcelor, has become the world's largest steel producer with still another European combination, LNM, now probably number two in the world of steel. All of this requires that the industry in Japan consolidate and rationalize facilities to achieve lower costs and the cash flows necessary to continue as industry leaders.

The steel industry has long had five integrated producers. Of them, Nippon Steel has been at the center of the stage in the steel dramas of the past century. It began operations as the government controlled Yawata Steel Works, not the first but very soon the largest of Japan's emerging steel operations. Yawata became the core entity in Japan Iron and Steel (Nihon Seitetsu) in the mid-1930s, with just over 50 percent of total production in 1945. The other four companies that are now major integrated producers – NKK, Kawasaki, Sumitomo Metals, and Kobe Steel – made up the balance. However, the postwar Deconcentration Law led to the breakup of Japan Seitetsu into two companies, Fuji Seitetsu and Yawata Seitetsu. The freeing up of competition meant that by 1970, when Fuji and Yawata were recombined into Nippon Steel Corporation, their combined share was 36 percent while the four other integrated producers held a total of 43 percent of crude steel output, and other producers, mainly electric furnace works subsidiary to the majors, held the balance of some 20 percent of output.

With the industrial crisis that followed after the oil shocks of 1973–74, it became clear that there would be no further growth in the total steel industry, and that company survival depended on capacity and cost reductions – and on careful controls of prices and of market shares. For the three decades following, Nippon Steel Corporation orchestrated a slow decline in its market share along with remarkable stability of share of the other majors. NKK stayed at about 11 percent, Kawasaki and Sumitomo at about 10 percent, and Kobe at about 6 percent as NSC went from 36 to 26 percent and electric furnace steel increased in share to around a third of crude output.

To deal with excess capacity and to reduce overall costs, NSC announced in 1978 its "First Modernization Plan," aimed to take capacity down from 47 to 36 million tons in only two years. Closures began and increased in scope steadily over the next ten years, with two subsequent modernization plans. Nine blast furnaces were shut down by NSC alone, with the industry total number doing from 38 to 25. Profits improved and industry confidence recovered.

This recovery was unfortunate in some respects. It coincided with the rise in the mid-1980s of Japan's "bubble economy." Instead of simply enjoying an improved steel business, NSC led the way into a frenzy of diversification signaled by its 1987 "First Medium Term Business Plan" and the establishment of such entities as the Electronics and Information Systems Division, the New Materials Division, the Life Service Business Division, and even a Biotechnology Business Division. Somewhere in all this NSC even established a retail catalogue division for mail order sale of sundries. Urban development and building construction businesses followed in establishment. In short, NSC (and its fellow integrated steel producers) indulged in an orgy of diversification – not in fact unlike the disastrous course of the major electronics companies.

Before evaluating the consequences of diversification from steel in the late 1980s, it is useful to look first at the steel business itself over the years. In 1970, when Fuji and Yawata merged into Nippon Steel Corporation, total employees in their combined steel operations numbered 79,000. The several "modernization plans" resulted in a reduction of steel employees to 61,000, and through continuing programs to improve productivity by 2002 the number of workers in steel at NSC was only 17,000. Over a 30-year period, steel employment was reduced in the company by more than three-quarters – yet steel output in 2002 was greater than output in the early 1970s. Production was up by a fifth and employment down to nearly one-fifth of those early levels. Labor costs, long about 13 percent of total costs, dropped to about 8 percent for NSC and for its Japan competitors as well.

In keeping with the "lifetime commitment" of Japanese employment, this reduction in workforce was accomplished without summary dismissals or mass discharge. Indeed, in 2002, average years of continuous service were 22.0 years for males and 14.0 years for females, nearly twice the national average. In an industry with little or no growth, and thus with no need for new hires, the workforce average age increases nearly one year each year. One consequence, overlooked in much of the discussion of the lifetime employment system, is that workforce aging and normal retirement allow a steady decline in the number of employees without resorting to dismissals. Workforce adjustment is largely automatic, a function of natural aging, of closing the front door and opening the back door of the company.

However, the reduction in numbers of steel workers in NSC was due to not only natural attrition but also the practice of reassigning workers from the steel operations of the parent company to subsidiary and affiliated organizations – shukko. Limited in the 1970s, there was a very great increase in the number of workers shukkoed in the mid 1980s as NSC launched into extensive diversification with a huge increase in the number of subsidiaries and affiliates. From 1985 to 2001, consolidated subsidiaries increased from 3 to 254 and those accounted for by equity method from 17 to 87, a total increase of 17 times in 16 years.

This extraordinary increase was driven largely by diversification programs. However, from the point of view of steel employment, these subsidiaries and affiliates provided employment berths for redundant steel workers. Shukkoed workers reached a total of nearly 15,000 by the early 1990s. Shukko, a traditional practice, provides a way of living up to the basic social contract – the commitment of employment – but is a way of doing so at a lesser cost since wage increases and benefits tend to be less in smaller subsidiaries than in the parent company.

Along with continuing respect for the social contract with the workforce, other key elements of employment practices were maintained as well. The seniority system of increased pay with increased length of service continues to age 60 and mandatory retirement. NSC now rehires certain workers and extends their employment to age 62.

Benefits include housing – the company maintains 14,000 houses for employees plus apartments and dormitories for more than 5000 persons. There is a company loan system for house purchase by employees, and a loan system in support of children's education. Continuous service of 15 years earns a travel coupon and 10 special holidays; 30 years earns a more generous travel coupon and another 10 special holidays. All the stresses of low growth and drastic restructuring have not damaged NSC's value system.

Most of the extensive diversification moves of the 1980s, seemingly doing well while the bubble period lasted, turned to failures as the economy entered a long period of very low growth and sustained price deflation. From a peak in 1989–90, sales and profits went into sharp decline. By 1993, all five integrated steel companies were losing money and, with the exception of NSC which cut capacity faster and farther, all lost money again in 1994. The crisis was well and truly on them.

Nippon Steel Corporation's new businesses were largely in trouble. As an example, a heavy commitment to semiconductor manufacture ended with the sale of Nippon Steel Semiconductor Corporation to Taiwan's United Microelectronics in 1998, NSC absorbing a considerable loss on the sale. A final exit from the sector was made with the sale to Wacker-Chemie in 2003 of NSC's 45 percent interest in a joint silicon wafer manufacturing joint venture. Still another and more successful venture was a systems integration business, NS Solutions Corporation, which was taken out on an IPO with NSC still holding a majority position. The diversification era is drawing to a close.

Total employment by NSC peaked in 1975 at 75,000 with steel employment less than half of the total and dropping sharply. As new ventures have been abandoned, total employment has declined, but even in 2002, two-thirds of NSC's 50,000 employees are in subsidiaries, only a fourth in steel production. However, most subsidiary activity now is steel-related, in fabrication, finishing, trading, and finance. The focus is on steel. There remains however a considerable position in urban development with extensive land holdings. The drop in land prices requires taking a major loss as book value prices are slashed. Land and housing prices are key to dealing with this chunk of diversification.

Table 2.1 compares the performance of the four integrated producers now with what were in 1989–90 five integrated producers. Total assets and total production levels now are similar to those in the peak year of fiscal 1989. With price declines, total sales are down 12 percent from the peak and operating profit down 17 percent compared with the industry's best year. Clearly, the redesign of these companies has been a success with the industry very nearly back to its peak performance.

There had long been a view in the industry that five integrated producers could not all survive indefinitely. In a study of the industry for an Australian client, we found a general conclusion that the five would go to three over the coming decade, with Kobe Steel and NKK seen as weakest and most likely to merge or be acquired. In fact, the process began earlier than expected. With the abolition of the anti-holding company act, a relatively healthy Kawasaki Steel joined with NKK to create JFE Holdings, now one of the world's five largest steel companies along with Arcelor and LNM of Europe, NSC and Posco of South Korea. JFE is about the size of NSC, has moved fast to rationalize operations after the merger, and is now rather more profitable than NSC, highly regarded in the stock market.

Partly in response to the JFE development and its competitive threat, NSC entered into discussions of various arrangements with Kobe Steel and with Sumitomo Metal Industries. In our meeting with him, the then NSC President Akira Chihaya told us of his proposal that Kobe Steel, a considerably diversified firm, spin out its steel business in which NSC would then invest (and presumably in time integrate into NSC itself). Kobe has not agreed to the proposal, at least not yet, but the two companies have some joint supply activities and modest shareholdings. Sumitomo Metals has also been a merger candidate, and agreement was

Table 2.1 The steel majors now compared with their FY1989 peak

	FY1989	FY2003	Difference (%)
Assets	¥12,617 billion	¥11,460 billion	−9
Production	110 million tons	112 million tons	+2
Employees	137,900	92,400	−33
Sales	¥8,767 billion	¥7,670 billion	−12
Recurring profit	¥576 billion	¥480 billion	−17

Source: Nihon Keizai Shimbun, 5 March 2004.

reached in 2002 to combine their stainless steel and welding materials businesses. Again, there have been modest share investments by both in the other. Finally, NSC is now the largest shareholder, with 9.5 percent of outstanding shares, in a sixth but lesser steel producer specializing in stainless steel and reporting substantial losses in recent years.

The timing of a final configuration of the steel industry is not easy to predict. The move has been toward integration into a single entity of Kobe's steel operations and much of Sumitomo Metals along with NSC, bringing the total in Japan of integrated operators down to two from the traditional five. Perhaps the industry's current successes are the cause of a delay in these developments. A renewed period of industry trouble would no doubt speed a final restructuring that seems now remote.

Worldwide oligopolistic trends both in suppliers to the industry and customers of the industry dictate further consolidation. In recent years, mergers of iron ore suppliers have led to three companies holding a 75 percent share of world capacity, a formidable concentration when ore prices are being negotiated. In the key customer category of auto-makers, eight companies have moved to a 67 percent world share of output, with resulting pressure on prices.

In contrast and at disadvantage, NSC, Posco, and JFE each account for 3 percent or so of world steel production, with Arcelor, the largest company in the industry, holding only 5 percent of world output. Consolidation is required in simple self-defence to deal effectively with suppliers and key customers.

The arena in which NSC's future will be decided is Asia. Exports to North America and Europe are only a tenth of total exports, a mere 3 percent of total output. The key customer category in North America and Europe is the auto industry, the more so now that Japanese auto producers are shifting production to those countries. NSC has dealt with the issue of steel for autos with a joint venture with Ispat Inland in the United States and an agreement with Usinor of France, now part of Arcelor. These cover those flanks adequately, while East Asia becomes the main concern. Industry exports to East Asia are 20–25 percent of total production. And the importance of East Asia is increasing rapidly as Japanese production moves there and as the region becomes factory to the world.

In terms of steel production, East Asia divides into two. Integrated steel production is entirely in the Northeast, in Korea (Posco), Taiwan (China Steel) and mainland China. China is the world's largest steel-producing country with some 70 crude steel producers, arguably the world's least efficient. The China leader is Baoshan Iron and Steel of Shanghai, with about 20 million tons of output, which has already a tie-up with Thyssen Krupp of Germany to produce stainless sheet. NSC has negotiated a joint venture with Baoshan to produce steel sheet for autos in an effort to circumvent Chinese "safeguards" against steel imports.

The main player in Asia outside Japan is Posco. NSC has been involved with Posco from that company's beginning since the engineering of both Posco's original plant and subsequent expansion was by NSC's engineering division. The two companies have minor share interests in each other, and there is a "strategic cooperation" agreement between the two signed in 2000. The two companies are beginning joint procurement of parts for their mills and are considering joint purchasing of coal and other raw materials to increase negotiating leverage as coal and ore supplies merge.

A Posco executive said, "By tieing up with NSC, we can stabilize the Asian market and mutually achieve growth." A former NSC executive adds, "If we build an alliance of Asia's big four – NSC, Posco, Baoshan and China Steel, we can put in place a controlling position in Asia's market."[5] There are echoes in that of NSC's cartel history. Still, an alliance is possible. NSC engineered Baoshan and has close relations with that company. Sumitomo Metals has a joint venture in Japan with China Steel. Posco and NSC are much involved with each other. Perhaps an alliance of sorts could be negotiated.

The economies of Southeast Asia do not now, and will not for a long time still, warrant investment in integrated steel production. The front end capital costs are very great and the size of market to justify economic scale of production is not yet there. However, NSC already has investments in three joint ventures in Thailand, with its major auto production operations, as well as an investment in Indonesia. The steel game in East Asia will be an interesting one, and one unlikely to have non-Asian players in significant position in it.

The Nippon Steel story remains a fascinating one. The company is in all respects the most powerful steel producer in Asia and one of the leaders in the world, standing squarely in the middle of the world's fastest growing steel market. NSC will remain a world leader as the Asian game plays out.

Thinning over-populated service sectors

While the economic advantages of consolidation in the materials industries are very clear, these are by no means the only sectors in the economy that are over-populated with the numbers now being diminished through mergers – and in some cases through bankruptcy. Ekonomisuto magazine reviews the *banking* sector and finds that an original total of 22 major banks has been reduced to 7. Mergers are not new to banking. Sanwa Bank, now part of UFJ, was itself the result of long-ago merger. Daiichi and the Kangyo Bank merged in 1971, and Taiyo and Kobe in 1973. However, the big wave of banking mergers began in the 1990s and reached a climax in 2001 when four dominant bank groups were created – Mizuho, Sumitomo Mitsui, Mitsubishi Tokyo, and UFJ. Risona, Mitsui Trust and Sumitomo Trust are the three others. In addition, two bankrupted government banks were taken over by foreign investors, while Hokkaido Takushoku bankrupted and disappeared.

The merger of the Sumitomo and Sakura (formerly Mitsui) Banks, centers of the two Japanese business groups of longest history and great power is of special significance. The Sumitomo interests began in 1590 in Kyoto and shortly after in Osaka while the Mitsui zaibatsu dates from the opening of a shop in Tokyo, then Edo, in 1673. Sumitomo interests have generally focused on mining and manufacturing, with a family law that frowned on trading. Mitsui began in retailing and its trading company pre-World War II had the world's greatest sales volume, while the group was especially active in textiles.

I have not been given, nor yet found in publications, a thorough statement of how these two groups managed to merge some of their interests. There are stories of some, rather minor, financial and family links in the past. It is even argued that they could combine since one is Kanto-centered and the other Kansai-centered, with no regional rivalry between them – a very Japanese view of merger issues.

In any case, the two banks combined, Sumitomo being the stronger of the two and dominant in the relationship. Since, Mitsui-Sumitomo Construction has come into existence, and the two groups' casualty insurance companies have merged. As noted, an attempt at merging the chemical interests did not come off, but it seems likely that there will be further combinations across the two groups given the important role of the combined bank in group company affairs.

The *insurance* industry has gone through major reorganization as the collapse of asset values and the dropping of the interest rate to zero put the life insurance industry of Japan, committed to returns on annuity type policies, through a surge of bankruptcies and near bankruptcies. Foreign insurance companies moved in and acquired the failures at distress prices and moved the foreign share of the business in Japan to nearly 20 percent. Insurance companies have combined as well, since with deregulation casualty and life insurance can be handled by the same firm. Using the holding company umbrella, combinations have become frequent and the process continues.

Retailing too is going through some consolidation although there are still 1.4 million retail shops, half with one or two employees and owned by individuals in the classic mom-and-pop store pattern. The Bank of Japan listed M&A in retailing in 2002 and found 16 significant cases involving department stores, supermarkets, and convenience stores for the most part. Half involved bankruptcy or near bankruptcy, and one involved the purchase of Seiyu shares by Wal-Mart. Tesco made an acquisition in 2003, and Germany's Metro is also in the Japan game now. (France's Carrefour entered but later sold out and fled Japan after only a few years.) With these powerful foreign entrants making major investments, we can expect consolidation of retailing to accelerate in the near future.

Bankruptcy, curiously, has played a very minor role in all this restructuring and consolidation. Given the several years of deflation and generally severe economic environment, bankruptcies in both numbers and scale might be expected to reach new extremes. In fact, the historic peak in numbers of bankruptcies was in 1984 with a total of nearly 21,000 cases. The year 2002 nearly reached that level with 19,500 cases, but by 2003 the number had fell back rather sharply. Bankruptcies are high in number in the past few years but are only at levels reached earlier in the mid-1970s and mid-1980s.

There is a difference from earlier years in the amount of liabilities of bankrupted companies however. A historic peak was reached in 2000, when the liabilities totaled an enormous ¥23 trillion, with liabilities per bankruptcy nearly ¥1.3 billion. The amount of liabilities per bankruptcy sharply increased in 1991 as the bubble period ended and rose steadily to the 2000 peak. However, the total has since fallen to less than half of the peak, with individual bankruptcy liabilities in the last few years around ¥700 million, a rather small amount it would seem.

The huge total of liabilities in 2000 was due almost entirely to bankruptcies in the financial sector, due mainly to two very large insurance company bankruptcies in that year. Foreign investors bought both of these. Overall, bankruptcies occur mainly in the construction industry and in retail and wholesale distribution. As in all economies, these are low entry cost businesses with low exit costs, with bankruptcy an attractive exit mechanism. Over 60 percent of Japan's bankruptcies are in these sectors with very few in finance, a small proportion in real estate companies, and about 20 percent manufacturing companies.

However, the average liabilities of manufacturing bankruptcies are only ¥4 to ¥5 million per case. The conclusion is that many bankruptcies involve mostly small businesses, with an occasional large company bankrupting. Bankruptcies are not a significant factor in industrial restructuring.

Redesign III: Industries in crisis

Among the numerous false impressions of Japan, its economy and its companies, a persistent error is the view that the systems are rigid, that Japan's is a society and economy in which little changes. The view is the more surprising given the very great differences in income, output, and wealth since the mid-1950s. Obviously, to move to so large an economy with so high a standard of living there must be a very great shift in the economic structure from low technology, labor intensive, low value-added industries common to less developed economics to high value-added, high-technology industries requiring high levels of capital investment.

The shift in the case of Japan has been rapid. Perhaps the most dramatic example of industrial change is coal mining. Japan has few natural resources in any abundance. Coal is an exception. But Japan's coal is of low BTU content, and is difficult to mine.

Nonetheless as I was first studying Japan, the coal mining industry was the nation's largest industrial employer, with 374,000 employees at its 1957 peak. There were then 864 working coalmines in Japan. As of 2002, there were no coal miners and no active coalmines. Imported coal, LNG, and petroleum, cheaper and more effective, took the place of high-cost, low-quality domestic coal. There are few if any parallels in world economic history to industrial change of this magnitude and speed.

Much has been made in the academic literature of the high cost of government policies aimed at dealing with the decline of coal mining. With characteristic 20:20 hindsight, policies are critiqued and the role of management in the process ignored as government is the focus. A typical view is,

> The decades of continuous public policy support for coal mining were clearly the result of industrial policies. Given the strong political ties enjoyed by the firms in the industry and the strong voice of labor, policy makers were compelled to capitulate to the industry's political demands. As Samuels sums up, "The political benefits of providing unlimited state subsidies to coal producers seemed always to outweigh the staggering economic costs."[6]

One wonders how the industry managed to close down! The accuracy of academic hindsight is extraordinary.

However, not all academics take so negative a view. One concludes after a close study of the coal mining experience, "Japan's industrial policy for depressed industries fulfills all the market-oriented theorists' criteria for the correct response to restructuring. In addition, it follows OECD guidelines, provides a comprehensive package of assistance, and is given all-around high marks by most policy analysts."[7]

There has of course been in the case of coal mining and others of declining industries an active part played by government, using tariff devices, subsidies, and other means to ease the pains of transition. And no doubt there is waste in the process on many occasions. But all of this is hardly peculiar to Japan and indeed there is good evidence that Japan has managed more skillfully than most. Has any other nation managed the process as quickly or as thoroughly? Mrs Thatcher should have been so fortunate.

The cotton spinning industry is a case of the industrial restructuring driven by the shift to higher value-added, less labor intensive industries as Japan became an economic power. Cotton spinning has a long and important history in Japan. Like most developing countries, Japanese companies found entry to cotton spinning relatively easy technologically, and with low wage levels, made even lower by extensive use of young, unmarried women, Japan's cotton spinning industry thrived. In 1950 Toyo Boseki, now Toyobo, was Japan's largest manufacturing company followed closely by Kanegafuchi Boseki, now Kanebo, and Kurashiki Boseki, now Kurabo. While textiles dropped below half of total sales for Kanebo in 1991, it was not until 2001 that textiles were less than half of the sales of Toyobo, a stubborn survivor. Through its long period of industry change, it is a proud boast of Toyobo's management that no one was fired while the labor force shrank – all adjustments were through re-assignments, retirements, and transfers.

Cotton spinning employment peaked in 1952, with 111,000 employees in a total of 122 companies. By 2000, employment had dropped to 7400 workers in 30 companies – and the decline of course continues. As recently as 1965, imports of cotton goods were only 0.2 percent of consumption. Japan is now one of the world's largest textile importers, with nearly 90 percent of cotton goods imported. In terms of the government's role in all this change, "Despite the well-publicized interventions by MITI in Japan's economic direction, I find that industry rather than government played the major role in the restructuring of the textile industry."[8] Here as in much else, the role of Japan's government is often made the center of analysis, while it is in fact corporate management who are the key movers.

These are examples of constructive change, change that makes for reallocation of labor and capital resources to higher value-added sectors in order that economic growth might continue. The case of aluminum smelting however is one where a capital intensive industry went into sudden decline in what must be seen as an economic misfortune. As background, aluminum smelting became a major growth sector for Japan's chemical companies in the late 1960s. I remember meeting with the then president of Sumitomo Chemical during that time to discuss corporate strategy and Mr Norishige Hasegawa held forth at some length on how important aluminum smelting would be in his company's future. His enthusiasm was shared by Mitsubishi Kasei and Showa Denko, along with Alcan-related Nippon Light Metal. Japanese companies took their smelting capacity to more than 1,600,000 tons, about 12 percent of total world capacity, all of this in new and capital intensive facilities.

Alumina and aluminum are sometimes termed "canned electricity," since electricity is the largest single-cost component in bauxite smelting. Japan has had for a long time very high electricity costs. But the oil shocks of 1973 and after, with petroleum a main source of electricity in Japan, drove electricity costs to a level about four times that in the United States and perhaps ten times that of Canada where hydropower is widely available. By 1978 industry and government announced capacity reduction targets with a stockpiling plan, tariff refunds and exemptions, and an authorized production cartel in an effort to limit the damage to the industry. Companies saw the inevitable earlier and had already in 1976 restructured by spin-offs to minimize the damage to the parent company and began investing heavily in overseas projects as future sources of alumina.

By 1988, the game was over. Japan's domestic aluminum smelting industry had shut down. Capacity went from 1.6 million tons to 10,000 tons as one smelter using captive hydropower remained in operation. Industry employees went from 9500 to about 500 in the single operating smelting plant. Overseas investments went mainly to Indonesia, Australia, Venezuela, Brazil, and North America and by the mid-1990s were the source of a third of ingot imports, the balance divided between spot imports and long-term contract imports.

I remember a dinner meeting with Mr Nichiro Amaya, the brilliant head of planning at MITI, during the aluminum crisis period. He argued that Japan must retain 350,000 tons of smelting capacity for strategic reason, so as not to be over-dependent on imports from what might be unstable supplying nations. Despite MITI's best efforts, the industry disappeared. Governments do not prevail over economics. They might choose to delay the effects of economics, but they cannot stop the process.

Of these and other earlier restructurings of industries, perhaps the closest parallel to the challenges of the 1990s was the situation of the shipbuilding industry in the late 1970s. Japan had become the leading shipbuilding nation by the early 1970s, its share of world output equal to the combined share of Europe's traditional shipbuilding nations. However, the global demand for ships declined sharply with the oil shocks and by 1978 was only 10 percent of the 1973 level. Prices were forced down to below cost as builders fought to keep their facilities operating. Industry and government together set a target of 35 percent reduction in total capacity, with reductions steepest for the largest companies, the seven majors. Capacity cuts continued, with all manner of government assistance with special programs of re-training and support for displaced workers. Shipbuilding employment went from 137,000 in 1975 when the restructuring began to 53,000 by 1989 and the number of shipbuilders from 104 to 26 over the same period. Some companies, like Mitsubishi Heavy Industries, were reasonably diversified. Shipbuilding's collapse hurt but was not fatal. Others like Mitsui Shipbuilding and Hitachi Zosen were very heavily dependent on shipbuilding and were through very hard times indeed with several years of major losses. All survived however until recent mergers, noted below. As this and other earlier restructuring cases are considered, it needs to be remembered that these were years of high overall economic growth and low unemployment, making restructuring a good deal less painful that it became in the low growth, higher unemployment 1990s.

With all the world industry problems through the late 1970s and through the 1980s, Japan's industry was able to hold and improve world position, with a 53 percent share in 1985 while Europe's share halved and Korea began to emerge as a factor. One author describes the changes.

Competition between shipbuilding countries has always been there... The European countries led the way in the beginning and it is hard to believe that the UK once built 80 percent of the world's new merchant ship tonnage. By the mid-1950s Japan, through the strenuous efforts of its shipbuilder and their dedicated work forces, took the lead... and remained the leader for some 35 years. Then came Korea, with huge new shipyards, cheaper, and it seemed unlimited labour to challenge the Japanese position. Today we can see China beginning to go down that same road as a challenge to Korea, as that huge country's industrialization begins to gather pace.[9]

In fact, Japan and Korea have been trading first and second share positions for some years, with Japan having a higher share of new shipbuilding than Korea in 2001 and 2002, with Korea taking first place again in 2003. However, Japan's shipbuilding majors reported a tripling of orders in 2003 to a 30-year high, the best year since the 1973 crisis. The China rise is a real change however, its share of world shipbuilding going from a mere 2 percent in 1998 to 11 percent in 2003. Japanese companies are helping the China process; Kawasaki Shipbuilding for example is 50 percent shareholder in a shipbuilding joint venture in Jiangsu Province. Interestingly, the three Asian majors in 2003 accounted for over 90 percent of total world new shipbuilding – and help each nation's steel industry greatly in the process.

Despite greatly improved market conditions, the industry continues to reorganize. Hitachi Zosen and NKK combined their shipbuilding divisions into a new venture, Universal Shipbuilding. Sumitomo Heavy Industries spun off its shipbuilding division, now Sumitomo Marine Engineering. The shipbuilding division of IHI and the warship division of Sumitomo Heavy became IHI Marine United. The seven majors are now six, and no doubt there will be further consolidation in the coming years.

These many industry restructurings provide a vivid reminder that Japan's is a highly dynamic economy with a long history of reorganization industries and redesigning companies. Indeed, that is a requirement for a successful economy to develop and to continue to be successful. The process is less difficult when growth is high, offering both corporate management and the labor force a good range of options. The process is much less difficult when the economy is rather small allowing government to play a part – sometimes constructive, sometimes not. In any case, government's role in this past decade of massive restructuring and redesigning has been to clear the way for management decision by easing restrictive regulations. Direct intervention has been largely limited to banking supports where asset losses and deflation have wrecked havoc.

However difficult and painful it may have been for industries, companies, and the people in them, the redesign of Japan's business community has gone very far indeed and, with deflation ended and growth resumed, clearly has been in the end a great success.

Notes

1. *Financial Times*, 8 March 2004, p. 16.
2. *Bank of Japan Quarterly Bulletin*, Vol. 11, No. 4, November 2003, p. 187.
3. *Development Bank of Japan Research Report*, No. 34, November 2002, pp. iv, 2.
4. *Bank of Japan Quarterly Bulletin*, op. cit., p. 187.
5. *Nikkei Business*, 25 February 2002, p. 56.
6. Robert M. Uriu, *Troubled Industries. Confronting Economic Change in Japan*, Ithaca: Cornell University Press, 1996.
7. Suzanne Coulter, *Managing Decline. Japan's Coal Mining Restructuring*, Honolulu: University of Hawaii Press, 1999, p. 185.
8. Dennis L. McNamara, *Textiles and Industrial Transition in Japan*, Ithaca: Cornell University Press, 1995, p. 4.
9. Keith Wilson, "Shipbuilding – Where to Now?" *Ship & Ocean Newsletter*, 5 April 2002.

3
The Graying of Japan: The End of Growth?

Among the wrenching transitions that are changing the very basis of the Japanese economy, none is more dramatic and none more certain than the transition from a rapidly growing and youthful population to a rapidly declining and aging population. Having nearly tripled in the 20th century, Japan's population may reduce by half in the 21st century. For very long, the conventional Western view saw Japan as over-populated, a terribly crowded country suffering from lack of space for living, for farming, and for recreation. Now, in nice irony, Japan's decline in population is being viewed with alarm.

Decline in population is regularly equated to decline in economic growth rate, with labor shortages, diminished energy levels in laboratories, factories, and offices, heavy burdens of pension obligations, and increased health care costs among other negatives. In splendid disregard of both need and consequences, the glib solution offered all too often is that of mass immigration. The arguments for mass immigration are nonsense. Japan's labor shortage is at least for a generation still not a real issue – and the social and political costs of mass immigration into so integrated a society as Japan's are quite simply unbearable in any case. Japan is becoming very rapidly demographically mature, as it very rapidly became industrially mature. There is no crisis inherent in this maturity; handled with reasonably thoughtfulness, maturity brings with it stability and well-being.

The graying of Japan

Something unprecedented and irreversible is happening to humanity. This year or next, the proportion of people aged 60 or over will surpass the proportion of under-fives. For the rest of history, there are unlikely ever again to be more toddlers than gray heads. Already those aged 65 or over, who throughout recorded time have rarely accounted for more than 2 or 3 percent of most countries' people, make up 15 percent of the rich world's inhabitants.[1]

The graying of Japan provides a dramatic example of this great change in structure of the world population. In Japan, youngsters under 15 years were more than a third of the population as recently as 1950. A few years ago the proportion 65 years and over became greater than the proportion aged under 15 years, with persons 65 years and over becoming rapidly a third of the total. Japan is not unique in having a rapidly aging population. Its pattern of population decline and aging is much like that of Western Europe, but is taking place rather more rapidly and to a greater extreme. Like Europe, a key factor is the low fertility rate, now only 1.3 children born per woman for Japan and for much of Western Europe as well, Germany, Spain, and Italy included (Table 3.1).

The forces at work driving this change are similar for Japan and Europe. The shift from rural to urban locations and from agriculture to industry makes large families economically dysfunctional rather than useful. The emphasis changes from having helping hands in the family to ensuring that children can be well provided for. For Japan especially other factors in reducing the birth rate include later age at marriage, now 27 or 28 years. In addition, more women now are not marrying in Japan, 14 or 15 percent. This is important since there is in Japan's case a very low rate of births to unmarried women, only 1 percent compared with more than 30 percent in the United States and 50 percent in Sweden. Also in the Japanese case there is still limited governmental and corporate support for working mothers. All this, along with a desire to invest in the care and education of children and therefore to limit numbers, brings the birth rate down despite a general view that a larger family is ideal.

At the same time, Japan's death rate has been falling dramatically, driven by fast-rising incomes and universal health insurance. There has been a massive increase in postwar Japan in the numbers and quality of professional health delivery systems. The World Health Organization ranked Japan first in the world in the attainments of its health care systems (the United States 15 and Germany 14) and tenth in the effi-ciency of its health care systems (the United States 37 and Germany 25). Powerful evidence is the fact that life expectancy in Japan is longest in

Table 3.1 Population and age structure, 1950–2050, Japan, Germany, United States

	Japan				Germany				United States			
	Total (million)	0–14 (%)	15–64 (%)	65+ (%)	Total (million)	0–14 (%)	15–64 (%)	65+ (%)	Total (million)	0–14 (%)	15–64 (%)	65+ (%)
1950	83	35	60	5	65	23	67	10	152	27	65	8
2000	127	15	68	17	82	16	68	16	282	21	66	13
2050	100	13	53	34	76	13	57	30	420	19	60	21

Note: Japan's total population 1900–44 million.
Source: US Census Bureau. IDB Population Pyramids. *Suji de miru Nihon no Hyaku Nen*, Daiyonhan, ed. Yano Tsuneta Kinnenkai, Kokuseisha: Tokyo, 2000.

the world for both men and women. Since the mid-1950s, life expectancy for Japanese women has increased by 22 years from 63 to 85, and for Japanese men by 18 years from 60 to 78. It is this combination of factors – low birth rates, low death rates – that has given rise to the dramatic shifts in population structure for Japan and to a lesser degree in much of the developed world.

It might be noted here that in these respects, the United States, along with Canada and Australia, is an exception to this general condition of the populations of the developed economies. Driven by massive immigration, with the immigrants often not well educated and from high birth-rate regions, the population of the United States is expected by its Census Bureau to continue to increase much as it has for the past half-century. An increase in the population of 65 years and more is expected, but the older group will still be a much lower percent of the total than in Japan and Germany. Of special note, the United States, Canada, and Australia can and do deal well with mass immigration. All three countries have massive space available and substantial natural resources to support the economics of mass immigration. And all three are without a national culture, and are also without the degree of social integration that makes for the high social risks and costs of mass immigration.

For most of the developed world – Japan and Western Europe – mass immigration poses major problems of social integration along with major difficulties in physically accommodating large scale inflows of new residents. And in any case, the prospect of population size stability at some future point need not be a daunting prospect. The current obsession with economic growth, and thus population growth, as the only relevant measure of success needs to be corrected; maturity and stability are desirable conditions.

What of the future? Is there no room for change – for increased birth rates, more youngsters, for a trend toward a larger population? The answer looking at the next several decades must be no. Even a significant increase in birth rates beginning very soon would not much change the total population projections for 2030 or even later. However, there might well be changes out toward mid-century, with a possible increase in birth rate. A positive factor is the continued view that the ideal number of children is two to three (statistically 2.56) per family, a view that has changed very little since the mid-1980s.[2] There has been some increase in birth rates in, for example, Sweden, after a long-sustained decline, and Japan might well prove to be another case.

While most Japanese believe a larger family is better, they do not now intend to have nor do they plan for a larger family. To realize the ideal of a family with two or three children, there must be major programs introduced to supply child care and other supports for working mothers – tax relief and extended parental leave for example – and these programs must be supplied no less by the private sector than by government. In the case of France and also Germany, as in Sweden, efforts to deal with declining birth rates are beginning to result in increases in the fertility rate. Japan's companies and government must do no less. Some programs and approaches are now being introduced as the government determines that an increase in birth rate would be economically useful. However, very much more is needed and in any case the results would be seen only after a full generation, toward the middle of the 21st century. We can assume that the population projections to mid-century are reasonably accurate.

As noted, there is a certain irony in this concern over population decline. For long, Japan has been seen by many as terribly overcrowded, its quality of life lessened by a lack of space. True, much of this view is from Americans and Australians whose pride in open spaces compensates for other quality-of-life problems in those countries. Japan has now about the same population density as Belgium, rather less than the density in the Netherlands, and much less than in its neighbors Taiwan and South Korea. In any case, the anticipated reduction of the population over the next decades by about one-quarter will finally put paid to the long-held view of Japan's "overpopulation." A new cliché will be required.

An end to growth?

Perhaps the greatest concern over population change is the impact on the labor force. The number of working-age people, those aged 15–65 in the usual definition, peaked in 1995 at 87 millions. The total in this age group in 2050 will be about 54 million, a reduction in labor force size of about 40 percent. Since total GDP is a function of the number of labor units employed and the output of these units as a result of capital used by them, the expected reduction in labor force would lead to zero or negative GDP growth as mid-century approaches – all else being equal. A basic question therefore in considering the future of Japan and its economy is the issue of labor force size and effectiveness over the next decades.

The population data is clear. The age group making up the labor force is in decline and that decline will continue and even accelerate. What is likely to take place over the next years that might offset the projected decline in labor force size and thus in GDP? We need to note first that labor shortage is not now an issue. Unemployment at around 5 percent is very high by Japanese historical standards; there is labor available in ample supply now and for some years still. No doubt labor shortages will be a future issue; they are not a problem now.

Underlining the fact that labor is currently in ample supply is the dramatic reduction in hours worked. Another of the many incorrect views of Japan is that Japanese work hours are especially long – "workaholics in rabbit hutches" was one vicious description. In fact, from a peak of total hours actually worked in the poverty-ridden Japan of 1960, annual hours worked have declined by 25 percent. It helps to get rich – not surprisingly, with increased incomes has come increased leisure. The average Japanese worker now works fewer hours per year than the average US and British worker – although German workers still hold first place in fewest hours worked. Put another way, increases in hours worked, through overtime especially, are available as one more offset in the near term to a potential labor shortage.

Increased employment and longer working hours are minor, short-term responses to the problem of a diminishing labor force. There is however a number of more basic adjustments that need be allowed for when gauging the impact of the labor force decline. One is retirement age. As noted, Japan has now the longest life expectancies in the world, for men 78 years and women 85 years. Yet for the great majority of companies the mandatory retirement age is 60 years. This is up from the customary 55-year retirement age of the mid-1950s, but still leaves a considerable room for additional change.

Retirement policy for companies is complicated by the continued emphasis on seniority as a major factor in compensation, with the result that the older employee is the more expensive employee. With real pressure on costs, early retirement programs are widespread and extending retirement age unattractive financially to the company. However, with pressure on pension financing, the government seeks to establish a later retirement age. The compromise has been retirement at age 60 (with retirement benefits provided) and then, in the majority of companies, programs to provide continued employment but at lower wage rates and with limited benefits.

As the pressure on costs eases, and as labor in fact moves to short supply, it is quite clear that the labor force size can and will be expanded by much longer working lives for both men and women. One view on this was provided by Peter Drucker: "Politicians everywhere still promise to save the existing pensions system, but they – and their constituents – know perfectly well that in another 25 years people will have to keep working until their mid-70s, health permitting."[3] Since Dr Drucker was still active while in his 90s, he may have taken a somewhat sanguine view of the strengths of older people, but no doubt working lives will extend substantially over the next decades as he suggests. Japan has already the highest labor force participation among persons 65 years and over for both men and women, and this will continue and increase, thus adding to the effective labor force.

Changing retirement practices to add to the labor force is a rather clear and straightforward process. A changing role in the labor force for the women of Japan is a considerably more complex matter, yet one that offers considerable opportunity.

Women in the labor force

At present, of a total employed labor force of 64 million persons about 40 percent are women. Social change and legislative measures aimed at enforcing equal employment opportunity have increased that percentage from around 35 percent in the mid-1980s. However, it is still that case that of the potential female labor force aged 15–64, only about half are in fact in the labor force, compared with three-quarters of the male group. Thus, simply in sheer numbers, the opportunity for increased labor supply by engaging more females in employment is substantial, apart from the opportunity to make more effective use of the women who already choose to work.

Law now dictates equal opportunity. Custom and habits tend to work otherwise. The traditional view of "men at work, women at home" remains a real factor. Here there is still a very real difference between Asia and the West, with a quarter to third of Japanese, Taiwanese, Koreans, and Indians agreeing that the woman's place is caring for the home and children. The contrast is with the West where only 2 or 3 percent of Europeans and 10 percent of Americans hold that view.[4]

In Japan, views regarding women's employment are changing to a great extent, as indicated in Table 3.2. Over a 30-year period, there has been a massive shift in attitudes on the part of both men and women. The earlier view that women should not work, or if they did, work only until marriage, has largely changed. Attitudes now are largely divided between the view that women should be free to work even while caring for children and that women should reenter the workforce only after children are older. This view that women must be at home to care for young children remains a very powerful factor in shaping the patterns

Table 3.2   Views regarding women working

	1972		2002		
	Men (%)	Women (%)	Total (%)	Men (%)	Women (%)
Continue working even after having children	10	12	38	38	37
Stop working after having children; work again as they grow older	21	39	37	41	32
Work until having children	16	12	10	9	1
Work until marriage	26	19	6	5	8
Women should not work	16	8	4	3	6
Other	–	–	1	1	1
Don't know	11	10	4	3	5
Total	100	100	100	100	100

Source: *Danjo Kyodo Sankaku Shakai ni kan suru Yoron Chosa*, Naikakufu Daijin Kanbo Kohoshitsu, Tokyo, July 2002.

of employment of women in Japan. However, these survey results show quite clearly great changes in attitudes on the part of both men and women, with the views of men and women moving quite closely together over time.

The good news is that there has been real change. The bad news is that change is still slow. Women in parliament are 5 times as numerous now as in 1975 – but are still fewer than in any of the Western nations. The proportion of women in such occupations as medicine, dentistry, pharmacy, law, and accounting has increased steadily – but remains at a low level. Only 20 percent of civil servants are women, a very low level compared to most other countries. Women are in supervisory positions in three-quarters of Japan's large companies, but in only a third of all companies, with smaller firms still promoting few women.

Curiously, this is not simply a glass ceiling. In the political sphere, for example, a woman serves as head of a major political party, and earlier was Speaker in the Lower House of Parliament. A woman serves as foreign minister and another, formerly a senior UN official, is now head of the foreign aid program. Several other Cabinet positions in addition to the foreign ministry are held by women. In daily life, as an example, the writer's tax accountant is a woman, as is his attorney, and so was the supervisory doctor during a recent hospitalization, and the occasional taxi driver.

Still, the situation is a mixed one. Despite great changes in views, despite reasonably vigorous legal measures toward equal opportunity, despite very able women in high and highly visible positions, discrimination remains an all-too-common reality. "Japan stands out as the country with the largest gender wage gap, at 39.2 in 1999."[5] More than in any other of the OECD member countries, the wages of women compared to those of men are low in Japan. This is tempered to a degree by the fact that, with Germany, labor in Japan is the highest paid in the world; wages of women are not absolutely so very low – but are very low relative to the wages paid men.

The barrier to career advancement is not education – as many women as men in Japan go on to higher education, about half of the age group, now a third to university with a diminishing proportion going to junior colleges. However, attitudes held by women themselves remain a major factor, as suggested in a rather amusing poll result reported a few years ago in *The Economist* (Table 3.3). Japanese women seem not so bent on entire equal treatment as in other countries – but have no illusions regarding the extent of equality provided.

The key to more effective involvement of women in Japan's labor force is the issue of the care of children. There remains the very general opinion that women should leave the labor force at marriage or on the occasion of the birth of a child. It is a tribute to the strength of the Japanese family system that this remains the dominant view. The child is reared in a family where a parent is in place. They do not return from school to an empty house. Currently in the United States 70 percent of families are headed by two working parents or a working single parent. Little

Table 3.3 Women's views compared

Country	% of women who think they	
	Should have all the same rights as men	Do have all the same rights as men
Japan	21	0
United States	62	8
Germany	70	7
Britain	73	9

Source: *The Economist*, 9 October 1999.

time is available for the care of or attention to children. The social costs of the US parentless home are clearly high; these kinds of social costs are largely avoided in the Japanese system of parent care.

The economic costs of the Japanese system are no less real, however. Female employment by age has an M-shaped curve. That is, the proportion of women working aged 20–29 is quite high, more than 70 percent. However, the proportion at work aged 30–39 drops to 57 percent as women leave the workforce to care for their children. Then the proportion again rises to over 70 percent for women aged 40–55 years, falling off after. The steepness of the M-shape has lessened over the past decades, but the pattern remains, as women drop out of the labor force to care for their children and then seek to return as the children grow. Were they to remain in the labor force, if the M-shape were to flatten, the addition to the employed, active labor force would be some 1.1 million persons as of 2003 by reckoning of the Ministry of Health, Labor and Welfare, a significant factor in helping to ease any future labor shortage.

The Ministry reported that two-thirds of all working women give up their jobs upon the birth of their first child. The process is a costly one for these women.

> Women who wish to return to work after leaving the work force face a very harsh reality. In 2000, some 70 percent of women between the ages of 35 and 44 who re-entered the labor market only found part-time work. The wage gap between female part-time workers and female full-time workers (regular employees) is increasing, with the hourly wage for female part-time workers only 66.9 percent that of regular workers. . . . If bonus payments and retirement allowances are included, the gap widens further.[6]

It seems clear enough that there is a pressing need for significant investment in first-class child-care facilities nationwide both to address the labor supply issue and to supply much needed relief to those women who would like to continue working but feel they cannot in order to care for their children properly. Professional child care can work. The writer's step-daughter, devoted to the care of her two-year-old child but divorced and wanting to work, has been able to use a fine child-care facility very nearby, with a well-trained staff, and as a single woman, this is available at no cost to her. First-class child care can be available – and, for the sake of all concerned, needs be done, soon.

This would increase the labor force by more than one million. Assume that with these programs of parental support and with continuing changes in attitudes, the percent of women in the active labor force were to increase from the current 50 to 60 percent. Such an increase seems quite possible, even low, since the percent for men is 76. An increase to 60 percent for women would add some 6 million additional persons to the labor force. As the economy continues to move toward an expanded services sector, where women can be quite readily employed, and as labor moves to short supply, the opportunities and indeed need for women in the labor force will grow rapidly – and with reasonable planning the need can be met to the advantage of all concerned.

There are real efforts now to remedy this problem of lack of child-care facilities. As one private sector example, NEC Corporation has announced it will provide up to ¥600,000 in child-care assistance to workers with newborn babies. It will also increase support for dependents, and roughly 6000 workers, a quarter of NEC's total labor force, will be eligible for the new programs. NEC is not only moving on this matter. Legislation was enacted in 2003 making it mandatory for companies with over 300 employees to formulate action plans to help workers in raising their children, and to have plans in place by 2005. Thirty major companies have joined together, including IBM Japan, Canon, Toyota, and Sony, to devise child-care programs as will be required by law. Real relief is near at hand, therefore, to make increased female participation in full-time career employment a reality on a wide scale.

Robots to the rescue

During Japan's high growth period, the need for increased labor in manufacturing was met by the very fast migration out of primary industry – agriculture, forestry, and fisheries – into the secondary sector – mining, manufacturing, construction, and utilities. In 1955, as high growth began, over 40 percent of the labor force was in the primary sector which now makes up less than 5 percent of the total. There will be some further migration out of the primary sector since the total value added by those businesses is only 1.5 percent of the economy's total. But much of the reduction in the primary labor force will be from retirement – half of Japan's farmers are 65 years of age or older. There will be little gained by future transfers out of the primary sector.

Instead, as an alternative of sorts, automation in its many forms and notably through application of robotics will provide a new source of supply of labor to manufacturing. Japan now has in place about half of the world's total supply of robots, nearly 400,000, about four times as many as in either the United States or Germany. Robots take no tea breaks or holidays, seek no wage increases, and provide output of exceptional reliability. Assume each robot is equivalent to perhaps two human laborers. Thus the labor force of Japan has already been increased by nearly a million workers by robotics alone, leaving aside the impact of other forms of automation.

The factors favoring the application of automation and robotics in Japan are many. Japan has high labor costs – with Germany's, Japan's is the best paid labor force in the world; labor prices are high. Capital costs in Japan have historically been low and with current interest rates near zero, continue to be low. Therefore, economics dictates substituting machinery for labor. Moreover, with job security in the manufacturing sector still very high, automation is not threat to employment. And with the world's best-educated labor force, Japan's workers are not only willing but also able to make full use of the most sophisticated manufacturing systems. No surprise then that research and development in robotics is by far the most advanced in the world, including now robotic pets and robotic care for the bedridden and the elderly, the so-called "partner robots." Using advanced electronics, these partner robots will go far to reduce the need for staff for nursing and caring for the aged.

One of Japan's biggest robot makers, and technology leader, is Fanuc, a spinout from computer pioneer Fujitsu. Former British Prime Minister Thatcher, on seeing its manufacturing, described it as the "factory where robots make robots." Four hundred production workers work with 1000 robots to produce $2 billion in sales, for a very profitable company that has no debt on its balance sheet, and that plans a 37 percent increase in robot sales in fiscal 2004 over 2003.

One of Japan's largest machine tool makers, Yamazaki Mazak, is installing assembly lines for its complex products that can be operated entirely without human workers for up to 72 continuous hours, using intelligent robots with visual functions and three-dimensional sensors, with an unmanned system for product transfer to warehouses. It is adopting this unmanned system to compete against labor-intensive producers with low wage costs in China and elsewhere.

Canon has announced automation of its camera and printer production, and will bring production back to Japan from overseas as a result. With a fully automated output system, Canon can produce in Japan both low-end and high value-added products, and will achieve higher cost efficiencies in Japan than in China where labor costs are about 5 percent of those in Japan. While Canon's overseas production share has climbed to 40 percent, the company now expects to raise its domestic output ratio. Its facilities in China making low-value products will produce only for sale in the Chinese domestic market. Given the rate at which optico-electronics and computer applications are developing in Japan, it seems quite clear that we are only at the beginning of the massive shift to unmanned facilities producing the full product range, the ultimate answer to the issues of labor price and labor availability.

With all these sources of reinforcement for the labor force in Japan, a focus on labor shortage as a key issue over the next several decades seems misplaced. Leaving out current unemployment and underutilization, which certainly do not suggest labor shortage in any case, the potential for ready expansion of labor force capacity is clearly substantial. Extension of retirement age to better use capable older people, extension of child-care facilities and other supports to expand the role of women in the labor force, and the continued increase in extent of automated production and in degree of sophistication of automation – all these suggest that much discussion of labor shortage is simple over-reaction to crude population data.

Nonetheless, population projections provide regular opportunities for the many Cassandras whose preoccupation is to chant of fatal weaknesses in Japan's economic armor. The aging and declining population will reduce demand, it is argued, and thereby cause the economy to shrink. Yet projections indicate a population in Japan at mid-century of 100 millions of persons, a good deal more than that of most nations and surely a large enough group to provide a considerable demand – which in any case is more likely to be determined by income levels rather than crudely by numbers of persons. Demand patterns will of course change with an aging population – from kindergartens to adult education, from teenage entertainment to adult pastimes, from new housing to home improvement and luxury, with more leisure and much increased medical services. Rather than demand reduction, demand change.

Note too that a reduced population need not and almost certainly will not lead to reduced incomes. Assume Japan's population reduces by 25 percent by 2050, as is now projected. Assume that Japan's economy is only able to continue at present levels of output and income generation. Then by 2050, the income of the average person will have increased by 25 percent despite no economic growth. Assume modest growth as befits a mature society, and one must assume rather handsome increases in per capita income and hence in demand. Note too that older people will not be saving for an old age that has already arrived, but will be spenders too.

Still, the view is offered frequently and in utmost seriousness that Japan can and should deal with what is seen as its population problems by undertaking massive immigration from abroad. The United States, Canada, and Australia are offered as examples of the splendid workings of immigration. A headline in a British paper catches the cliché, and offers the argument in all seriousness. "Japan faces a choice between open borders and slow decline."[7] What is not noted in most of these discussions is that these are nations without a common culture, with a very low level of social and cultural integration, and thus persons of quite diverse backgrounds can rather readily move into – and out of – these nations, at relatively little social cost to themselves or the nation. The United States at least is held together, it appears, by an elaborate apparatus of nationalistic symbols – flag and anthem are central – along with a very elaborate apparatus of police, courts, and jails – the world's largest prison population for example. The system is mechanical rather than cultural. It is hardly a model for the future of Japan, where common values control communal behavior.

Most of the nations of the developed world have integrated domestic cultures, and it has become clear in recent decades that large-scale immigration into Italy, Germany, Sweden, and France has very high social costs and becomes a national political issue of some intensity. This is more true of Japan, with a very long history of separate identity and with a high degree of cultural and social integration. It is nonsense to speak of large-scale immigration into Japan. If cities in Britain flame up from racial/cultural disputes, if the government of Denmark wins election on an anti-immigration platform, one can from these and many other examples catch a glimpse of the cost to Japan of large-scale immigration.

Movement of labor into Japan is in fact increasing. From1996 to 2001, the number of foreigners entering Japan for the first time for the purpose of work roughly doubled – but was still only 141,000. The Ministry of Justice also reports a total of 33,000 illegal foreign workers – although since they are illegal, it is not at all clear how the Ministry is able to count them.[8] In any case, the numbers are low. The World Bank reports that only 0.2 percent of Japan's total labor force is foreign born. The total for Germany is 8.8 percent and for the United States 12.4 percent.

This is not a matter of legalities. As the writer can attest, becoming a Japanese citizen is a quite straightforward and rather simple matter. Of course there is the usual hurdle of bureaucratic paper work that would be encountered anywhere. But the law is not the barrier to entry. Japanese social custom, and foreigner's expectations of problems in seeking entry, are the barriers to immigration, not policy or law.

Indeed, if labor supply and labor cost is the issue, why in the world should the desired solution be immigration? Why incur the social costs and political risks of importing large numbers of inexpensive – and thereby rather poorly trained and educated – laborers? Why not take the jobs to them? And that is in fact precisely what is happening. In 1992, about 6 percent of total Japanese manufacturing was in overseas locations, a very low level compared to the quarter of US production and a fifth of Germany's already off-shore at the time. Only a decade later, Japan's companies had nearly tripled their proportion of off-shore production to 17 percent, with the increase expected to continue rapidly.

About one in seven of Japan's manufacturers already have production sites off-shore. To an overwhelming extent these are located in East and Southeast Asia, about 80 percent of the total, with 40 percent in China alone. Production is machinery products, with about a third of the total electrical machinery; we may assume these are largely familiar consumer electronics. Of special interest is the fact that half of the total overseas production is for local markets, the markets in which the plants are sited, with an additional third of production for export to Japan.[9]

There are limits already reached however in producing abroad. "After two decades of shifting production overseas to cut costs, domestic manufacturers are starting to return. Led by electronics makers, the homecoming is being driven in part by a fear of technology secrets slipping into the hands of foreign rivals. Companies also need workers with higher skills to compete."[10] An example from the experience of Matsushita Electric is cited, with a new production facility in Japan to replace one in use in China. The work had previously been done by a staff of more than 200 in China, but the Japanese plant needs only 20 workers to operate the new, fully automated lines. Automation can in fact substitute effectively for labor and make overseas production less necessary and less cost-attractive.

Hollowing out?

This process of shifting production abroad is carelessly termed "hollowing out." The term is a stupid one, not at all helpful in gaining understanding of the situation. Moving routine and labor-intensive work abroad is in fact a hollowing out of Japan's industry only if industry in Japan stands still, making no progress forward to higher value-added products. Japan's economic success has depended until now, as it must in the future as well, on a steady movement from low technology, labor intensive, low value-added production up the ladder to higher value-added products. Witness the demise of such major industries in Japan as coal mining and cotton spinning, as first steel, then autos, and then electronics each in turn took center place. Shifting production of mature products to factories abroad is in fact economic development, Japan providing developing economies with the capital and technology required for their economic progress and Japan in turn focusing its efforts on the next generation of technologies and products. Calling this "hollowing out" is a grotesquerie.

In fact, Japan's industrial leaders are fully aware of these facts and are shaping their companies' strategies accordingly. Vice Chairman Nishigaki of NEC: "Since labor costs in China are one-thirtieth those in Japan, we aim to use China for production and parts procurement. We will continue to develop and produce cutting-edge products in Japan, but we have no choice but to consign mass production to other countries." Honda Motors President Yoshino: "From now on, it will be an ongoing cycle of developing and manufacturing new products in Japan, and shifting production overseas when the markets for the goods mature." Sharp President Machida: "We will disband manufacturing operations in Japan if we cannot continue developing cutting-edge technology and products."

In fact, a number of companies are now building up production facilities in Japan where labor prices are high but labor costs – given high skill levels and high capital investments – may well be lower than in less developed economies. Labor is now only 8 percent of steel production costs in Japan, and for a good many highly sophisticated products, labor is only 2 or 3 percent of total costs. Moreover, production bases in Japan are vital for developing original and high value-added products, where R&D and manufacturing must be close together. "Hollowing out" is not a useful notion in thinking through labor supply policies and problems.

The issues posed by investment abroad, especially into China and Southeast Asia, are complex and go well beyond questions of labor supply alone. However, in this context of the issues posed by an aging and diminishing population, the conclusion must be that investment abroad is simply one more approach to handling the issues of a smaller labor force. Immigration is not the answer, certainly not for Japan nor yet indeed for most countries and societies. Investment abroad is part of the answer, along with changing roles for women, longer careers, and capital intensive automation. It is not at all obvious that the aging and diminishing of population do in fact pose major problems for Japan over the next generation or so. Rather, Japan's will be a demographically mature society, focusing economically on new technologies and products, and enjoying the absence of the population pressures it has historically experienced. For at least a generation, the issue of labor supply is no threat to the continued improvement of the quality of life for Japan's citizenry.

Notes

1. Frances Cairncross, "Forever Young. A Survey of Retirement", *The Economist*, 27 March 2004, p. 3.
2. *Dai 12 Kai Shussei Doko Kihon Chosa*, Kokuritsu Shakai Hosho Jinko Mondai Kenkyusho, Tokyo, 1 June 2002, p. 19.
3. Peter Drucker, "The Next Society", *The Economist*, 3 November 2001, p. 3.
4. *Dai Go Kai Kachikan Kokusai Hikaku Chosa*, Dentsu Soken Report, Tokyo, March 2001.
5. Lawrence Mishel, Jared Bernstein and Heather Bousley, *The State of Working America 2002/2003*, Ithaca, NY: Cornell University Press, 2003, p. 409.
6. "Working Women: Current Situation and Perspectives", *Japan Labor Bulletin*, Vol. 41, No. 6, June 2002, p. 1.
7. *Financial Times*, 4 January 2003.
8. *Japan Almanac 2003*, The Asahi Shimbun, Tokyo, 2002, p. 81.
9. *Nihon Keizai Shimbun*, 7 February 2002, reporting on a survey by the Ministry of Economics, Trade and Industry.
10. "Japanese Makers Return from Abroad", Asahi Shimbun, 13–14 November 2004.

4
Japanese Style Management

The great achievements of the companies that make up Japan's economy are the result of a brilliant blending of the technologies of the West into a management system built on the special characteristics of Japanese society. There is no need to debate whether these characteristics – an emphasis on age-grading, a high degree of group consciousness and identification rather than a focus on individualism, a general egalitarianism in compensation and privileges – are unique to Japan. They are, instead, stronger in Japan than in the Anglo-American world, rather closer to some of the characteristics of German society for example. It was the development of these original management methods that allowed Japan to become the first fully industrialized non-Western society. The classic Japanese phrase *wakon yosai* (Japanese spirit; Western learning) captures something of the nature of the management approach that has made for Japan's industrial success.

The management patterns that distinguish the kaisha center on the relationship between firm and employee, and make up what is called *nihonteki keiei*, Japanese style management. I first described the system based on my research in Japan in 1955 and 1956, studying large and small Japanese companies throughout the country. It was quite clear even then that successful Japanese management depended on building systems of recruiting, training, and compensating personnel that were built on distinctive aspects of Japanese culture.[1]

My early studies noted three key characteristics of nihonteki keiei, that came to be called the three pillars of the management system. The basic pillar was – and is – the social contract between firm and employee, a commitment to work as a community to achieve economic security for all members of the workforce. The second pillar was the seniority system that dominated compensation and promotion decisions. The third was the system of trade union organization, *kigyonai kumiai*, by which all employees of a given firm were together members of a single union, a single negotiating organization. (Over time, other aspects such as group decision-making were added to the list by some. But the "three pillars" remained the key elements of Japan's management systems.)

I termed the firm–employee social contract a "lifetime commitment." In translation, this became *shushin koyosei* – translated back as "lifetime employment," a rather different concept from "lifetime commitment." However, the words "lifetime employment" became standard in both languages in describing Japan's employment system. As is rather often the case, the original source of the term was ignored and the re-defined phrase took on a life of its own with a rather incorrect implication.

The concept of a career commitment to a single employer was seen as strange, and indeed seen as quite unworkable by most Westerners. How can you motivate workers if you have only the carrots of promotion and pay raises and no sticks of the threat of a pay cut, of demotion, or of discharge? Because this employment system was seen as peculiar and unworkable, and because it was and is different from the Anglo-American systems, any change of any sort or scale in employment relations was taken as evidence that the system was at an end. Reports of "the end of lifetime employment" became standard features of newspaper and magazine stories almost from the beginning of use of the term, and have persisted, even increased in incidence, annually since the mid-1960s.

The end of lifetime employment?

Has lifetime employment in fact ended? Is Japanese style management a relic of the past? The question is critical, and is all too often answered with splendid disregard of the facts. We need to look closely at the realities.

First, note that even in 1955 there was job change. Even then, some industries were phasing out, and even then companies were often in real trouble. So even then there was "voluntary retirement," then as now a tap on the shoulder with a modest reward for leaving. Then, as now, workers could be assigned to subsidiaries or to unattractive locations as encouragement to leave the firm. All this happened regularly. However, each year from 1958, when my book was first published, I would be told that the system had ended – Suzuki San or Watanabe San or whomever had just moved from one company to another.

None of this, then or now, bespeaks a change in the underlying system. On the contrary, all evidence indicates that the lifetime commitment, or social contract, is as well-recognized and honored now as it was when I first studied management in Japan 50 years ago. Table 4.1 shows the results of a study done under the auspices of the International Labour Office comparing job tenure in Japan, the United States, and the European Union of 14 countries over the period 1992–2000. This is a period during which Japan's companies have been under severe cost and financial pressure. Despite the difficulties of this period, job tenure in Japan did not shorten. On the contrary, employees are kept on their jobs even longer than before, with job tenure patterns in Europe similar but not increasing as rapidly as in Japan. The United States in this as in a great many management aspects is the odd man out, the outlier, with very much lower job tenure, about half the Japan average, and job tenure in the United States is even shortening still.

Few workers in Japan are in short-tenured jobs, and the proportion – less than 10 percent – is still diminishing, while in the US more than a quarter of the labor force are in short-tenured jobs and the proportion is increasing. At the other extreme, only a quarter of US workers have been in their jobs for ten years or more, while the proportion in Europe and Japan is over 40 percent. Despite the widespread view that job security has lessened, all evidence is to the contrary. Long-term employment relationships have increased in proportion and duration in nearly all OECD countries except in the United States, the outsider in management of personnel. Not surprising then that US observers of Japan assume that the employment system is changing. Rather than studying the reality of Japan, they generalize from their own country's exceptional situation.

Table 4.1   Employment tenure, Japan–United States–EU, 1992–2000

		Japan	**United States**	**EU**
Average job tenure (years)	1992	10.9	6.7	10.5
	2000	11.6	6.6	10.6
Change (%)	1992–2000	6.4	−1.5	1.6
Tenure under one year	1992	9.8	28.8	14.2
(% of labor force)	2000	8.3	27.8	16.6
Change (%)	1992–2000	−15.3	3.5	17.0
Tenure ten years and over	1992	42.9	26.6	41.7
(% of labor force)	2000	43.2	25.8	42.0
Change (%)	1992–2000	0.7	−3.0	0.6

Source: *Employment Stability in an Age of Flexibility*, Peter Auer and Sandrine Cazes (eds), Geneva: International Labour Office, 2003, p. 25.

Other studies confirm these findings.

> Contrary to the popular rhetoric of the end of lifetime employment, evidence points to the enduring nature of this practice in Japan.... Large firms have been trying to accomplish their restructuring and downsizing targets by relying heavily on transfers of their employees to their subsidiaries and related firms and hiring cuts, and thus avoiding layoffs.[2]

Again,

> The tenure of Japanese male workers has not declined, but has increased, especially for older workers in larger corporations. And the increase is especially prevalent between 1992 and 1997 when the economy was in a slump. Thus, contrary to the expectations based on the argument for declining job security, the cyclical downturn did not have a negative effect on employment.[3]

Why assume lifetime employment is ended?

Lifetime employment – at least in the sense that I originally used the concept – has not ended. Nor is there any evidence that it is in process of ending. Question: Why the assumption that the system has changed?

The ILO study makes an interesting point relevant to this question. "The Japanese paradox: acute perception of job insecurity in a context of job stability." Japanese employees, by most reckonings enjoying a high level of job security feel at the same time very unsure of their jobs. In a recent study, Tetsuo Ebato provides an amusing – and insightful – example of the quite general Japanese characteristic to be pessimistic about the future, however satisfactory the present.

> "People today, especially present-day salarymen, when looking at the future, take a very pessimistic view. (Our research shows that) with respect to employment practices, salarymen hold a dark view of the future compared with the present, now as they did earlier. In the study of 1985 beliefs regarding employment practices at that time, a high proportion – 90.0 percent – stated that they enjoy 'lifetime employment.' However, when asked about the future, 79.6 percent, a tenth fewer, felt that lifetime employment would continue into the future.

"When the same study was done thirteen years later, in 1998, after all the reductions and restructurings that had gone on as the bubble era ended, still as thirteen years before, 89.9 percent of the salarymen stated that they enjoy 'lifetime employment.' There was no change in views from the heights of the bubble to the depths of the period of restructurings.

"However, when the 1998 study asked about future expectations, only 66.1 percent stated that they expected the system to continue into the future. Pessimism regarding the future increased 2.4 times over the thirteen years, even though present conditions were seen as the same in both periods.

"All this is dramatic confirmation of the view that Japan's salarymen take a pessimistic view of the future, however comfortable they feel in the present situation."[4]

Convergence: Meeting of East and West?

When Western academics speak of "convergence," they do not mean a meeting in some unknown middle territory, in which different systems "converge." They mean instead a move to what we all surely know is the proper system, the Anglo-American system. US attitudes assume that differences need mending, and that change will take place to move Japan to the Anglo-American position in labor practices and management methods, self-evidently the best of systems.

Thus, for example, Moody's Investors Service, a stronghold of Anglo-American arrogance about finance, writes at length of how lifetime employment will impair the competitiveness and thus the creditworthiness of Japan's large companies. And Moody's gave full play to their arrogance by reducing the credit rating of what is by nearly all measures the world's leading automobile company, Toyota Motors. Toyota's management, not at all amused, replied that far from being a handicap, the skills of its labor force and its high level of loyalty to the company are a direct consequence of lifetime employment, "for Toyota an immense plus."

The chief executive officer of one of Japan's great companies, Canon, puts it as follows:

Managing a company has two aspects. While product development and financial strategies are universal, employment practices differ from country to country because cultures are different. If we employ people in countries where we operate, we have to respect their culture. For Japan, it is lifetime employment.

The advantage of lifetime employment is that employees absorb the company's culture throughout their careers. As a result, a team spirit grows among them, a willingness to stick to the corporate brand and to stick together to pull through crises. I believe that such an employment practice conforms to Japanese culture and is our core competence to help survive global competition.[5]

These attitudes concerning lifetime employment on the part of senior Japanese management are held generally. In a survey by Asahi Shimbun in July of 2003 of 100 major companies in a range of businesses, 88 percent replied that they will maintain lifetime employment, while 12 percent felt the system would be difficult to maintain. Continuation of the system is clearly the majority view, reinforced by the fact that Japan's most successful companies – Toyota, Canon, Hoya, Nippon Steel, Shin-etsu Chemical, Honda, and the like – all continue very much in the Nihonteki keiei methods of personnel management.

The importance of employment commitments

A powerful negative proof of the value of Japan's social contract in the workplace is provided by America's Boeing. Long the overwhelmingly dominant producer in the world of commercial aircraft, Boeing was as well the largest single source of exports from the United States for many years. However, aircraft purchases are cyclic, and in 1993, Boeing announced a cut in production of more than 40 percent because of order cancellations with the labor force to be cut by a full 35 percent. In addition, a special early retirement program stripped out 9000 more workers who had special skills. The retirement program alone cost $600 million, with a major strike by 32,500 workers increasing costs and losses. All of this to deal with a predictable turndown in orders over a two-year period.

By early 1996, the entirely predictable increase in orders began as the order cycle changed direction again as it had often in the past. Production delays and missed deliveries at Boeing mounted as the lack of trained assembly workers meant parts assemblies needed to be reworked, with newly hired managers simply unfamiliar with building airplanes. By late 1997, overwhelmed by thousands of production foul-ups, production of the 747 and 737 aircraft was temporarily halted, while the company reported a $1.6 billion third quarter loss, with another $1 billion expected. The company report for 1997 spoke of "raw material shortages, internal and supplier parts shortages and productivity inefficiencies associated with adding thousands of new employees."

The *New York Times* spoke of Boeing's competitor Airbus being "hampered by European restrictions on laying off workers," showing steady expansion of production.[6] "Hampered" indeed! Boeing should have been so "hampered." "After laying off 30,000 workers during an early '90s slump, Boeing hired 32,000 new workers in just 18 months. Many of the new workers did not have the same refined skills as the journeymen they replaced," said *The Times*. By early 2004, Airbus took the market share lead in commercial aircraft away from Boeing, won more gross orders than Boeing in four of the five earlier years, and established a much bigger order backlog, with a much higher R&D budget and a percentage return on sales similar to Boeing's. With scandals over government contracts, buffeted by shifting to Chicago from its long-time Seattle headquarters, Boeing terminated first its finance director and then its chief executive officer. It looks now to the defense business for its sales as its commercial aircraft position continues to decline.

Boeing might have followed the Japanese practice. It might have kept virtually all its staff as business turned down in 1993. It might have accepted lower share prices for a year or two, cut its dividend payment, reduced executive compensation, and tightened operations instead of blowing away tens of thousand of employees. A $600 million retirement program expense would have been unnecessary, and massive losses from failed production efforts would have been avoided if Boeing would have opted for continued employment, absorbed the cost of temporarily unnecessary workers, kept its head down through the slump, and retained its commanding share position as the market recovered.

It is hard to conceive of a more dramatic proof of the value of lifetime employment than this self-inflicted disaster at Boeing. The outcome is in very much the terms used by Toyota management in reply to Moody's rating reduction – skills and company loyalty are of vital importance and result from the employment commitment. Leaving aside the human costs of savage workforce reductions in the US manner, in sheer business and management terms lifetime employment offers critical advantages that Japanese companies like Canon and Toyota can take full advantage of – as Airbus did in the Boeing case.

High turnover means that human and organizational capital may be quickly eroded or transformed by newcomers. Even with respect to physical capital, turnover of employees plays a role, because utilization of physical capital depends on the experience of the workforce. The more firm-specific capital a worker has, the bigger the loss for the firm if the worker quits.[7]

It is to the advantage of firms in all types of businesses that the skills, experience, knowledge of suppliers and customers, and identification with the company be kept intact to maximize profits. Lifetime employment ensures the presence of that experience and those skills to help ensure the health of the firm.

As a footnote to this review of lifetime employment, it should be noted that there is no statutory law guaranteeing employment in Japan. However, there are court decisions that allow legal protection against "abuse of dismissal rights."[8] Certainly labor forces can be reduced. I have participated in several projects where redundant sales forces were cut in half without employee protests, negative publicity, or other disturbances. But these reductions in numbers of employees must be well planned, done over a considerable period of time, with generous termination allowances.

However, while layoffs and firings are the major labor adjustment methods used in the Anglo-American economies, "Japanese firms accomplish adjustments in personnel over a longer period, and circumvent dismissals for economic reasons by using internal buffers against aggregate changes in demand, reducing overtime hours, reassigning employers, hiring fewer new employees, and transferring employees who are temporary or permanent regular staff to affiliated firms."[9]

Note too that in the system of lifetime employment, fast-growing firms are hiring numbers of young workers, with labor costs dropping, while firms in low-growth, sunset industries have hired few if any new workers. These low-growth firms have increasing labor costs as the workforce ages, thus further slowing growth. The effect is to spur overall economic growth by rewarding the growing firms and punishing the slow-growth firms. At the same time the members of the aging workforce of the slow-growth companies move steadily to retirement age. By opening the back door for retirees and closing the front door to new hires, the workforce can be reduced steadily but without dismissals. A few years ago, half of the workers in Japan's steel industry were reaching retirement age within ten years, offering the steel companies an easy way to cut their labor force size in a zero-growth industry that they took full advantage of.

The revolution in non-core employment

The employment pattern based on career commitment continues as the core of the system in Japan. However, about one-quarter of Japan's workforce are quite outside that system, termed generally "part-timers" – although that includes a number of types of non-regular employees. The phenomenon is not new. Part-timers have a long history in retailing and wholesaling, sales activities, and services. Indeed, Japan's manufacturing industry too has long relied on part-time employees, seasonal workers, and subcontractors for labor in addition to regular, full-time employees. However, the total number of part-timers has gone through an extraordinary rate of increase, from less than 5 million in 1985, 11 percent of the workforce, to nearly 12 million by 2000, 21 percent of the workforce, and still increasing. Thus, while part-time and temporary employees are by no means an unusual category in Japan, the expansion is startling.

A number of forces are at work. One is the continued shift in the employment structure from once dominant primary industries – agriculture, forestry, and fishing – to manufacturing and now, with Japan having reached economic and demographic maturity, the tertiary industries the main sources of employment. More than half of all part-timers work in the wholesale, retail, and food and drink businesses, and part-timers make up almost half of all employees in those businesses. Part-timers are very few in construction and in utilities, and are about 12 percent of all employees in manufacturing. Clearly, the shift to services in the overall economy is a main driving force in this part-timer phenomenon. A corollary of this emphasis on services is the fact that in Japan, as in many of the OECD economies, three-quarters of all part-time workers are women. Many need to work flexible hours, as in personal services and retailing, where as well special skills are not required. Aeon, Japan's largest supermarket chain, has nearly 80 percent of its staff on part-time status, no doubt mainly women.

Another force at work in recent years has been deflation and low economic growth, with great pressure on companies to cut costs and reduce employment. One result has been increased unemployment to about 5 percent of the labor force. With increased unemployment, the willingness of workers to accept part-time work is increased. Another result has been the interest of companies to limit fixed costs by using temporary employees.

Still another factor in this expansion of part-time work is increased affluence. The "freeter" phenomenon, discussed further below, is due in part to the reluctance of many younger people to commit early to a career path while still wanting to explore alternative lifestyles. For many of these younger people – and for a good many career professionals as well – there is an interest in maintaining flexible working hours and circumstances. With affluence, younger people can draw on family support without the compulsion to find immediate and full-time employment.

The Ministry of Labor White Paper of 2000 made an important point regarding the expansion of part-time employment. "...If we look at patterns in the increase and decrease of employment, fewer than 10 percent of cases involve reducing the number of ordering workers and increasing the number of part-time workers in a so-called replacement."[10] Rather than taking the place of regular employees, the part-timers fill supplementary roles. The Ministry White Paper notes, "Because of the expansion of industries and employment patterns that use part-time workers, the rate of non-regular employment has grown at an unprecedented rate. Yet replacement of regular employees by part-time employees within a single company has been relatively rare."

A real change: Dispatching of workers

What is in process of greatly changing Japanese companies' approaches to staffing is the explosive growth of the business of dispatching workers. Until 1986, Japanese law prohibited the labor supply business whereby companies supply other companies with their own personnel. With the passage of the Worker Dispatching Law, the placing of a firm's own employees with third parties was approved as a business. Limited in initial application, the range of work allowed by dispatched workers has steadily broadened with the final extension in 2004 to manufacturing workers.

The growth of this temporary staffing business has been extraordinary. There are now in Japan more than 10,000 dispatching agencies. The largest is the Japan subsidiary of Switzerland's Adecco, with annual revenue in 2002 of ¥135 billion. Persona and Tempstaff Co., join in the ¥100 billion league, with Manpower Japan and Recruit Staffing also majors in the ¥70 to ¥80 billion range. Some of these companies, like Manpower Japan, go back several decades well before the change in the dispatching law, and the leading position of foreign companies is a striking phenomenon. But most of the agencies stem from the mid-1980s and the change in the law. The most recent Ministry data, for FY2003, estimated the revenues of the industry at ¥2250 billion, involving 2,130,000 workers, an increase in the year of 22 percent. And the business is not yet 20-years old.

There are two categories of workers at dispatching agencies. One is termed "registered" workers who are hired by the agency only when a job is available to be filled by dispatch. Most of these workers operate office equipment or work in the financial/clerical field, with fees to the agency around ¥16,000 to ¥17,000 for eight working hours. The other category is that of "regular-base" dispatched workers who are employed continuously by the agency, who work in software development, equipment design, and other highly skilled tasks, and for whom the agency receives fees of ¥30,000 to ¥35,000. These are all temporary workers, the largest number contracted for less than three months, and nearly all for less than six months.

A Ministry White Paper notes that dispatched work is especially common in IT-related operations – software development, operations of business machines, and instruction in office automation. It seems clear that dispatching of temporary workers will provide a means for Japan's companies to bring in specialist workers for projects that have a finite life. The dispatch agency takes the risks regarding staff competence and bears the costs of recruiting and handling personnel, a real saving for the purchaser who is spared the burden of providing permanent employment to individuals carrying out what may well be a one-time task.

So Japan's employment system has a major new component. Around the core of permanent employees it is now possible to add supplementary skills, on a temporary basis. This new approach to staffing is not replacing the traditional hiring of regular employees for career employment. Rather, it is adding a valuable dimension of additional flexibility to labor management in Japan. The high and increasing incidence of part-timers in the labor force may not be a permanent feature, but the dispatching agencies look like being here to stay.

As the economy renews steady growth and deflation ends, pressure on company finances and pressure for cost reductions eases. Unemployment is reduced. The labor force continues to decline in numbers, and continues to age. Labor shortage rather than labor surplus becomes the prevailing rule. With all these forces at work, how much of the current emphasis on temporary employment will continue? Will the part-timers become full timers? Outsourcing has its merits, but full command of the time and interest of employees, the ability to invest in their training, their focus on quality of output all require full timers. The current phase of the Japanese economy is a difficult time to predict how permanent all of this part-time frenzy will be. Dispatching of specialists is an important new development that will expand in scope in coming years. Continued large-scale hiring of part-timers seems much less likely as labor shortages begin to occur and regular employment, with its greater income and much greater security, becomes easily available.

Freeters: The odd fellows?

"Freeters" as a term is a combination of the English "free" and the German "arbeiter" – "arbeit" having a long history in Japanese as a term for part-time or occasional jobs. Freeters are young people who are voluntarily working as part-time or marginal laborers. Freeters are said to have increased from some 500,000 in 1982 to over 2 million in 2002, with increases continuing, although any estimate must rather arbitrarily distinguish between part-timers and true freeters. Perhaps we should consider freeters a sub-case of the increased population of part-timers, a precise number not possible given the rather vague definitions of freeters.

However many they may be, it is clear that true freeters switch jobs often, staying in one job at most for a few months. Thus a large part of recent reported increases in job separation is due to the frequent job changes of the freeters. Freeters are defined as employees between the ages of 15 and 34, who graduated from or dropped out of an educational establishment, who in the case of females are unmarried, who are termed "part-timers" by their employers, who neither undertake house-work now nor are enrolled in an educational establishment, and who wish to work as part-timers.[11] Freeters are less well educated than the average in Japan, most with no more than a high school education. Most are women, and estimates are that two-thirds of the freeters live at home with their parents.

The Japan Institute of Labor concluded that there are three types of freeters. Some have no immediate future plans or goals, the so-called "parasite singles" who depend on their parents for basic living necessities. Some freeters are young people who are planning and preparing for work in such professional areas as theatre, the arts, animation, and game software and want to avoid the constraints on their time and interest of regular employment. And some freeters simply have failed to find or qualify for regular work but would like to find such a job. It is a very mixed group in motives and behavior, and lumping all freeters together under a single term is not accurate nor is it helpful in under-standing the labor force situation.

Economics are a force in creating some types of freeters. Companies have held down employment of new staff, who would be younger, while continuing the employment of older persons. Thus unemployment rates of younger people have become high in Japan since the mid-1990s. As a result, even younger people who would like a regular job find themselves freeters. This situation like the broader issue of part-timers will change substantially with economic growth and renewed inflation.

However, there is an important category of freeters who are serious in their career pursuits, and do not seek a regular job. Japan as an affluent society now has room for such youngsters who, thanks in part to family support, can take several of their years of youth to pursue ideas and activities outside the normal industrial routine. My generation of Americans, children of the economic crisis of the Great Depression who lost their youth to military service, came out of World War II bent on starting their income producing careers as soon as possible. But our children had no such compulsion, seeing a few years of exploration after college as reasonable, even necessary. The drive to start earning immediately was not there for a generation born into affluence. And so now for Japan. Some of the freeters are no doubt simply irresponsible persons. Some are no doubt victims of a punishing employment environment. But some are able, sincere, and important for Japan's future as they develop new concepts and new skills. Grouping all these together as "freeters" and condemning them all as economic burdens is a mistake.

Seniority pay and promotion: Redesigning the second pillar

The first pillar of Japanese style management, the lifetime commitment, has survived largely intact, with some important embellishments as dispatch workers take the place of seasonal and other temporary employees. The second of the three pillars, seniority pay and promotion, is undergoing extensive, but still incomplete, redesign.

Two notes are useful when discussing seniority systems. First, every society tends to recognize seniority in promotions and in pay. Older persons tend to be in higher ranks; the very young executive is still an oddity almost everywhere. And the curve of average compensation tends upward in all economies from the early 20s to around the mid-50s, falling off then toward retirement age. Second, Japan's nenko joretsu, or seniority-based system was never pure. The age escalator did not carry one automatically to the top; the rise of most stopped early on. And often a younger person would exercise authority even though not yet holding high rank. Pay went up automatically with age, but such pay elements as the bonus were in most companies made subject to performance to a degree.

That said, the very strong connection between tenure and pay in the Japanese company is changing. Various surveys provide evidence of the change, with increasing differences between the basis for executive compensation and general employee compensation. For example, the Asahi Shimbun survey of 100 major companies noted earlier found that when deciding compensation of supervisors, 61 percent used performance as the basis, while 31 percent used mainly performance with some weighting for seniority. Only 8 percent used seniority as the main factor with a lesser weighting for performance.

However, the compensation of general employees according to this survey is more seniority based. Only 13 percent of the companies use performance in deciding pay, while 56 percent use mainly performance with some seniority weighting, and 31 percent use mainly seniority with some consideration to output. An extensive survey by the Japan Productivity Center for Socio-Economic Development presents a very similar picture with ability and performance the key factors in supervisors' compensation, with tenure a minor factor, while for general employees tenure remains a major consideration in pay.

Reviewing survey data, Professor M. Morishima concludes:

> A slightly larger proportion of firms used employees' age and tenure to determine their base pay in 2001 than in 1997! These results seem to show that employers are not simply shifting to a new determinant. They make the wage determination system more complex than before by considering a larger number of factors. Employees' performance has become important but other factors such as employee age and tenure have not been abandoned.[12]

However, real changes are occurring, company by company. Toyota is to end seniority pay for all employees and a similar decision has been announced by Hitachi Ltd, Matsushita Electric, and Canon. These are four of Japan's most powerful companies, and also four of Japan's most "traditional" companies in terms of management practices. We can assume seniority pay is phasing out, rather rapidly perhaps. No surprise really. In a rapidly aging Japan it may well prove to be the case that younger people, fewer and thus more valuable, will receive higher pay than older people at some future point.

While not strictly related to the seniority pay and promotion system question, a few other aspects of compensation in Japan can be noted here. First, while exchange rate changes make comparisons hazardous, generally in recent years the hourly pay of Japanese workers has been amongst the highest in the world, about at the German level and above the US level. This is the case while actual hours worked per year by Japanese labor, well above the low level of Germany, are now rather less than hours worked per year by US labor.

Second, while a topic for discussion of corporate governance, it should be noted here that income distribution in Japan is notably egalitarian, Japan's Gini Coefficient at the level of the Scandinavian countries, unchanged since the mid-1990s. Since Japanese tend to compare their country with the United States, it needs be noted that income distribution in the United States is similar to that in Cambodia and Ethiopia, according to World Bank data, extremely unequal.[13] In the Japanese industrial company, the chief executive receives in total income about 10 times more that the average employee, a ratio quite like that of Germany. In the United States the ratio in recent years of top management pay to that of the average employee has been over 400 times, and this appalling inequality is increasing still. Management compensation in the United States actually increased in 2002 while share prices and profits fell sharply.

Overall, the role of seniority in the Japanese company is fast diminishing. It seems likely that this reflects and interacts with a more general tendency in Japanese society of a weakening of the age-grading system. The changing population structure and the shift to the nuclear family living in an impersonal urban setting no doubt are factors in the change. Older persons do still command respect, in language and in actions. But the very special role of older people is lessened – witness the enforcement of an age limit for parliamentarians by the current prime minister, despite great protest from a distinguished predecessor of advanced years who was summarily displaced, the Koizumi-Nakasone confrontation.

The hardly noticed third pillar, the enterprise union

The enterprise union, kigyonai kumiai, is the third of the three so-called "pillars" of Japanese style management. The union is made up of the employees of only a single company, taking in all employees up to supervisory ranks. There are almost no craft or industry trade unions in Japan; worker identification has been with the company he or she is part of rather than with the skill category in which he or she works. The contrast with the Anglo-American pattern is again complete. It has been the case that a single British company management might have to negotiate with a dozen or more unions representing different skills. And the US union movement is dominated by the auto workers union, the steel workers union, and the like, as well as having skill-based unions. None of this applies to Japan, where the individual company is the unit.

Curiously, this system has two diametrically opposing effects. One, if all workers belong to the same union, the strength of the union is very great indeed in negotiations. It is not possible for management to set one group against another in bargaining. However, if the union exercises its strengths, through strikes for example, too vigorously, it risks damaging the company and thereby, in Japan's employment system, the well-being of all its union members. The enterprise union is another instance of how the Japanese company is an integrated social system, a community in which all cooperate in the common interest. It is a powerful concept.

In any case, the trade union movement in Japan surged mightily under the Occupation authorities at the end of World War II. It was clear that Occupation policy favored unionization – which had a previous history in Japan but was largely destroyed in the military regime's run up to the war. As a result of this perceived encouragement, union membership in 1947 included 45 percent of all employees, an extraordinarily high proportion. Much of the leadership of unions at this time was well to the left on the political spectrum, indeed often Communist, and some fierce battles took place in the late 1940s and early 1950s for control of the workplace. As the battles for control were ending, by 1955 unionization was at about a third of the labor force. It remained at this level through to the mid-1970s. It began to decline then and is now about 20 percent of the workforce, the decline in unionization continuing.

It is hard now to remember how very important the trade unions were in every aspect of management decision-making in this earlier period. All discussions of corporate plans and policy in the 1950s paid major attention to the attitudes and reactions of the trade union to any proposed decision. The "spring struggle" was a major event for the nation as the unions fought for higher wages and better working conditions, in an annual, nationwide effort. Railroads were struck, and commuters walked the long miles to work. Political issues had the union leaders as central figures in the debates and battles. Companies like Nissan made it through the period by essentially giving their union control over major corporate decisions (now it is the French, not the union).

Now in our interviews with the CEOs of Nippon Steel and Sumitomo Chemical, they see the union as even more committed to the long-term interest of the company than is management. Far from confrontation, the relationship now is one of close cooperation. The head of the Japan Business Federation notes that shunto, "spring struggle," is an obsolete word as fierce negotiations over annual wage increases have come to an end. The union concern now is job security rather than wage increases, and to this end labor–management cooperation must and has taken the place of confrontation.

Take the decline in the role of the union, once so very important, to be due to several factors. One is the fact that much of what the unions were earlier fighting for has by now been achieved, through improved laws governing working conditions, and through winning the wage battles with earlier management. The data suggest that the effect of unions on salary and earnings is by now virtually non-existent. "We've won. No need to fight longer." And no need for union membership. The other factor no doubt is the shift in the industrial structure and the changes in the employment system described above. New companies appear in new industries; growth takes place in service and other tertiary industries where unionization has been and is limited.

The enterprise union of Japan, the third pillar of Japanese style management, has not disappeared. It remains the entirely dominant form of union organization, and commands still about a fifth of the workforce in membership. But it is now quietly cooperative, eager to work with management to improve the company's results, focused on job security rather than pay, avoiding confrontation – and playing a steadily lesser role in the affairs of Japan's companies.

*   *   *

Over the past half-century of dramatic economic and technological change, has Japan's employment system changed? Basically, it has not. The underlying values on which it was built – the concept of community in which all fully and fairly participate as one does in family, village, and neighborhood – remain the foundation. Key practices – an emphasis on continuity, on group integrity, and on egalitarianism – remain in effect.

Change is taking place, as it always must. Technological change dictates bringing specialist skills into the organization as needed rather than permanently. An aging workforce dictates reducing the part of seniority in compensation and promotion. Changing industry structure reduces the role of the union. These are not changes toward some hypothetical, Western model. They are adaptations to changing conditions whilst leaving intact the values and practices that have characterized Japanese management and that are the key source of the system's continuing strength.

Notes

1. James C. Abegglen, *The Japanese Factory*, Glencoe, Illinois: Free Press, 1958. In Japanese, *Nihon no Keiei* (translated by Urabe Kuniyoshi), Tokyo: Diamondo Sha, 1958.
2. Takao Kato, "The End of Lifetime Employment in Japan? Evidence from National Surveys and Field Research", *Journal of the Japanese and International Economies*. 15, p. 512.
3. Yukari Matsuzuka, *Changes in the Permanent Employment System in Japan Between 1982 and 1997*, New York: Routledge, 2002, p. 69.
4. Ebato Tetsuo, *Seika Shugi o Koeru*, Tokyo: Bungei Shunju, 2002, pp. 9–13.
5. *Nikkei Weekly*, 18 March 2002, p. 3.
6. "Boeing Problems Help Airbus Narrow Gap", *New York Times*, 3 December 1998.
7. Auer and Cazes, op. cit., p. 3.
8. *The Labor Situation in Japan 2002/2003*, Tokyo: The Japan Institute of Labor, 2002, p. 43.
9. Auer and Cazes, op. cit., p. 162.
10. Ministry of Labour, *White Paper on Labour 2000*, Tokyo: The Japan Institute of Labour, 2000, p. 33.
11. *Jiyu no Daisho/Furiitaa*, Kosugi Reiko (ed.) Tokyo: Nihon Rodo Kenkyu Kiko, 2002, p. 26.
12. Motohiro Morishima, "Pay Practices in Japanese Organizations: Changes and Non-Changes", *Japan Labor Bulletin*, 1 April 2002, p. 9.
13. "The United States suffers from greater earnings and income inequality, higher poverty rates and lower poverty exits than almost every other OECD economy. Due to the highly unequal distribution of income in the United States, low-wage workers and low-income households are almost universally worse off in absolute terms than their low-wage, low-income counterparts in other, less affluent OECD countries. . . . There is less mobility out of poverty in the United States than in other nations. Poverty is deeper and harder to escape . . . and much less is available in the way of adequate social policy relative to other OECD countries." Mishel Lawrence, Jared Bernstein, and Heather Boushey, *The State of Working America 2002/2003*. Ithaca, New York: Cornell University Press, 2003, pp. 430–431.

5
A Perfect Financial Storm

The changes in Japan's economy as it has moved from historic high growth to full industrial and demographic maturity are nowhere more striking than in the sourcing, structure, and management of corporate finance. These changes, taking place from the mid-1990s, were driven by an extraordinary combination of low and erratic growth rates of the economy, long-continued deflationary price drops, massive declines in asset values, and sharp changes in accountancy rules – in finance, a perfect storm. Companies have weathered the storm by a focus on reducing debt, with bank borrowings very much lessened and other sources of finance more widely used. Careless and unmanaged proliferation of subsidiaries and affiliates has been corrected. Holding company structures allow establishing financial structures for separate businesses. Pension obligations are fully recognized and asset values marked to market value. All this at considerable cost; all made necessary by a brutally difficult economic environment and changed regulations; all now largely accomplished as a new era begins.

Japan's companies, in all sectors, have been on a severe diet for a number of years. Low demand levels, virtually no growth, and continued price deflation have forced reductions in labor costs, in numbers of competitors, in overstated asset values, in excessive diversifications and over-grown capacity. By 2003, the results of the diet were becoming evident as the economy was regaining its balance. Japan's companies, across the economy, were becoming lean and vigorous, recovering confidence and profitability.

Some of the changes in financial management in the difficult years were been driven by the economic situation, and are not likely to be permanent as growth resumes and balance sheet pressures are relieved. Cross-shareholdings between banks and clients, now very much diminished, are likely to be renewed in some degree. Indirect financing through bank borrowings is likely to increase again with renewed capital expenditure. The institution of the main bank will have a lessened role, but the main bank in a more limited role is to continue. Corporations in 21st century Japan will not be funded and governed through securities markets as in Britain and the United States. The emerging Japanese pattern is a complex one, with a great deal of change, but largely within the broad and familiar patterns of the past.

Financing historic high growth

Financing of corporations in Japan from the mid-1950s was driven by – and was driver of – the very rapid growth of the economy. To appreciate the impact on finance, the magnitude of the growth achievement needs be kept clearly in mind. In the 45-year period from 1955 to 2000, the economy grew in yen terms about 65 times, and in US dollar terms about 210 times. This massive shift from real poverty to significant wealth resulted from very high levels of investment. Gross domestic investment as a percent of GDP averaged 32 percent from 1960 to 2000, half again as much as in the cases of the United States and Germany during the same period.

These overall figures are the sum of countless corporate decisions regarding financial management, decisions shaped by the compulsion to grow assets and sales to hold and try to improve competitive position. Under conditions of very rapid growth, a failure to match competitors' growth rates would mean in short time a brutal loss of market share and thus of profitability. Markets during this long period of high growth not uncommonly doubled each year for several years. Failure to double manufacturing capacity by indulging for a single year in a focus on profitability would mean the instant halving of market share, with a commensurate disadvantage accruing in production costs. The name of the game became market share/growth.

However, in a capital-short economy, this growth could not be funded by sale of new shares. Nor could it be funded through high prices/profits since the high prices would block market share growth. The solution was, inevitably, high levels of debt borrowed from commercial banks. Not only was bank debt more available than direct debt or new equity, but it also was low-cost since the central bank was prepared to provide money supply through the banks to meet growth requirements. Debt is always less expensive than equity in any case, since interest is a tax deducible expense while dividend payments for equity are high and are only after-tax.

No surprise then that the growth was debt-financed in Japan (as it is in all fast-growing economies like Korea and China in their turn). Debt-equity ratios reached a high in post-oil shock 1975 of nearly 6:1 in all businesses and about 5:1 in manufacturing. At this kind of debt level, US commentators were prone to see Japanese companies as having an unfair advantage, these levels of debt not available from US banks.[1] Asset growth reached a maximum in 1990, when it was at an index of 164 with 1975 as 100, according to the Ministry of Finance Policy Research Institute. Capital investment similarly peaked in the 1990–92 period, having climbed steeply through the bubble period of the mid- to late-1980s.

Partly because of the high debt levels, returns on equity were rather good, generally in the 8–9 percent range through the 1970s and 1980s. Dividend policy was fairly consistent over time, with the dividend payout ratio around 35 percent. It might be noted here that despite all the mythology about Japanese managements' indifference toward shareholders, dividends have been paid at a quite consistent level whatever the profitability might be – which can mean a more than 100 percent payout rate in a loss year.

The shareholders in Japanese companies have done well in the long run. The return on the NRI 350 index (Nomura Research Institute stock market index of 350 Japanese stocks) since the early 1970s is about the same as the return on Standard & Poor's 500 during that period. (From the first quarter of 1971 until the third quarter of 1995 the annual growth rate of the NRI 350 was 12.16 percent. Over the same period, the annual growth rather of the S&P 500 was 12.17 percent.)[2]

The main stakeholder in the Japanese company is the employee. The share in the company held by whoever now has it represents a capital investment. That investment is entitled to a return, and that return is provided when at all possible. But there is no further obligation to, nor right held by, the shareholder. (The United States and the United Kingdom have somehow developed the curious view that the shareholder has total entitlement to the company.)

Recent changes in law have made possible share buybacks and stock option programs. Both changes are aimed presumably at supporting and increasing share prices. Neither program has achieved any significant role in Japan's financial management. Share options are confined almost entirely small, start-up companies, and are not part of the compensation of management in most large companies. (Employee share ownership programs have a long history in Japan, but these are in no sense stock option programs.) Share buybacks do occur but in amounts very far below what is termed "share buyback ability," available surplus cash totals. Cash surpluses like Toyota's $20 billion, Takeda's $10 billion, Fuji Film's $10 billion are reserved for presumed future business needs – and are not used to support share price by reducing shares outstanding or by increasing dividends greatly. Share price remains a marginal goal, and is not the measure of corporate performance in Japan.

The role of the shareholder has been, not surprisingly, a lesser one since the great majority of corporate funds has been sourced from banks rather than through issues of equity. The bank provided most of the money; the bank could if it chose have the louder voice in affairs. This flow of funds through banks, indirect financing rather than financing directly through bonds and other capital market instruments, led to the phenomenon of the "main bank."

> There is no single agreed definition of the term "main bank," but in cases where a number of banks have made loans to a particular firm, it generally refers to the bank that has a particularly long and continuous record of business relations with the firm and has advanced the largest loans. In some cases a comprehensive range of business dealings, including shareholdings and directorships in the firm, and handling its pensions and financial settlements, are considered the characteristics of a main bank. Currently many firms in Japan have this sort of special relationship (though not always of the same type) with their "main bank", and the arrangement is said to serve a variety of beneficial functions with regard to monitoring the firm, spreading associated risks, and so on. The link between Japan's post-war economic success and Japanese-style firms has long since been pointed out. The distinctive features of these firms are summed up in the long-term harmonious relations that exist between the different levels within each firm, and between firms that do business together. The main bank system is regarded as a fundamental component of this so-called Japan-style capitalism.[3]

As part of the financial structuring of Japanese companies, cross shareholdings between the corporation and its main bank became a key part of the share ownership structure. These often had long histories, as the companies in the historic groupings – Sumitomo, Mitsui, Mitsubishi – used the group's bank as main bank with the bank holding shares in the company and the company shareholder in the bank. These mutual shareholdings, or "cross holdings," came to as much as a third of total group company shares in the case of Sumitomo group companies at the 1987 peak of cross-holdings. Thus not only the debt portion but the equity portion of the company as well was dominated, indeed largely controlled, by the main bank. And thus the risks associated with the very high debt levels incurred to fund rapid growth were greatly tempered by the deep relationships between lender and borrower, with the Bank of Japan and Ministry of Finance providing the essential assurance that there would be no bank failures.

This in general was the dominant pattern of corporate financing through the period to the early 1990s: a focus on growth and market share driving massive capital investments, these funded by bank borrowings to a very high level, borrowed against collateral values, the bank borrowings largely from "main banks" with mutual shareholdings. High debt helped in the achievement of very good returns on equity, all this providing attractive returns to shareholders, even with modest levels of dividend payouts. The system was based on high growth – and required high rates of growth to continue as a viable approach to financing.

The grand climax – and denoument

Rapid economic growth had as its corollary rapid growth in exports. Japan has never been a large exporter; exports are generally around 10 percent of GNP, well below the average for other major economies. However, exports did keep pace with growth, exports coming after high growth in domestic demand and output. The United States was for long the dominant export market. The US economy went through a difficult period in the early 1980s, and in the usual US fashion, the cause was argued to be foreign plotting. Japan was seen as a major cause of industry problems, much as China is being made villain in more recent years. In 1984, Japan's exports increased considerably, this time by 16 percent, this while the yen had for several years been weakening against the dollar – from a 201 rate in 1978 to 252 in 1984. The low yen value was seen as cause of the export increase.

Not surprising then that at a meeting of finance ministers of the major economies in 1985 there emerged the "Plaza Accord," an agreement to adjust exchange rates, and in particular to move the yen up substantially. And in fact the yen did move, dramatically from 252 to 122 to the US dollar in only three years, doubling its exchange value. To meet US demands, and as well to deal with the deflationary potential of so rapid and drastic an exchange rate shift, Japan's money supply was increased explosively, by 10 percent annually through 1990. Along with this, naturally, went a drastic drop in the discount rate of the Bank of Japan to a low in 1988 of 2.5 percent, half the earlier rate levels.

All of this triggered Japan's nearly fatal "bubble," the extraordinary increase in the values of real estate and corporate shares in the 1985–91 period. The causes are not unlike those that led to the US "bubble" of the late 1990s, with the Federal Reserve greatly expanding money supply, holding interest rates at a moderate level. In both cases, asset values took off, while consumer price levels increased rather little, asset inflation rather than the usual price inflation.

The magnitude of the "bubble" was astonishing. Land prices in Japan tripled in only six years from 1985 to their peak in 1991. Share prices nearly tripled in four years from 1985 to a peak in 1989. Nominal GDP growth reached 8 percent in 1990. Total national wealth doubled from 1984/85 to a 1990 peak. One hazardous myth born in this period was the conviction that in land-short Japan land prices would rise forever. Golf club memberships soared in value and became major financial instruments as investments. Price: earnings ratios of shares went over 60:1 as prices far outstripped earnings, even while earnings were doing well.

As asset values rose, corporations were able to increase borrowings with equal rapidity as banks lent with these increasingly valuable assets as collateral. This was the case through the period of high growth, and the pace even accelerated from the mid-1980s as the "bubble" grew. Then, quite suddenly, financial policies changed drastically as fears over asset inflation took command. The increase in money supply, 10 percent annually up to 1990, dropped to 0.6 percent in 1992. Money supply was simply turned off. The central bank discount rate, 2.5 percent in 1987, went to 6.0 percent in 1990. No surprise then that share prices plunged, losing over the next decade more than three-quarters of their value on average. Urban land prices dropped even more drastically, to a mere 15 percent of their earlier level.

The resulting situation is summarized by Richard Koo of Nomura Research Institute as follows:

> During the 1970s and 1980s, Japanese companies took out massive loans with which to expand their businesses.... The value of the assets, which should be at least as large as the size of their debts, has

collapsed. As a result, the balance sheet, or the financial health of the companies, has deteriorated drastically. The sheer magnitude of the decline in assets prices suggests that perhaps there are hundreds of thousands of businesses in Japan whose liabilities exceed their assets, or whose financial condition is close to it. For these companies, the excess liabilities mean that they are actually bankrupt.[4]

This is the crisis situation that Japanese companies found themselves in as the bubble burst and asset values plunged. Financial managers could hardly have imagined so severe a set of problems. The like has in fact not been seen in the world since the experience of the United States in the Great Depression of the 1930s. That period of US deflation ended only with the outbreak of World War II and the massive government expenditures that resulted. Japan's government did not have so dramatic a remedy for deflation and lack of growth ready to hand.

A long-continuing deflation was in fact a critical outcome. There is a certain fashion to blame the deflation on government policy failures in terms of money supply, interest rates, and fiscal policy. No doubt perfect moves in each of these aspects could have mitigated the problem. But policies – clever or clumsy – were not the cause, nor remedy. Deflation was the consequence of long-sustained massive capital investment, continuing far longer than basic demand warranted. The extent of investment can be gained by observing, as noted above, that through the entire period from 1960 to 2000 gross domestic investment as a percent of GDP was half again greater in Japan through the entire period than was the case for the United States or Germany. With high demand growth, so high a level of investment made excellent economic sense. As demand growth slackened and as the economy matured, over-capacity became all-too-commonly the rule.

With money supply down, interest rates up, and share and land prices dropping sharply, demand inevitably began weakening. Especially given overcapacity in any case, production needed to be cut back and costs reduced. This in turn further reduced demand as wages began to fall and job security lessened. And this in turn made for further cuts in capacity and capacity utilization – and so on down the vicious deflation cycle. GDP real growth went from 5.6 percent in 1990 to 0.5 percent only two years later, with negative real growth in 1998. Demand plunged; growth stopped; companies were in crisis. The magnitude and abruptness of change can be gauged from the Bank of Japan's report in its Quarterly Bulletin of November 2003 (page 200) that the increase in real business fixed investment averaged a very high

8.4 percent from 1981 to 1990, and averaged precisely 0.0 percent from 1991 to 2002.

Stated asset values of Japan's companies peaked in 1991, after a rapid run up in values from the mid-1980s, and began to decline in 1992. A decade later, in 2002, corporate asset values had declined by nearly 60 percent from the 1991 peak. Banks had been lending aggressively against the ever-higher asset positions of companies that served as attractive collateral for loans. And quite abruptly the backing for those bank loans began to disappear rather rapidly. Shareholder equity, at 100 in 1991, was only 42 by 2002. That is, the average Japanese company shareholder lost well over half of their share's value in a decade. For larger companies the decline was to 80 – small- and medium-sized enterprises took the major beating.

Koo of Nomura describes this cycle in financial, rather than in industrial capacity terms.

> A balance sheet recession typically emerges after the bursting of a nationwide asset price bubble that leaves a large number of private sector balance sheets in need of serious repair. In order to repair their balance sheets, the affected companies are forced to move away from their usual profit maximization to debt minimization.... When everyone moves in that direction at the same time, aggregate demand shrinks and worsens both the economy and assets prices. This, in turn, forces the companies to pay down debt even faster, resulting in a vicious cycle.[5]

And pay down debt they have. Even against the sharp drop in equity values, the ratio of debt to equity for manufacturing firms, the usual measure of a company's financial strength or lack of it, went from 5.8 in 1975 to 2.9 in 1990 to under 1:1 in 2002 – and continues to decline, according to the Ministry of Finance Policy Research Institute. "In 1997, corporate debt in Japan and America was nearly equal at $900 billion each. By 2002, however, total American corporate debt had risen to more than double that of Japan."[6] And Japan's companies continued still to reduce borrowings – causing considerable grief for Japan's troubled banks. There is a certain irony in all this since throughout the 1980s, as Japan grew mightily and the United States stagnated, it was customary in the United States to view with self-righteous alarm the very high levels of Japanese corporate debt – "You cannot have that much leverage and still be a company," said one US investment banker, looking at average D:E ratios of 6:1 and higher. There has been a nice reversal of circumstances and views from that decade through the next one.

Indeed, a good number of Japan's leading companies now have no debt. This is true not only of top manufacturers like Canon, Takeda Chemical, Murata, and Rohm, but of the top retailer, Seven-Eleven Japan, as well. This reduction of leverage – and especially its total absence – makes devotees of return on equity numbers unhappy as that measure of profit is depressed when leverage is low. One group of ROE devotees, the staff of Goldman Sachs, state,

> In a low interest rate environment like Japan's where the cost of equity is well above the cost of debt, companies that can afford to do so should in fact be raising financial leverage rather than reducing it – i.e., indeed, the exact opposite of what most firms have been doing over the past several years.[7]

Not only is this a quite extraordinary reversal of earlier US conventional wisdom, but it is also a statement seemingly oblivious to the crucial factors that have driven debt reduction by Japan's companies. So long as deflation continues, there will be a drive to reduce debt levels. Inflation pays off debt; deflation magnifies it.

Recognition of the need to repair balance sheets and regain financial stability did not come early nor yet easily. Neither government nor business fully realized the changed nature of the economic environment and the shift from growth to maturity that the ending of the bubble signaled. The initial downturn was generally seen as simply another cyclic change, a temporary condition to be remedied in the usual fashion with reduced interest rates and increased government expenditures. When that failed to work in the first year or two of downturn, the conclusion was to try again, with more. And when that too failed to deal with the increased problems, there was finally a realization that this was and is a new era, needing new measures, a structural crisis requiring structuring change. On the level of government policy, the Hashimoto government's move in 1996 to the financial system "big bang" was a clear indicator of the conclusion that real changes were required. The mid-1990s was the time when restructuring plans began to be put in place by Japan's companies as well as they too realized the basic change in the nature of the economy.

Weathering the perfect financial storm

As Japan's companies began facing up to the greatly changed environment, a series of accounting changes hammered the problems home with a vengeance. Through what has been called the "Accounting Big Bang," new accounting rules were put in place beginning in 1999, implemented in stages over the next several years, bringing Japanese accounting practices into line with international standards in several key respects. A first major change in rules was the requirement that companies report on a consolidated basis, corporate results to include all firms in which the parent has control – not simply majority share owner-ship but effective or substantial influence on subsidiaries and affiliates.

The impact of this change has been substantial. For a long time, it was the practice in Japan for companies to report only the results of the parent company itself – consolidated corporate returns were not required nor yet even customary except for those rather few companies subject to the US Security Exchange Commission rules for reporting. Businesses doing badly could be spun off as subsidiaries, with losses not reflected in the parent's reported results. And indeed very promising businesses could also be spun off, to free them from the parent's bureaucratic tendencies and to allow promising young executives a field to practice in.

Generally around the mid-1980s, the numbers of subsidiaries of Japa-nese companies increased rather suddenly. Even in 2003 both Hitachi and Sony reported more than 1000 subsidiaries, Mitsubishi Shoji nearly 600, Sumitomo Trading more than 500, Toshiba and Matsushita Electric more than 300. And so on and on. It would seem a remarkable achieve-ment for the management of Sony and Hitachi to remember the names of all those subsidiaries, much less keep track of or discipline perform-ance. And these numbers include only subsidiaries, and do not include the considerable numbers of affiliates accounted for by the equity method.

Now, many of these subsidiaries no doubt serve marketing purposes in foreign jurisdictions. And for some companies, subsidiaries served as well as locations for relocating personnel deemed redundant in parent operations. But in any event, whatever their purpose, the sudden requirement of consolidating balance sheets of so vast a number of odds and ends of businesses placed enormous pressure on what were already precariously balanced corporate results.

As an example of magnitude of the problem subsidiaries can present, a news report on the subsidiaries of Mitsui & Co., in the English edition of the Asahi Shimbun of 15–16 September 2003 provides an interesting and no doubt representative example.

> Mitsui & Co. said Friday it will cut the number of its consolidated subsidiaries and affiliated firms by nearly 30 percent by the end of March 2005 to reduce negative effects on group earnings from

poor-performing units. The trading house selected about 190 of the 702 consolidated units in Japan for liquidation, sale or merger with other firms.... Mitsui's consolidated units booked losses totaling 71.1 billion yen in the year ended March 31, and the company hopes to reduce the losses to around 10 billion yen by the end of March 2005.

There is a real question of management competence when problems of this magnitude are allowed to fester unattended for a long period. In any case, the change in the accounting rules to require consolidated reporting is in turn requiring that management move to bring order to these sprawling complexes of subsidiaries, used all too often in the past as a device to move business mistakes from the front steps to the rear alley. Economic performance can only be improved as a result of cleaning up these odd bits and pieces. And, in fairness, a great many leading companies have had little or no resort to the subsidiary device – Fanuc 17 subs, Takeda Chemical 54, Rohm 48, Hoya 52, Murata 52. No surprise – these are among Japan's most profitable companies, clearly more tightly managed than many.

The second major change in accounting rules was market value accounting, or "mark-to-market." Investment portfolios and real estate holdings, previously valued at either acquisition cost or the lower of acquisition cost and market value have now to be stated at current market value. In a growth environment, with rising share prices and increasing land prices, this accounting requirement would make for very positive balance sheet results, the number getting steadily better. In Japan's economic environment of 2001 when the new rule came into full effect, the impact was disastrous. Share prices and land prices were dropping as GDP growth went negative. Assets acquired at peak prices in the 1980s reached new lows in market value in 2001 – and these values had to be reflected on company balance sheets.

Closely related to the change in asset value accounting was the change in accounting for pension obligations. Like market value accounting, this was introduced in fiscal 2000. The new rule required that pension obligations be fully accounted for and valued at current market value. It became an extremely punishing accounting requirement in the context of falling interest rates and steeply declining share prices.

An appreciation of the impact of these changes in accounting rules in the context of declining share prices can be gained by looking at the case of NEC. A \$40 billion sales company founded in 1899, NEC has been Japan leader in telecommunications equipment for more than a century. But with the telecom and semiconductor markets collapsing at home and abroad, with NEC involved in a government procurement scandal, and with some mistaken diversifications dragging down results, NEC struggled for several years in a massive effort to reconstruct. In the midst of this effort, the accounting rule changes made problems distinctly more difficult.

In fiscal 2003,

> NEC incurred a loss of ¥132.2 billion ($1,120 million) from the minimum pension liability adjustment due to a falling investment returns on pension plan assets reflecting slumping stock prices and a reduction in the discount rate for calculating benefit obligations, and losses from marketable securities of ¥45.2 billion ($383 million), reflecting the realization of the unrealized gains due to the sale of marketable securities and an increase in unrealized losses on marketable securities due to worsening market conditions.[8]

Despite heroic restructuring efforts, the shareholder equity ratio fell to only 8.7 percent. NEC's is an extreme case in some ways, but not unique by any means, as more rigorous accounting standards were introduced at an especially difficult time for companies already struggling with distressed balance sheets and near enough to bankruptcy.

Certainly Japanese accounting standards needed to be brought into general conformity with international practice. Certainly increased transparency regarding corporate affairs and results is highly desirable. And equally certainly, these changes in accounting practice came at an especially difficult time for Japan's companies. The impact on financial management was very great indeed. Companies had been already making frantic efforts to avoid balance sheet bankruptcy as asset values fell and debt levels were still high, though falling. Consolidated returns, mark-to-market pricing of assets, and acknowledgement of pension liabilities very much compounded the problem and did so in the 2001 period when the economy was in especially bad shape. One might reasonably wonder how companies managed to get through all this alive.

It is something of a tribute to Japanese financial management that companies did in fact weather this almost perfect storm. Increased cash flow became the name of the game – not increased sales, and certainly not increased profits. Instead, to deal with the mountain of debt, made even more towering by accounting changes, the focus was on maximizing cash flow to reduce debt. A first measure was handed to the companies by the central bank, as nominal interest rates dropped by

70 percent over a ten-year period to a historic low. Personnel cost was cut, most easily by taking out overtime and slashing bonus payments, then by early retirement and much reduced recruiting, along with seconding staff to subsidiaries with less generous benefit terms. A major factor in personnel cost reduction was the closing of plants abroad, in Europe and the United States.

Cash flows were also much increased by quite drastic cuts in capital expenditure. For example, capital expenditure at Toray, Japan's leading synthetic fiber producer, peaked in 1997 at more than ¥140 billion and then dropped rapidly to only a little over ¥50 billion in 2002. Cash flow was not down but capital expenditure (capex) was way down, by nearly two-thirds. (Note that the Accounting Big Bang required that there be cash flow statement disclosures, so cash flow data is now ready to hand.) The reductions in capex showed up not only in reduced bank borrowings but also in aging plant and equipment. By mid-2003, nearly half of Japan's manufacturing companies were operating at full capacity. No surprise that capital expenditures finally began to rise, rather sharply, as 2003 played out. The long, painful, deflation-ridden era of massive over-capacity moved toward an end finally. But the reductions in capex and increases in free cash flow served their purpose. Along with all this went of course efforts to speed inventory turns and to shorten the times of trade receivables, also contributing to increased free cash flow available to reduce debt – and in time, and as appropriate, to increase capital investment.

The lifting of the ban on establishing holding companies in late 1997 allowed such combinations as JFE Holdings, a combining of Kawasaki Steel and NKK, with attendant rationalization of facilities and reduction of personnel. With holding company structures and a subsequent revision of the Commercial Code facilitating spin-offs of businesses, it became possible to separate out pieces of the company as separate corporations. Thus Hitachi set up Hitachi Display and NEC separated out NEC Electronics, realizing cost improvements and equity income as well when the spin-offs went public.

All of these, and other measures, took cash flow levels up in order to deal with the balance sheet and accounting crises. By 2003, free cash flows were at their highest since reporting began in 1999, with the beginnings by that time of increased dividends, increased share buybacks, and increased capital expenditure. Some companies began further repairs on balance sheets by the issuing of new equity and convertible bonds in substantial amounts in 2002/2003 – Fujitsu ¥250 billion, Mitsubishi Shoji ¥150 billion, Nikon ¥56 billion. Sony sold

¥250 billion convertibles and Casio Computer ¥20 billion. Other, rather less secure companies, not surprisingly many in the deeply troubled construction industry, chose to issue preferred shares, for example Haseko with ¥142.8 billion in preferreds. With major balance sheet repairs well underway, the crisis was nearing an end; the storm had been weathered.

End of the main bank system?

There has been a considerable trend to place the blame for the bubble and its aftermath on the banks of Japan, and to attribute slow economic growth to the failure of the banking system to deal with enormous amounts of non-performing loans. There is a curious arrogance in much of this commentary. The banks during the bubble were doing as they always had and were expected to do so – making loans against client asset collateral. As the value of collateral rose, so did the amounts of the loans. Were there unusually large numbers of errors in credit evaluation? Only if one argues that the banks should have realized what no one else seemed to realize – that this was a bubble with a brief, spectacular life and abrupt and ghastly aftermath. The banks simply acted as did nearly everyone else, including Japan's government agencies.

It seems only fair to Japan's financial institutions to note that despite the horrific effects of the bursting of Japan's bubble, sheer theft by collusions of banks and clients was not the kind of problem that was revealed by the bursting of the US bubble.

> Investment banks...all too often trafficked in distorted or inaccurate information, and participated in schemes that helped others distort the information they provided and enriched others at shareholders' expense. The offenses of Enron and WorldCom – and of Citigroup and Merrill Lynch – put most acts of political crookedness to shame....The scale of theft achieved by the ransacking of Enron, WorldCom, and other corporations in the nineties was in the billions of dollars.[9]

Japan has its scandals. However, none are of the magnitudes of the appalling US thieveries, nor yet involving theft from shareholders by bank and management conspiracy.

The Japan bank problem was non-performing loans. With the unpredicted and in some ways unpredictable deflation, and with client companies in very deep financial trouble, non-performing loans not only were very large indeed, but became larger with each reckoning as deflation continued to drive down the value of collateral and companies' capacity to pay on the loans continued to diminish. Of course, the loans could be called, immediately, as many outside commentators proposed. And then of course there would be mass bankruptcy, mass unemployment and widespread economic chaos – surely too high a price to pay for financial tidiness. Better a period of working through the problems, even if that period is a long one and exacts an economic price of its own.

The banks were not the basic cause, but only a part of and participant in the cause of the terrible storm. And the banks are not the entire remedy, only part of the process of remedying the ill effects of the bubble. Indeed, a case can be made that the banks of Japan are more sinned against than sinners. The fact is that for several years now Japan's corporations have steadily reduced their bank borrowings, and that process continues. Japan's banks were built on the business of lending to companies. They were not built on consumer finance, home mortgage loans, or the like. And the business of company loans has dried up – except of course possible loans to those companies so troubled that no bank chooses to lend to them. Outstanding bank loans in Japan declined steadily for a number of years. Will there be some revival of corporate borrowing? Certainly. However, clearly, the role of the banks in Japanese financial management has changed. There will be no return to the pattern of the past with banks virtually the entire source of funding. Management will exercise options in sources and types of funds.

As noted, a special characteristic of Japanese financial management has long been the "main bank system." Much discussed, it is variously described as a residual and partial restructuring of prewar holding company relations, as a result of the way credit was allocated during World War II, and as a result of capital shortages through the early postwar period. Whatever the causes, the main features of the system include a long-term relationship between bank and client, substantial mutual shareholdings between bank and client, and the bank as the instrument for corporate control as the client might become financially at hazard.

Of these special features of the main bank system, the one that has most changed over recent years – and one that has been basic to the system – is that of mutual share ownership, or cross-shareholdings. Aoki describes the development of mutual shareholding as a post-World War II phenomenon.

The event that first triggered mutual shareholding was a takeover attempt in 1952 by an individual investor against Yowa Fudosan (predecessor of Mitsubishi Estate), which owned and managed Mitsubishi real estate of the former Mitsubishi zaibatsu in Tokyo's Marunouchi District. As an emergency measure, eleven major former Mitsubishi firms joined together and devised a way to increase holdings of Yowa Fudosan stock among the group. As this episode clearly shows, the primary direct incentive for mutual shareholding under managerial leadership was the need for a defense strategy against hostile takeover. When stock acquisition by non-Japanese nationals was liberalized in the mid-1960s, the mutual shareholding rate rose even more rapidly. Thus, the neoclassical market for corporate control was eliminated as the prevailing system in Japan. What took its place was stable stockholding by corporate stockholders centered around a main bank.[10]

Survey data confirms this view of the role of cross shareholdings.

Firms were asked to specify the single most important benefit of cross shareholding. The result of this (1993) survey shows that three kinds of benefits, namely "preventing hostile takeover" (36.2 percent), "providing the stability of firm's transactional relationships" (27.0 percent), and "long-term stability of share price" (22.8 percent), stand out as the most important functions of cross shareholding.[11]

Cross shareholdings were as high as 18.4 percent of the value of all share traded in 1987. The total value of cross shareholdings remained at the 16–17 percent level until the mid-1990s. Then as corporate efforts to deal with weak balance sheets intensified, the cross shareholding percent dropped rapidly to 7.4 percent in 2002 and seems likely to decline even further.[12] As part of the massive effort to reduce debt that has been noted, both banks and companies sold off shares. With bank share prices dropping most sharply, bank shares became a main target for selling share investments by Japan's companies. Banks too have needed to raise cash and have been selling off their investment portfolios as have the companies, although to a much lesser degree, presumably in hopes of retaining companies as clients. Strengthening share prices will slow disinvestments, but a rebuilding of cross holdings to the earlier levels seems unlikely, still another factor that will diminish the power of banks over their clients.

What about cross holdings as a defense against hostile takeovers? It seems quite possible that in fact cross holdings have not really been needed as a defense, whatever the general view. Even with the sharp decline in cross holdings there have not yet been any hostile takeovers. There have been agreed-on takeover bids, both by domestic and foreign interests. These have to date involved companies in some trouble, with the takeover an agreed-on rescue operation. There have been some well-publicized efforts at hostile takeover. So far, all have failed. It is not clear that cross holdings have played a critical role in limiting takeovers, hostile or friendly. The fact that relatively few Japanese shares are traded for most companies, with "stable" shareholdings a considerable and non-traded proportion, may be the actual defense against hostile bids, since obtaining a majority of shares through open market operations is difficult, even impossible.

Much has been made about the main bank role as providing a corporate control mechanism, as a delegated monitor. It is said that the main bank system is important in times of financial distress, but of little significance when the client is doing well. But surely banks everywhere, when they find that a firm to which they have lent very large sums is in danger of non-payment, will make every effort to intervene in order to protect the bank's vital interests. And as noted by Allen and Gale, "[it is suggested] that close relationships with banks – the hausbank in Germany and the main bank in Japan – provide a substitute for control by the market. Although there has been a lot of theoretical support for these ideas, the empirical evidence is weak."[13]

The real change in the bank and financial management is the shift away from bank borrowings described above, along with a related move to direct debt. As an example, Sumitomo Chemical's debt since 1996 has changed little in total. However, the majority of debt is now direct, as corporate short- and long-term bonds, with bank borrowings sharply down. Equity has nearly doubled. Sumitomo Electric is rather similar. While total debt is up for Sumiden, bank borrowings are about flat while debt in the form of bonds has nearly doubled. Perhaps more important, for both of these companies, equity has nearly doubled since the mid-1980s. All this despite the fact that both companies consider themselves part of the Sumitomo group still, and as such are close to and much involved with the reasonably strong Sumitomo Bank (now Sumitomo Mitsui Banking Corporation).

There are other indicators of this shift to more complex financing than simple bank borrowings. The increasing use of new equity issues and convertibles was noted. Bank borrowings were a third of total assets in the early 1980s, and are now about a fifth of total assets. The Bank of Japan reports that bonds and commercial paper (much of course still in bank management) has increased in proportion in six years by 10 percent to over 40 percent of total financing in 2002. And we have seen how drastically total debt to equity ratios have shifted. All this means of course that the central role Japan's banks once had in all aspects of corporate finance is very much diminished while a range of other financing channels is available and is being utilized.

Some caution is in order before deciding to write off the main bank as a major factor in Japanese financial management. *Nihon Keizai Shimbun* in September 2003 surveyed the corporations that make up the Nikkei 500 Stock Average. A total of 343 companies responded and nearly all – 96 percent – cite one or several specific banks as their "main banks." Only 14 respondents stated that they had no main bank or banks, including Toyota and Sony, telecomm and power utilities, and non-bank financial institutions. About a fifth of the companies had increased their ratio of main bank borrowings as they were reducing overall interest-bearing debts while maintaining their main bank involvements. There seems a kind of bimodal development since about the same proportion of the total sample, one-fifth, reported a reduction in main bank borrowings.[14]

In any case, it is clearly much too early to refer to the main bank phenomenon in the past tense. Okabe notes,

> It is true that banks did sell off shares of such firms that had a low dependency on bank loans, or firms with poor financial performance, for instance, firms in construction and real-estate industries. But they retained or increased the shareholding of client business firms, large and small, with which they expected to maintain or increase transactional ties in the future.[15]

We might assume too from the persistence of main bank relations by the vast majority of companies that these companies will re-purchase main bank shares as their balance sheets fully recover, in order to confirm what they clearly see to be a useful, even necessary, financial relationship. The full majesty of the main bank's earlier position with its clients will not be regained. But the main bank institution will, in modified and lesser degree, continue. In Japan's economy, as in the wider society, relationships remain highly valuable, to be maintained and reinforced.

Notes

1. For a detailed discussion of these matters, see Chapter 7, "Working with Banks and Shareholders for Competitive Advantage", in *Kaisha, The Japanese Corporation*, by James C. Abegglen and George Stalk, Jr, New York: Basic Books, 1985.
2. Franklin Allen and Douglas Gale. *Comparative Financial Systems*. Cambridge, Massachusetts: MIT Press, 2001, p. 16.
3. Juro Teranishi, "The Main Bank System", in *The Japanese Economic System and its Historical Origins*. ed. Tetsuji Okazaki and Masahiro Okuno-Fujiwara, Oxford: Oxford University Press, 1999, p. 63.
4. Richard C. Koo, *Balance Sheet Recession*, Singapore: John Wiley & Sons (Asia) Pte Ltd, 2003, p. 4.
5. Ibid., p. 269.
6. *The Economist*, 20 September 2003, p. 101.
7. Goldman Sachs Global Strategy Research, 3 July 2003, p. 9.
8. *NEC Corporation Annual Report 2003*, p. 33.
9. Joseph E. Stiglitz, *The Roaring Nineties*, New York: W.W. Norton & Company, 2003, pp. 167–168.
10. Masahiko Aoki, *Information, Corporate Governance, and Institutional Diversity*, Oxford: Oxford University Press, 1995, p. 64.
11. Mitsuaki Okabe, *Cross Shareholdings in Japan*, Cheltenham: Edward Elgar Publishing Ltd, 2002, pp. 37–38.
12. *Nissei Kikenkyu Report*, October 2003.
13. Allen and Gale, op. cit., pp. 8–9.
14. *Nikkei Financial Daily*, 3 September 2003, from Nikkei Net Interactive.
15. Mitsuaki Okabe, *Cross Shareholdings in Japan*. Cheltenham: Edward Elgar Publishing Ltd, 2002, pp. 37–38.

6

The Research Imperative

The future of Japan's economy, for better or for worse, depends on the research output of Japan's scientists and engineers. Japanese industry is now at rough parity with the best of the world in technology – ahead in some sectors, lagging in others, as would be expected. Economic growth has depended on a steady and rather rapid shift of industry to ever-higher levels of value added. As labor-intensive industry moves off-shore, as the economies of Taiwan and Korea and eventually of China become fully competitive in established sectors, as Japan's limited labor force must move to highly sophisticated manufacture and services, all progress comes to be a function of R&D.

As is too often the case, Japanese observers tend to take a negative view of the nation's situation, in this as in so many other matters. A government official directly involved in research policy matters speaks of "the trade deficit in technology transfer," speaks of the "universities' anti-patent approach," laments the limited number of Nobel science awards and lists the shortcomings of Japan's patent office.[1] The Science and Technology White Paper of 2001 spoke at length of Japan's low R&D productivity, citing relatively few numbers of patent applications and low levels of exports of R&D among other indicators.[2] However, Japanese observers have a special capacity to detail the failings of their nation and its systems. We need to examine these matters in some detail in order to reach accurate conclusions. As we shall see, most of these complaints are simply wrong, with no basis in fact.

The advances in Japanese R&D over recent decades have been very great indeed. Resources devoted now to R&D compare very favorably with the levels in other nations. Patent applications are very numerous, and Japanese patents have a strong position abroad. There is now taking place in large scale a historic move bringing industry and universities together in R&D efforts, which can only provide further major impetus to research output.

There are problems. One is the currently seriously understaffed Patent Office, causing delays and confusion in patent registrations. Second, there has been a too general neglect of the value of and need to defend intellectual properties. Further, graduate study facilities at universities are under-funded. And Japan suffers a considerable degree of intellectual isolation with few resident foreign researchers and few foreign patent applications in Japan that further limits research progress.

All of these problems do not sum up to a serious shortfall in either effort or output. A sweeping conclusion of relative failure is not in order. Still, nothing, absolutely nothing, is more important for the nation's future than world-class science and technology producing a steady stream of new concepts and products. Prime Minister Koizumi in his policy statement of 4 February 2002 stated,

> Japan already possesses some of the best patents and other forms of intellectual property in the world. I will set as one of our national goals that the results of research activities and creative endeavors are translated in various forms of intellectual property that are strategically protected and utilized so that we can enhance the competitiveness of Japanese industries.

One can only hope that political leaders will in fact do what is needed in the economy.

The level of effort

Japan spends more on R&D than any other nation in the world, in proportion to its economic size, in 2001 about 3.3 percent of GDP compared with 2.8 percent for the United States and 2.4 percent for Germany. This high rate of spend relative to economic size goes back to the late 1980s and the proportion has been growing steadily. The great majority of these funds are from private sources. Both in Japan and the United States two-thirds or more of all R&D funding is from industry. In Japan's case, the expenditure by industry has held up through a sustained period of economic difficulties; the research commitment is a fundamental one for Japan's companies, not to be tampered with to pretty up short-term profits. No doubt as a result of the heavy industrial funding component, both Japan and the US trail France and Germany in the proportion of spend on what is defined as "basic research." The emphasis has been more on the D than on the R.

While much is made often of the central role of government in Japanese business, government research funding is low, just over 20 percent, a lower percentage than in the other major economies. However, the US R&D numbers are much increased and their direction shaped by massive military expenditures. Government R&D spend in the United States in 2002 was 29 percent of the total but this percent drops to 14.5 when "national defense related" is excluded. For Japan the national defense proportion is less than 1 percent, and for Germany about 2 percent. A major driver of US research is war and preparations for war. The contrast with Japan is a sharp one – and surely to the benefit of Japan's industrial prospects.

As with funding, so with staffing – Japan's research establishment appears to be as fully staffed as it is fully funded. No doubt there are problems here with definitions. Just who in fact is a researcher? Still, using the OECD sources, Japan's researchers are about three times as numerous as Germany's, about 60 percent of the US staffing numbers. It appears that researchers in the United States and Japan are about the same in proportion to the size of populations and economies. Researchers in Japan are 96 persons out of 10,000 while the proportion is 81 for the United States. One must conclude that resources of funds and staffing for research in Japan are quite adequate by world standards.

Measuring research output

Measures of research productivity are various; none are definitive. At what may be the crudest level, patent applications and registration provide one index to output. Patents applied for in Japan have increased by nearly 4 times since 1970 to a total of more than 400,000 currently, while patent applications in Japan from abroad have not even doubled. There is a first indication here of the relative indifference abroad to the situation in Japan. In 1970, foreigners accounted for nearly a quarter of patent applications, but the proportion now is only 12 percent. Patents by Japanese reaching registration have increased more than five times since 1970, to over 100,000 annually while foreigners' patents registered are now less than 10 percent of the total.

The issue of foreign patent awards is of interest when countries are compared. About half of all patents granted now in the United States are granted to foreign persons or institutions. In Germany it is a rather high 60 percent. And in the United Kingdom for long the birthplace of new products and scientific developments, there are only 40,000 patents approved annually and a full 90 percent are awarded to foreign applicants. Like empires, it appears that science too has its period of glory and then declines.

Note that the very high number of patent applications in Japan – some 440,000 per year compared to some 300,000 in the United States is due in some part to the fact that the scope for patent definition in Japan is a good deal more limited than in the United States. To achieve a similar degree of coverage, more patents must be applied for in Japan, explaining some of the differences in numbers.

Another way to look at R&D productivity as measured by patents is to look at the patents granted in the United States over time and by country of source (Table 6.1). Given the critical economic importance of the United States, it is not surprising that patent awards there become a quite sensitive indicator of national R&D positions. Japan's companies have for some years now received about 20 percent of all US patent awards, three times more than the nearest competitive economy, Germany. Note too that in the most recent numbers available, Taiwan and Korea receive a great many more patents in the United States than do France and Britain, with Hong Kong and China now taking their places on the list. Asia's greatly increasing role in the world economy is now reflected in technology as well.

Still another measure of research output is the balance of payments for technology. The change for Japan over the half-century is most

Table 6.1 Patents granted in the United States

	1980		2001	
	number	%	number	%
USA	37,124	60.6	87,670	52.8
Japan	7,136	11.7	33,223	20.0
Germany	5,802	9.5	11,260	6.8
France	2,096	3.4	4,041	2.4
UK	2,416	3.9	2,695	1.6
Taiwan	69	0.1	5,371	3.2
Korea	10	0.0	3,538	2.1
Hong Kong	28	0.0	237	0.1
China	1	0.0	195	0.1
Other	6,625	10.8	17,809	10.7
Total	61,227	100.0	166,039	100.0

Source: US Patent and Trademark Office.

striking. In the early 1950s, annual technology imports – contracts entered into for transfer of technology – totaled fewer than 200. However, the balance of receipts to payments was 1 to 100. Imports were rather few since controls over imports of any sort were rigorous in the immediately postwar years, but import values exceeded exports by 100 times. The demand in that period for imported technology was nearly insatiable while output was trivial. It was not until the early 1990s that receipts for "royalties and license fees" reached even half of payments.

But the gap closed fast, and in 2003 the balance of revenues for Japan was positive for the first time ever. Leading companies like Canon, Hitachi, and Toyota had very substantial incomes from technology transfer, and such companies as Takeda and NEC are working vigorously to increase patent revenues. Of course for Japan as for other exporters, payments for copyrights and technology by overseas subsidiaries can be an important part of total revenues. Nonetheless, the change is a very great one, a tribute to R&D output. Germany remains a net payer on technology trade, with only a limited improvement in payment balance. The United States, massively in surplus for very long, with exports more than 10 times imports, is seeing its surplus diminish rapidly, although the United States is still well in the black with exports now twice the value of imports. The two sectors in which Japan remains in heavy payments deficit are software and pharmaceuticals, where Japanese companies are not yet competitive in world markets.

In sum, all measures of R&D output related to patents show exceptional progress by Japan, with Japan's position in research output measured by patent performance comparing very favorably with all other nations.

"Innovative capacity"

An interesting measure in comparing technological position is the concept of "innovative capacity," and its measurement as developed by Professors Porter and Stern in the United States.[3] Their analysis is intensive and its conclusions of real interest, highly relevant to a discussion of R&D output. "Innovative capacity" is defined as "a country's potential – as both an economic and political entity – to produce a stream of commercially relevant innovations." Table 6.2 provides the results of this research with Japan assigned top position in innovative capacity over recent years, with the United States losing relative position and the Nordic countries and Switzerland in increasingly strong position.

Table 6.2   Innovative index: Top 10 countries

1995	1999	2005
USA	Japan	Japan
Switzerland	Switzerland	Finland
Japan	USA	Switzerland
Sweden	Sweden	Denmark
Germany	Germany	Sweden
Finland	Finland	USA
Denmark	Denmark	Germany
France	France	France
Canada	Norway	Norway
Norway	Canada	Canada

Source: Porter and Stern, op. cit.

The most striking finding of this analysis is the convergence in meas-ured innovative capacity among OECD countries over the past quarter century.... Our results do suggest that both Japan and Scandinavia have already established themselves as important innovation centers.... Each of the countries that have increased their estimated level of innovative capacity over the past quarter century – Japan, Sweden, Finland, Germany – have implemented policies that encourage human capital investment in science and engineering (e.g. by establishing and investing resources in technical universities) as well as greater competition on the basis of innovation, for example through the adoption of R&D tax credits and the gradual opening of markets to international competition.[4]

Company spend; company output

As would be expected from the overall level of R&D investment, the amount spent on R&D by individual Japanese companies as a percent of total revenue is similar to that of US companies. The data in Table 6.3 on company spend are only indicative, but do reflect similar levels by similar companies in a range of industries. In Japan, as no doubt every-where, the spend in the pharmaceutical industry is especially high as a percent of sales. However, this is an industry in which Japan has almost no world-scale companies. No surprise then that foreign firms have a very strong position in the market with Japanese firms at both a techno-logical and sales disadvantage. Three of the top five pharmaceutical companies in Japan market share are foreign owned, with Pfizer the

Table 6.3   R&D expenditure by companies, 2002

Company	R&D as % of sales	Company	R&D as % of sales
Hewlett Packard	5.9	Intel	15.1
Canon	7.9	Tokyo Electron	12.9
Eastman Kodak	5.9	Procter & Gamble	4.0
Fuji Photo Film	6.4	Kao	4.5
du Pont	5.2	General Motors	3.1
Sumitomo Chemical	6.6	Toyota	4.1
Pfizer	15.9	Caterpillar	3.3
Takeda	12.5	Komatsu	4.3

Source: *Financial Times*, "R&D Scoreboard," 20 October 2003, p. 22.

leading firm in the industry in total sales. Japanese electronic firms help take up some of the slack; even while going through a very difficult period of deflation and low growth, research budgets for the likes of NEC, Toshiba, and Hitachi were not reduced. But the temptation to repair profit statements by cutting research must have been considerable, and these are hardware, not software, producers.

Regarding output/patents, as we have seen, Japanese sources account for about 20 percent of patents granted in the United States, a much greater proportion than from any other country. However, given the costs of the patent approval process, minor patents tend not to be filed abroad, helping to keep the total number down. It is of interest therefore to look not simply at the total number of patents granted, but to look as well at the corporate leaders in US patent awards. In 1978, some 25 years ago, of the ten leading companies in terms of US patent approvals, six were US companies, three were European – Siemans, Philips, and Bayer – and only one was Japanese – Hitachi. By 1990, only 12 years later, five of the top ten were Japanese companies. Throughout the 1990s and now, still five or six of the top ten corporate recipients of US patent approvals were Japanese each year; indeed in 1996, nine of the top ten were from Japan.

Table 6.4 lists the top twenty companies in number of US patent approvals in 2003. Of the top 20 companies, 10 are Japanese companies, seven are US companies, two companies are from Europe, and one from Korea. These companies are all in the electronics industry, the center of technological change in recent decades, and all are in some fashion competitors. Japan's companies are in strong, even leading, positions.

Table 6.4   Number of US patents awarded, 2003

Rank	Company	Number of patents	Rank	Company	Number of patents
1	IBM	3439	11	Samsung Electronics	1316
2	Canon	1997	12	Mitsubishi Denki	1265
3	Hitachi	1906	13	Toshiba	1217
4	Matsushita	1821	14	NEC	1198
5	Compaq	1763	15	General Electric	1139
6	Micron Technology	1708	16	Advanced Micro	908
7	Intel	1595	17	Fuji Photo Film	809
8	Philips Electronics	1355	18	Seiko Epson	779
9	Sony	1354	19	Texas Instruments	771
10	Fujitsu	1338	20	Robert Bosch	758

Source: IFI CLAIMS Patent Services.

The issue regarding Japanese company patents is whether these companies defend and exploit their patent positions to full advantage. Most do not. As an example,

NEC has been slow to utilize its intellectual property. Since 1999, it has had the second-largest number of registered patents in the U.S., following IBM Corp. But its annual licensing income is only in the 10 billion yen range, about US$100 million, compared with IBM's total of around 1 billion dollars. The electronics giant aims to earn about 50 billion yen in revenue, about US$500 million after three years by marketing some of its 68,509 patents.[5]

At issue here is the effective managing of intellectual property, still in a quite primitive state in most Japanese companies, a real and painful weakness.

This is changing, especially under the pressure of copying by Korean and Chinese producers. In what has been until now a rarely used defensive weapon, Matsushita Electric secured an order from Tokyo Customs to exclude from the Japanese market for two years LG-made plasma display products as infringing Matsushita patents. Defense of technology is becoming a major strategic move by Japanese companies, at long last.

Question of quality

That the effort and output of R&D in Japan is very great can hardly be disputed. However, there remains a question still of the quality of that output. All too often, foreign businessmen in Japan, especially American businessmen, simply dismiss Japanese patent achievements by claiming that the value of the patents is less than significant. Since the speakers are in no position to compare patent quality, this all-too-frequent remark can be put down simply to a combination of arrogance and stupidity, a combination rather frequently seen in Western business comments on Japan.

More substantial questions of the quality of research output are seen in two major dimensions. One measure of R&D performance is the number of scientific papers published in science and engineering. Here the overwhelming leader in numbers of papers is the United States, although its very high share has been falling recently. In this regard, Japan is second in the world, with a quite steady increase since the mid-1980s – a pattern consistent with the patent output data.

However, the impact of these scientific papers must be examined as well. One measure is the frequency with which scientific papers are cited relative to the number of papers published. By this measure Japan's scientific papers have a very low ranking. The second of these measures is the citations of scientific papers in patent applications to the US Patent Office. Here too Japan ranks well below the United States, although in second position with citation rates increasing, a mixed outcome.

Still another index to the quality of scientific achievement, very crude but often cited, is the number of Nobel Prize winners by nationality in the fields of the natural sciences. Japan ranks very low, with only nine science Nobels to date, all awarded since 1946. (Japanese scholars received no Nobels in the pre-World War II era.) In the post-1945 period, compared to the 9 awards to Japanese, French scientists have received 10 Nobels, the Germans 28, British scientists 45, and Americans a stunning 189.

These two sectors in which Japanese scientific achievement seems to fall short of the highest of world standards may have a certain common cause. Note that pre-1945, the United States too had rather few Nobel science prize winners, half as many as Germany, about the same as France. The United States was much given to adopting and commercializing European developments (called "Yankee ingenuity" rather than the more accurate "copying"). Fast-growing, newly developing economies like the United States earlier and Japan more recently are more likely to be engaged in engineering than in basic science. Indeed, a member of the Nobel Prize committee once pointed out to me that the burst of US Nobel awards owed mainly to Hitler and Mussolini who brought about the emigration to the United States of the best of Europe's scientists. So time, or rather the economy's stage of development, may be key to level of scientific output. It takes a good degree of wealth for a nation to be able to devote substantial resources to pure science.

Perhaps more basic is the question of the degree to which Japan's research centers and research staff have been – or are today – a part of the world community of science. The deep connections between German, British, and US research institutes and research staff, for training and for joint projects, has little parallel in the Japan case. Add to this the rather special aspects of written and spoken Japanese, and it seems quite possible that Japan's researchers and research output have a much more limited visibility and circulation in the world research community, which is dominated by the nations of the West. Thus, some part of the questions of quality of research output may rest on relative isolation still of Japan's researchers and research output.

Problems/weaknesses

The patent office

The most obvious, and most readily remedied, problem for Japanese R&D is the long delays and costs involved in dealing with the Patent Office. As noted, Japan has annually well over 100,000 patent applications more than is the case in the United States. Yet there are only two-thirds as many patent screeners in Japan to deal with this hugely greater number of applications. It takes at least a half-year longer to get a patent granted in Japan than in the United States, a particular problem for startup companies whose viability depends very much on early patent coverage, in terms of getting financing as well as achieving competitive advantage. One newspaper report put the backlog of pending applications as a staggering 500,000.

The solution seems utterly obvious. Staff up as needed. Yet it is only in fiscal 2004 that a serious effort to step up application screening, with 100 new employees to be added each year for the next several years. The target is to become the first country to eliminate the waiting period, typically two years prior to the start of screening. All this has the sense of "too little; too late," and is hardly commensurate with the grand goals set by the prime minister at the time of writing. But at least there is now some action underway.

Intellectual property rights

Through the decades of high economic growth rates, a main driver was the application of the world's best technology, purchased often at fire-sale prices. Japan's economy was small and remote, its companies no competitive threat. Sale of technology to one of Japan's companies could provide a decent down payment and perhaps some years of royalty income seemingly at no cost. Why not sell? From the buyer side, government surveillance ensured that prices and terms were reasonable and that by careful planning, no Japanese company would obtain a clean monopoly position. (Toray in nylon was an exception, an expensive one for Japan's nylon users.)

The result was a strategic disaster for Western companies who by licensing gave up the lever that would have made a position in the Japanese economy possible, and who by licensing put in place companies that all too often improved the technology and became formidable competitors.

The story has many implications. An important one now is the fact that this early and long experience in which technology became something of a commodity seems to have left Japanese companies unaware of or careless regarding the values of intellectual property. This has meant that Japanese companies have failed to realize the potential earnings from valuable intellectual property. More critical now, as Japanese production moves off-shore from Japan, transferring intellectual property in the process, failures to secure patents and otherwise protect and defend intellectual property becomes life-threatening. China, with a splendid reputation as vigorous copier of everything that can be copied, with no significant courts nor yet patent or copyright laws, makes that country at once a most promising factory site and a very real business life threat.

With all this, no surprise that at this stage in Japan's development cycle, intellectual property issues have moved to center stage. New legislation is in the works, new courts are being proposed, and cooperation with law agencies elsewhere in Asia on these matters is being strengthened. The real efforts here however will not be governmental. Governments can perhaps help. The private sector must lead.

An illustrative case is that of Hitachi, in many ways a prototypic Japanese company – very large indeed, proud of a history of generating its own technologies, very widely diversified in electronics and electrical machinery, most recently third in patents granted corporations by the US Patent Office. In fiscal 1982, Hitachi paid out in licensing costs a third more than its licensing income. However, by 1986, licensing income exceeded outgo, and in fiscal 2003, income from technology licenses was 3.5 times greater than expense – ¥44 billion. In only two decades, Hitachi's balance of licensing payments have shifted from heavy deficit to major surplus. It is noteworthy too that Hitachi has recently set up a special business group to focus on patent licenses and royalty fees. In another case, the management of NEC noted that despite massive patent approvals, NEC licensing income was trivial. The comparison with IBM was seen as especially painful by NEC and a corporate effort at gaining technology income was put in motion, rather like that of Hitachi.

Curiously, a significant number of company presidents believe that the company's interests are best served by keeping their technology confidential, maintaining competitiveness with proprietary technology. There may well be aspects of technology that can be kept secret from competitors – but that is not the way to bet. Defense of technology through strong action regarding patent infringement is a more reliable and powerful defense. And Canon, Takeda, Eisai, and others are now suing patent infringers in foreign courts, a rather new and long overdue development that is fast gaining momentum. It will serve the legal profession well, but should in fact prove important in defending intellectual property.

The issue here is not only one of vigorous defense of corporate intellectual assets. There is a real issue of compensation for corporate researchers, which came into sharp focus with a court award of ¥20 billion to the inventor of a commercially highly valuable diode. Traditionally Japanese corporations paid a nominal reward, an "honorary prize," for R&D achievements. Rather clearly, there is a need for improved systems to reward patent acquisition, already in place in some companies. With the sharp increase in focus on R&D, compensation systems of substance supported by contractual agreements will need to be put in place and soon.

Educational achievement

That education is the key to scientific discovery is obvious. Measuring, comparing, and predicting educational achievement is a rather more challenging matter. There seems to be no nation in which the parental population is entirely satisfied with its educational system; Japan is no exception to the habit of complaint about its school system. And no doubt all systems can be improved.

Of Japan's educational system, a leading expert on education in Japan has remarked,

> Capacities for particular kinds of learning vary from society to society. In the Japanese case, the capacities for adaptive borrowing, broad knowledge promulgation, and continuous learning are particularly significant. They have allowed the nation to industrialize very rapidly. Furthermore, the level of learning that occurs in Japan today, both in schools and in companies, is arguably greater than in any other industrial nation.[6]

There is a good deal of evidence in support of this positive view of Japan's educational achievements, especially in mathematics and science. In a US-led study in 1996, involving a half-million students in 41 countries, Japanese students were in third place in math achievement, following Singapore and South Korea, with Germany 23rd and the United States 28th. In science achievement as well, Japanese students were in third place, with Singapore again first and South Korea 4th, the United States 17th, and Germany 18th. The report notes that US students spend more time in classes and are given more homework than students in Japan – no explanation for the huge achievement differences is offered.

Other surveys provide similar evidence of the exceptional quality of Japanese education. The 2000 OECD study of 15-year-olds in 30 countries, testing reading comprehension, mathematics, and science found Japanese students 8th in reading, first in maths and 2nd in science, with the United States 15th in reading, 19th in maths and 14th in science. In compilation of OECD data prepared by the United Nations Children's Educational Fund (UNICEF), country scores were established. In this "educational league table," South Korea rated first with a score of 1.4. Japan was second, with a score of 2.2. Finland was third, with a score of 4.4. The United States was in 18th place among the 24 countries rated, with Germany in 19th place.

Graduate study

Thus, the issue of general level of education is not a problem for Japan. On the contrary, Japan is a world leader, in contrast to the educational levels in economies with a longer history of industrialization. The educational issue for Japan in the R&D sector is twofold, it appears. The first of these is stated well by Rohlen: "A world leader needs institutions that can generate basic knowledge and provide guidance. Can Japan's quite conservative universities be changed in directions that emphasize basic research, meaningful instruction, and greater independence from government?"[7]

As one who has taught graduate courses in universities in Japan and in the United States, I find the issue a real one. The kinds of facilities for graduate study and research are superbly done at the best of US universities. Much investment in Japan is needed to reach those levels. One factor favoring the US university system, in addition to massive government research support, is a tradition of philanthropic giving that has made the best of American private universities near-on financial powers. My own university, Chicago, was founded by John Rockefeller, its first and greatest benefactor. Stanford grew out of a major philanthropy. And the gifts to the likes of Harvard, Yale, and Princeton are legend. There is no equivalent tradition or practice of private philanthropy in Japan. Nor are there the great differences in wealth and the favorable tax treatment of wealth in Japan that are all too common in the United States.

Rather than private endowments, Japan's universities must depend on governmental financial support. There is no other option. This need not be a bad thing – but it does require a higher level of neutral, purely academic support than is the case now, with Japan's spend on education rather less than that of other major nations. The real shortfall in spending on education in science is the low expenditure per student at the tertiary/university level. In 1998, in purchasing power parity (PPP) dollars, it was barely over half that of the United States – Japan under $10,000 and the United States over $18,000. Clearly this is a area that urgently needs budget increases of significant size.

Still, there is no visible shortage of trained scientists and researchers in Japan. And there is a curious balancing factor in the educational area. It was long argued that Japan had a "free ride" in the defense sector from the fact that the United States spent heavily on defense, some of this to Japan's defense benefit, while Japan itself spent rather little on military defense. An academic friend of mine once noted that the very real "free ride" for Japan at the expense of the United States was not the military "free ride," but rather the academic "free ride," the opportunity for Japan's best students to take full advantage of study and research at the very best of the US universities.

To be sure, Japanese companies have made helpful and generous gifts to MIT, Cal Tech, Chicago, Harvard, and the like. But these are not disinterested – they help keep entrance open to Japanese students – and these gifts in no way match the splendor of faculty and facilities available to Japanese students who enroll in these universities. At present, roughly half of all advanced science degrees awarded now by US universities go to students who are foreign nationals. Many chose to remain in the United States, but Japanese students have a history of returning to Japan to further their careers. In this fashion, quite without intending, the United States is at least for now helping to make up for shortfalls in foreign educational institutions.

At the same time, the structure of Japan's universities is changing, with the national universities and their faculties being made much more independent of government dictate, and with a quite striking shift to faculty business ventures and to university-business joint efforts. It is likely that some of the problems noted in the university system are moving toward resolution rather rapidly and in a highly constructive fashion.

Internationalizing study and research

Along with and closely related to the issue of the quality and reach of graduate study is the issue of foreign students and scientists attending Japanese graduate schools and are in Japanese businesses. Writing earlier about foreign students, Rohlen states:

> More and more foreign students are coming to Japan, especially from nearby Asian countries. Japan's graduate schools are filling up with foreigners, and every year more governmental fellowships are announced. A third of the graduate students at Kyoto University are foreign, for example, the great majority from Korea and China. Thus, Japan is becoming an educational and cultural center of an increasingly interdependent Asia...[8]

Moreover, the current paranoia-driven US barriers to visas for students and scholars provide an opportunity for Japan – and other countries – to redress the imbalance in foreign students and researchers.

During his tenure as prime minister in the mid-1980s, Nakasone Yasuhiro set as target for foreign students coming to Japan an annual total of 100,000, a highly ambitious goal for the time. However, as of 2003 there were indeed 100,000 foreign students in Japan, half or more from China, nearly all from East Asia. While there are stories of student visas used as a basis for working in Japan and indeed for thieving in

Japan, the increasing position of Asian students seems clear enough – and of great potential value for Japan's future as an Asian nation.

Consider the importance to the United States of the Fulbright and similar programs in furthering the role of the United States in world affairs. From that, one can gain some estimate of how important it is for Japanese institutions to go very much further still in providing support for foreign students in terms of access to good and reasonable housing, community acceptance and support, and financial aid. Again, in my own experience as university professor in Japan, a very much greater effort is needed by all to ensure that these visitors, potential leaders in their nations and in Asia, come away from Japan with a highly positive attitude of friendship and appreciation. The nurturing of those attitudes is all too often lacking today in Japan. This neglect is costly, and even dangerous in terms of Japan's future.

However, attracting and involving students from abroad looks to be a rather simple matter compared to the problems in attracting scientific personnel to come into residence in Japan even for relatively short periods. As noted, a very considerable part of the spectacular expansion of science in the United States resulted from emigration of distinguished scientists who were at some hazard in pre-World War II Europe. US universities made generous room for these émigrés – Enrico Fermi at my University of Chicago was only one of an extraordinary group. And after the war as well, US universities, research institutes, and companies sought out and welcomed the world's best.

We have in Japan nothing like this phenomenon – however important it will be for Japan's future. Japan itself – its geographic location, its language, and its culture – poses a real barrier. Japan is in all respects "insular," as a continental power will not be. Japanese institutions are not much given to seeking out and drawing in foreigners, however distinguished or promising; occasional visits, of course; the odd lecture or seminar, of course; financing for a research project in a foreign location, perhaps – none of these in any fashion provides the sort of deep involvement in the world scientific community that Japan must achieve. And none of these bring to residence in Japan the best the world has on offer in scientific teaching and research. And yet to move to and stay in world science leadership we must in Japan be able to bring and retain the best.

In this regard, it was most encouraging to learn that Nobel Laureate Sydney Brenner of Britain was selected to head the new Okinawa Institute of Science and Technology, a graduate school being set up by the government. Brenner is currently a research professor at the Salk Institute in San Diego, the kind of leader in world science that Japan needs badly to recruit in some numbers.

Perhaps some of the initiative will come not only from government but from the private industrial sector as well. Mitsubishi Chemical has named an MIT professor as head of their research operations, with a seat on the main board. But he is not resident in Japan, only traveling between his university and business positions. Hitachi has over the years had more than 200 foreign researchers visiting their Japan operations, an average in recent years of 10 per year. Again, however, these are visitors for various lengths of time. These are not fully integrated, resident scientists.

Even in business settings, bringing senior managers to Japan is not a simple process. International schools are needed for demanding children. International socialization is needed for demanding wives. Car, driver, club memberships, home leaves, cost of living allowances, and special housing are needed for demanding husbands/executives. The total price is a very high one; the impact on the Japanese organization is often a nasty one; and in any case long periods in Japan and taking Japanese citizenship seem generally not even considered by the "expatriate." Scientists are unlikely to be more accommodating.

So there is a good part of Japan's R&D problem – the need to integrate and the difficulty of integrating into the world scientific community. We have seen the isolation in the Nobel Prize awards and in the limited number of Japan patent applications from abroad, as well as in the scarcity of citation of Japanese scientific papers. Perhaps all this can be dealt with only as the center of world industry and then of world science moves from the West to Asia, with Japan the key factor in that shift to Asia. The shift is getting underway – but it will be a long, slow process, with Japanese science long continuing to be in relative isolation from the world research centers.

Given the importance of and the high regard for the US Fulbright fellowships in Japan, and their obvious value for Japan, it is greatly puzzling to find that a Japanese equivalent program has not been established by Japan's government. Bringing the best of younger students and scientists to Japan, providing them funds and facilities, and having them return to their home nations understanding of and sympathetic to Japan – while contributing to scientific development when in Japan – seems of priceless value to this isolated and not-well-understood nation. Why, in heaven's name, has nothing been done? A splendid example is right at hand. The nation has ample wealth – and has great need. Start a Japanese Fulbright program. Soon.

The university as venturer

The most exciting new development in Japanese R&D is the changing and fast-expanding role of the universities, and increased university–industry collaboration. The Technology Licensing Organizations Law of 1998 has led to the establishment of TLOs in universities and research institutions. This is broadly similar to the Bayh-Dole Act of 1980 in the United States, which drove universities to encourage patents and seek to commercialize research results. The results of the new law in Japan are being rapidly realized. In 2003, Kyoto University won 780 R&D contracts worth ¥5.5 billion. The University of Tokyo's 2003 results were slow in being announced but in 2002 Todai realized 3945 contracts worth ¥10.1 billion. Technology transfers from Todai in 2003 total 159 cases, with a value of ¥340 million, with Tohoku following with 82 cases. Patent applications through TLOs totaled 720 for Tohoku University, famous for leadership in semiconductor and IT sectors, with the University of Tokyo second with 696 such applications.

All of this has been in response to the changed law of 1998, and prior to the 2004 establishment of the national universities of Japan as self-sufficient independent entities, with the faculty members no longer civil servants, but rather employees of separate legal units. The pressure – and incentive – to improve finances and make the university more attractive to students and to faculty as the national university's status changes is a powerful force at work in invigorating Japan's university research community. The process of competitive response is only beginning, and is already impressive.

Of some special importance is the movement of the universities to establish "incubation facilities," to promote the launching of startup companies. Japan has long suffered by a low level of new company star-tups, a trend that began well before the economic problems since the mid-1990s. One move, a helpful one, has been to allow companies to incorporate with a capital initially of only one yen. Another factor however is university-related startups. There were almost none, only 17, as recently as 1997 – and even fewer before. By end-August, 2003, there were 600 startups in place.

As an example of what is happening in this university startup sector, Professor Y. Nakamura of the University of Tokyo's Institute of Medical Science founded a "university-origin startup" in 2001. The company, OncoTherapy Science, Inc., pursues proprietary technology for gene research to provide cancer therapy. OncoTherapy entered into various licensing agreements with a half-dozen top pharmaceutical companies and in December, 2003, went public in an IPO for some ¥8 billion. As a result, the 2000 shares in OncoTherapy held by Tokyo University's Center for Advanced Science and Technology Incubation have a market value of ¥3.5 billion. OncoTherapy is one of a group of startup companies from Osaka, Kumamoto, and Tokyo Universities in various biogenetic sectors. The list of major academic startups is becoming a long one, even before all the new legislation is in place, with an emphasis generally on biotechnology and on advanced electronics. In fiscal 2002, 531 companies were started based on university research findings, with a government goal of 1000 by end of fiscal 2004. The government is awarding grants to 56 colleges and universities in support of selected research programs.

As this goes forward, companies are lining up with research plans involving universities. Rohm, NTT, and others are in joint work with Kyoto University on nanotechnology. Matsushita Electric is contracting with the University of Tokyo for a wide-ranging IT program and with Kobe University on next generation manufacturing technology. NEC and Osaka University are jointly developing network technology. Osaka University and Mitsubishi Heavy Industries are in R&D partnership in a range of fields including fuel cells and aircraft engines. In sum, we appear to be entering a new era of university independence and industry–university collaboration, with faculty members as important entrepreneurs. These are new and potentially highly valuable changes in the Japanese R&D scene and its prospects.

As the Ministry of Economy, Trade and Industry (METI) looked at the issue of maintaining Japan's competitiveness, it cited seven fields as having priority in government policy considerations. These include biotechnology, the environment, digital consumer electronics, digital content, nanotechnology, fuel cells, and robots. All are likely to be on the priority lists of most countries' planners – with the exception of robotics. Yet in the Japanese case, robotics holds special position. Of the world population of some 750,000 robots, about half or about 390,000 are in use in Japan. Now of great and increasing importance in manufacturing, the focus is on "partner robots" for use in applications ranging from entertainment and nursing care to home security and construction work. The driving force is the cost and impending shortage of labor.

In one study, it was estimated that there were in 2002 some 3800 patents in the world covering robotic humanoid movement and some 600 patents dealing with artificial intelligence technology. Of the movement patents, Japan was calculated to hold 89 percent of the world total, the United States only 3 percent. In artificial intelligence, the Japan patent share was reckoned to be 70 percent, with Europe and the United States holding 14 and 16 percent respectively.[9]

METI have set up a panel of corporation and university representatives to provide a vision of a new society in which robots will be a feature of people's lives by 2025, with robots providing nursing care to seniors and carrying out other practical functions. With this Toyota, not much given to wild fantasies, is setting up a division specializing in the development of "partner" robots, combining the Toyota group of companies' resources and staffed with several hundred persons. So in this field at least Japan is moving from the science fiction of anime characters toward a very real role in the lives of Japanese to be played by robots. There may not be Nobel prizes for robot development, but the impact on daily living may well be great indeed.

* * *

Japan's economic future will be determined by Japan's scientific and technological competence and creativity. The Bank of Japan made an especially cogent statement regarding technology: "In order for Japan to survive as a technologically advanced country, its efforts must be deployed on several important fronts, including due cooperation between industry and academia, the nurturing of human resources, and an overhaul of the system protecting intellectual property rights."[10] Certainly the cooperation between industry and academia, long a real issue in Japan, is moving ahead very rapidly indeed now. The area of human resource development is in reasonably good condition, but graduate study facilities and programs need prompt and large-scale support. The protection of intellectual property rights has moved to a very high position on the agendas of both business and government.

There can be no guarantees. Predicting the future is a hazardous game in any case. But it is quite clear that Japan will be in the forefront of world science and technology progress over the next decades.

And thus will continue to be world leader in quality of life for all its citizens.

Notes

1. Hisamitsu Arai, "Japan's Intellectual Property Strategy", *JPO-IMPI Seminar*, 10 March 2003.
2. "Nihon no Kenkyu Kaihatsu Seisansei Hikui", *Nihon Keizai Shimbun*, 7 June 2002, evening edition, p. 1.

3. M.E. Porter and S. Stern. The New Challenge to America's Prosperity: Findings from the Innovation Index. Washington, DC: Council on Competitiveness, 1999.
4. Jeffrey L. Furman, Michael Porter, and Scott Stern, "The determinants of national innovative capacity", *Research Policy*, 31, 2002, pp. 929, 931.
5. *Nihon Keizai Shimbun*, 2 April 2002.
6. Thomas P. Rohlen, "Learning: The Mobilization of Knowledge in the Japanese Political Economy", in *The Political Economy of Japan*, S. Kumon and H. Rosovsky (eds), Stanford, California: Stanford University Press, 1992, p. 322.
7. Ibid., p. 360.
8. Ibid., p. 362.
9. *Nihon Keizai Shimbun*, 15 June 2002, p. 7.
10. *Bank of Japan Quarterly Bulletin*, Vol. 11, No. 4, November 2003.

7
Corporate Governance: US Model? Japan Model?

Just as fashions change and styles go in and out of favor, so ideas regarding corporate management change with the economic climate. In the 1980s, the great success of the Japanese economy brought about efforts to understand and copy Japanese management methods. With the end of Japan's boom and long-continued restructuring of Japan's economy, Japanese management methods went entirely out of fashion. US companies no longer seek to introduce quality control circles, or kaizen, and industrial policy concerns gave way entirely to a belief in the efficiency of the untrammeled market.

In much the same way, the great success of the US economy in the 1990s led to efforts to understand and copy the presumed causes of that success. The result was a widespread fashion for the study of what has come to be called "corporate governance," an odd term referring to the distribution of power in the company. And since Americans are not shy about instructing those they consider less well-informed, Japanese managers have been treated to much lecturing about how to improve Japanese governance by adopting US methods.

There are two very great problems in all this discussion of US corporate governance and its application in Japan. First, there is very considerable evidence that the US system of corporate governance, so loudly praised, has in fact been a considerable failure. Second, even supposing that the US system of governance is entirely effective (and it is not), it is quite clear that companies in Europe and Japan, with different histories, cultures, traditions, legal systems, and institutional frameworks, must develop their own systems of good governance. One size does not fit all. Just as Japanese management methods did not work in US companies – quality circles for example – so much of

US management methods cannot be applied effectively to Japanese companies.

The failure of US corporate governance

The Anglo-American view of corporate governance derives from the view of the company as the entire property of the shareholders. The OECD view is that "generating long-term economic gain to enhance shareholder value is the corporation's central function." In this view, managers are agents for the shareholder-owners of the company and the objective of management is to increase the value of shares. Thus the price of shares becomes the measure of management success in this view.

The US thinking about corporate governance resulted from concern over the separation of ownership and control that resulted from the shift from privately owned institutions run as private property to large corporations operated by professional managers. The remedy to the possible loss of property rights and values as control and ownership separated was to take the position that the corporation exists for the purpose of making profits for the shareholder. The apparatus of US corporate governance as we see it today has derived from this concern over defending ownership rights. In consequence, shareholder profit, that is increased share price, becomes the key objective of managers of the US corporation.

Leave for the moment the question of whether this position regarding company objectives is reasonable or not. It is necessary to appreciate that the primacy of the shareholder and shareholder interests is the basis for US corporate policies and behaviors. Thus, for example, the members of the board of directors are to be independent outsiders, representing the shareholders, not management or employees. They are to supervise and control the operating officers of the company, naming the chief executive officer, determining compensation of officers, establishing strategy, and ensuring accurate corporate accounting and reporting. They represent, act for, and defend the interests of the shareholders.

In practice, of course, much of this is simply fiction. The shareholders are owners of the company only by legal convention. There is, in this view of the shareholder as owner, the primitive notion of the company as a small enterprise with a founder-owner or owners taking all risk and reward. Modern corporations are very different. The shareholder-owners are participants in "casino capitalism." The buyers of shares are in fact purchasing lottery tickets, in hopes of a quick and handsome return, with average length of share ownership a mere eight months. They can hardly be considered owners of the company, either in terms of scale of investment or in terms of commitment to the future of the company. And now with massive mutual funds and pension funds, most shareholdings are by large institutional investors rather than individuals. The interest of the funds is in short-term profits from increased share price, with usually a three-month time horizon.

Outside directors

The notion of the board members representing shareholders implies nomination of candidates and election to the board by the shareholders. A nice idea but in actual practice, the boards of US companies are made up of friends and acquaintances of the chief executive officer, the CEO. All too often, the CEO invites executives of other companies onto his board, and they in turn invite the CEO to serve as a member of the board of their companies. This is true "crony capitalism," and ensures board support for the proposals advanced by the CEO – with little or no criticism or correction.

One example, and a surprising one, of this rigging of the board is the case of Berkshire Hathaway, the investment company led by the second richest American, Warren Buffett. Considered an exceptionally wise and able businessman, he has on his board his wife and his son – hardly "independent" directors. An extreme case, this does illustrate how the board in the United States becomes captive of the CEO. The notion of independent board members supervising the company's management is generally a fiction.

Even if really independent, the board member from outside will have little or no knowledge of the inner workings of the company, and indeed may even have little knowledge of the industry in which the company operates. He or she attends an occasional board meeting, perhaps a half dozen times a year, for a few hours each time, and may take part in a few committee meetings as well. It is hard to see how persons so limited in knowledge and experience of the company and its affairs are in a position to advise, supervise, or direct the management of the company.

It is argued that an outside director to do his or her job properly must devote at least 100 hours annually on the job. However, many directors serve on several boards and have in addition a full-time job of their own, and are unable to contribute that much time to the board of an outside company. One study showed that more than 20 percent of directors serve on four or more boards. Surely a busy executive cannot devote 400 or more hours, more than ten weeks per year, to his or her outside boards.

An interesting case is that of former US Secretary of Defense Frank Carlucci, who held a full-time job as chairman of the large and important Carlyle Group but in addition served on the board of no less than 20 corporations and a dozen non-profit organizations. It is said that he had an outside board meeting for every single working day. This is an extreme example, but illustrates how the notion of the independent outside director as solving the governance problem is a key element in the failure of US governance methods.

Stock options

The independent board member providing protection of the rights of the shareholder seems not to be a real solution to the problem. How then to make sure that management works in the interest of the shareholder? How better to do this than to tie the interests of shareholders and managers together in schemes involving share price? Out of this train of thought has come the cause of the most pernicious failures of US governance – the stock option.

On the face of it, the idea behind the use of stock options is a fine one if you accept share price as highest corporate goal. Ensure management focus on the shareholder's interest in a high share price by allowing managers to benefit from the share price increase as well. Provide an option price that requires improved performance and allow management who meet and exceed that improvement to profit directly as well.

However, since the US corporation is a purely economic structure, with no internal social sanctions on the CEO, and since the CEO has total control of his board of directors in nearly all cases, the CEO reigns as emperor over the company – "the imperial CEO." With little limits on his authority, he can in fact use the stock option as a device to increase his income, and the income of his close associates, while rationalizing this behavior in terms of shareholder interest. (In fact, of course, his increased income comes at the expense of the shareholders who would otherwise receive the money as part of dividend payments.) In addition, he can arrange that the price of the option be reduced if share prices fall, to make sure the option is profitable, even if the other shareholders are losing.

A Nobel award-winning economist comments on the US stock option system and its value in corporate governance:

By 2001, options accounted for an estimated 80 percent of the compensation of American corporate managers...In less polite circles, we might speak of stock options as corporate theft – executives stealing money from their unwary shareholders....Theft – taking something from someone without consent – is exactly what it was. The victims were in no position to give their consent, because, for the most part, they didn't realize that something had been taken from them....Options, it was said, made the interests of managers and the interests of shareholders the same. It was a seductive argument, but, as event proved, a deeply flawed one. In a stock market boom, most of the increase in the value of stock has nothing to do with the efforts of management, making executive compensation dependent chiefly on the outcome of the stock market casino.[1]

The amounts of money the US CEO pays himself have become huge, far beyond the level paid by managements in any other country. Some examples – Wang, CEO of Computer Associates $655 million, Case of AOL $303 million, Eisner of Disney $637 million, Weill of Citigroup $488 million – all of these within only three years. The average CEO in the United States has an annual income 450 times greater than the average worker in his company (up more recently to over 500 times). In the case of Japan and Germany, the difference is 10 or 11 times and has been so for many years. In the United States in the 1990s the payments to CEOs increased by 340 percent while the average worker's compensation increased by only 36 percent – or after inflation did not increase at all.

All of this greed that is allowed full play in US corporate governance is a substantial factor in the exceptional inequality of income distribution in the United States, reported by the World Bank to be at the same level as that in Ethiopia, Ghana, and Cambodia. Japan's income distribution is exceptionally equal, the same level as in Denmark, Sweden, and Finland. The degree of US inequality would seem to risk political and social instability over the long term, yet there is little thought given to the issue in America.

The imperial CEO

Compensation is made up of more than merely the results of exercising stock options, of course. US CEOs receive tax reimbursements, housing allowances, access to company cars and aircraft as desired, bonuses, and other special payments. Huge pension benefits are another plus (and not included in the compensation figures). CEOs are credited with many years more of service than they have actually incurred, and thus receive massive special pensions. For example, the president of Delta Airlines had in fact been with the company for only five years. However, the board credited him with another 22 years of service. If he retired immediately, he would receive about $1 million per year for the rest of his life, a special bonus for five years' work. The post-retirement payments to Gerstner of IBM and Welch of GE – both very highly paid before retirement – were of massive proportions, Welch receiving a pension of $357,000 per month plus an after-tax payment of "consulting fees" of $377,000 per month as well as many living expenses.

All of this serves to demonstrate the powers of "the imperial CEO." However, from a governance point of view, the stock option is an additional hazard. It builds in a very powerful incentive to distort company accounts in order to increase share price, and given the stock market's three-month time horizon, to take a short-term view as well. The special appeal to US management of stock options is the fact that they are a tax-deductible expense for the company, reducing the tax burden, but are not an accounting expense to the company so do not reduce the profit statement.

The result is enormous distortion and misstatement of company accounts. For example, in 1996 Microsoft reported earning $2.8 billion. However, if stock option costs had been included in the results, Microsoft in fact lost $10.2 billion that year. In 2002, if Cisco had expensed its stock option costs, its net income would have dropped 80 percent. A US Federal Reserve Bank study indicates that had stock options been treated as a cost the level of profit of US companies would be lowered by a full 2.5 percent, or nearly half of the widely reported profit margin.

Are they an expense in fact? The sage of Omaha, Warren Buffett, has best stated the issue:

> It seems to me that the realities of stock options can be summarized quite simply: If stock options aren't a form of compensation, what are they? If compensation isn't an expense, what is it? And, if expenses shouldn't go into the calculation of earnings, where in the world should they go?

One major effect of stock options on governance is a large overstatement of the actual profit level of US companies.

From transparency to rigged accounts

The second effect is that stock options act as a powerful incentive for the CEO to manipulate revenues and earnings in order to increase share price. An obvious and frequent tactic is to use available cash to buy back company shares from the market, increasing share price both by the effect of the purchases and also by reducing the number of outstanding shares. This is for short-term effect, and quite disregards the issue of whether the money would be better invested in the company's business for long-term benefits.

Another tactic is to exaggerate earnings. With the Enron and other scandals in US business putting pressure on companies to report more honestly, more than 10 percent of US companies restated their financial results to correct accounting frauds. The result was a $100 billion drop in the share prices of these companies. Put the other way, dishonest accounting was worth $100 billion dollars in exaggerated share prices. One example is the important telecomm company, Qwest. The CEO resigned under pressure in mid-2002 but in the preceding three years had made $227 million and the largest shareholder, a board member, made almost $1.5 billion selling shares. The new CEO found that revenues and costs had been misstated for those three years. The share price dropped from $40 to $1 as a result, greatly damaging innocent shareholders.

In a special study in mid-2002, the *Financial Times* concluded:

> Top executives and directors of the biggest US business failures amassed billions in salary and share sales while the stock market was still booming. In just three years, they grossed about $3.3 billion before their companies went bust, having wiped out hundreds of billions of dollars of shareholder value and nearly 100,000 jobs.

The list of such failed companies is long – Enron, ImClone, WorldCom, Tyco, Adelphia, Global Crossing, HealthSouth, AOL-Time Warner, JDS are only some of the largest involved in legal actions, bankruptcies, and restatements of accounts.

With all this have come as well major scandals regarding collusion between Wall Street firms and their analysts and the management of companies. Led by Citigroup, Credit Suisse First Boston, and Merrill Lynch, the top firms have agreed to pay a fine of $1.4 billion for fraudulent actions on company shares, and face even greater damages as clients bring individual legal actions. In addition, corporate management has engaged "independent" auditors, who in fact made most of their revenue from consulting fees paid by the company and thus overlooked or colluded in accounting irregularities. Acquisitions were widely undertaken – they generally increase share price in the near term – even though it is well known that the majority of acquisitions result in loss of value to the company over time. In another tactic, managements in many companies pushed the use of *pro forma* statements of accounts to present exaggerated earnings numbers.

Another approach to managing earnings has been "big bath" accounting. Accounting earnings are not economic earnings. Assume a company that reported earnings over the past five years of $10 a share per year, but in the sixth year announces a restructuring charge of $75 a share. During the entire six-years period, the company is deemed to be reporting profitably from an accounting point of view, and because this is a restructuring charge, in US reporting it does not alter "earnings from on-going operations" of another $10 per share. The company has lost money over a six-year period, yet shows a profit in each annual reporting. Even worse, many companies report non-recurring costs and losses a number of times, each time evading the impact on reported earnings, "recurring non-recurring costs."

Again, during the US bubble, pension funds showed substantial gains, and these can be taken in as company profits. These gains are fictitious. A high return is projected; the actual return is much less. Companies like General Motors are billions of dollars in misstatements/overstatements of earnings as a result. Still another and more dangerous device to increase earnings statements is the use of "special purpose entities," structures that can hold debt off the company balance sheet. Used most heavily by Enron, even Ford Motor has some billions of dollars of off-balance sheet debt through these devices. One conclusion of all of this can only be that the often displayed reports of high US returns on sales, on equity and on assets, as well as reported financial positions, must be viewed with caution and scepticism. And that corporate governance is all too often a farce.

It is impossible to escape the conclusion that the US system of corporate governance has failed in a great many cases and from basic weaknesses. The concept of an outside board has in practice meant a top management with nearly total powers, as the outside, presumably independent, board members are too often cronies of top management. The concept that shareholder interest is best served by basing management compensation on share price has in practice brought about major share price distortions that damage the company in both the short term and longer term as well, by providing top management very great incentives to distort results and inflate share prices. Greed has consequences.

The remedy offered to the scandals and the governance issues exposed as a result has been to enact new legislation introducing legal standards with penalties for malfeasance. American society is multi-cultural, lacking a common set of values and code of behavior. Instead, the apparatus of law – courts, police, prisons, and the like – define and enforce rules. When the economy is the pure and unrestrained market, the jungle, that is often held to be ideal by many in America, only law will bring about some semblance of order.

However, no law or set of laws can anticipate and forestall those persons whose objective is self-aggrandizement, whose motive is greed. Most of the losses of company value in the United States have been due to unchecked management excess, not to criminal action, due to greed rather than incompetence. Law can only limit the range of the application of greed. The result of the US governance system, dedicated to maximizing share price, with the CEO largely free to pursue his own interests, is short-term share price maximization, selling off the corporation's future, the future of everyone in the company except top management, and the future of much of the community as well.

Transparency prerequisite to governance

In evaluating management systems, it is useful to separate the concept of transparency from that of actual governance. By "transparency" in corporate terms is generally meant the availability of full and accurate accounts of the corporation's operating results and financial position. Transparency is not governance. However, transparency in corporate accounts is surely a prerequisite to establishing credible and effective governance.

For some years, the US system had been seen as preeminent in transparency, with US "generally accepted accounting principles" (GAAP) a world standard. As is evident from the discussion above, there are now reasons to be highly skeptical of the accuracy of US accounting reports. The treatment of stock option costs, the accounting of pension gains and losses, "non-recurrent restructuring costs" that repeatedly recur, off-balance sheet treatment of debt, misleading reporting of profita-bility through "pro-forma" devices, overstated revenue amounts – all of these and more raise very serious questions about the transparency of US accounting during the 1990s bubble period and after.

The situation of Japanese companies regarding transparency has been until very recently also highly questionable. Accounts were reported for only the parent company, assets were priced on the books with little relation to current values, losses (and gains) could be carried in subsidiaries off the balance sheet, pension liabilities were essentially unaccounted for, and cash flow positions were largely unknown to investors. Reported positions and results had no necessary relationship to actual fact, to the great hazard of investors and indeed to the disadvantage of management seeking good governance.

Fortunately, recent years have seen massive improvements in Japanese corporate transparency. Assets must be marked to market values, consolidated reporting is required, retirement liabilities must be accounted for, and cash flow statements are routine. Effective transparency has been largely achieved, and lack of transparency is no obstacle any longer to implementing effective corporate governance in Japan.

Japanese corporate governance

A discussion of Japanese corporate governance, and the question of whether the US model is relevant for Japan, must begin with an examination of the extent to which the corporation – the share-issuing company – is comparable in the two societies.

In *The Living Company* de Geus states,

> There are, in fact, two different types of commercial companies in existence today, distinguished by their primary reason for being in business. The first type is run for a purely "economic" purpose. This sort of "economic company" is managed primarily for profit. The economic company is not a work community. It is a corporate machine. Its sole purpose is the production of wealth for a small inner group of managers and investors. It feels no responsibility to the membership as a whole.
>
> The second type of company, by contrast, is organized around the purpose of perpetuating itself as an ongoing community. Return on investment remains important. But managers regard the optimization of capital as a complement to the optimization of people. The company itself is *primarily* a community.[2]

The US company is clearly an economic company, while the Japanese company is a community.

In similar fashion, Albert concludes, "Capitalism has two faces, two personalities. The neo-American model is based on individual success and short-term financial gain; the Rhine model, of German pedigree but with strong Japanese connections, emphasizes collective success, consensus and long-term concerns."[3]

These two analysts offer a view that is in fact widely accepted, that there are basic differences between corporations in different societies and cultures. The differences are often stated as differences between the Anglo-American model and that of other industrial economies. That there are real differences seems hardly in question. But then it must follow that a corporate governance system appropriate for one model is not likely to be appropriate for the other. Whether the US system of corporate governance is an effective one or not, it certainly should not be applied to the Japanese company – or to the German or French company for that matter – without major adjustments to ensure that its application will not do great damage. Even the OECD statement of its principles of corporate governance begins, "there is no single model of good corporate governance."

This appreciation of difference is especially important in the Japanese case. Japan, the only non-Western society to industrialize fully, achieved industrial success and national wealth more rapidly from poverty than has any other nation in history. It did so in critical part because it introduced advanced production methods and technology into a corporate system that was based entirely on Japanese social relations and Japanese value systems. These values and systems of relations change, but change slowly. To introduce systems of governance that are not in full compatibility with basic Japanese values and human relations is to put at risk the entire strength of the economy.

Comparing Japanese governance systems with those of the other major economies, a leading British analyst reported,

> To understand how corporate governance works requires us to know what the participants perceive their objective to be. In Japan there appears to be a general consensus (which is lacking in some other countries) that although profit is important, the long-term preservation and prosperity of the family (which is how companies are viewed) are and should be primarily the aim of all concerned, and not profit maximization or shareholders' immediate values.[4]

Slow growth in recent years has not changed this fundamental view of the company as a community. Dore speaks of "the community nature of a Japanese firm – partly predicated on the fact that it is not run primarily for the benefit of shareholders" when he compares Anglo-American governance with that of Japan and Germany.[5]

The recurring references to the Japanese company as a social organization – a family, a community, a village – provide a starting point for examining the special requirements of Japanese corporate governance in comparison with that in the United States. As seen above, the US governance system rests on the primacy of the interests of shareholders. The company objective is to maximize shareholder value. It is as simple as that. But this has come all too often to mean enriching the CEO as much as possible – inevitably at the expense of the shareholders and employees. It is interesting to note that the various US works on corporate governance make almost no reference of any sort to employees. "What is corporate governance? It is the relationship among various participants in determining the direction and performance of corporations. The primary participants are (1) the shareholders, (2) the management (led by the chief executive officer), and (3) the board of directors."[6]

The shareholder as entire owner and share value as the entire objective for the corporation is in fact rather recent. Even in the United States, according to so great a figure as Abraham Lincoln, "Labor is prior to, and independent of, capital. Capital is only the fruit of labor, and could never have existed if labor had not first existed. Labor is the superior of capital, and deserves much the higher consideration." This powerful statement by Lincoln would be agreed with in much of today's world – but it could not possibly be stated by or agreed to by a political leader in today's United States.

It is not at all clear as to how or when the peculiar role of the shareholder in the US scheme of things came into being. Law in most countries recognizes the shareholder as owner, and indeed nearly everywhere the company is seen as having an obligation to provide the shareholder a return on his or her investment. It is quite another matter however to turn over all assets, proceeds, and power to the shareholder or the shareholders' representatives as is now the case in the United States.

The shareholder position in the United States and the United Kingdom compared with other countries was recently stated by Peter Drucker in an interview:

> With the exceptions of the US and UK, no developed country believes that the corporation exists for the sake of the shareholder. This is a totally alien idea. Corporations exist in most countries for

the sake of social harmony, for employment. In Japan the social reality is that the employees come first, and in Germany too.[7]

Here again is the contrast between the Anglo-American model and the Japanese/German one, with the objective of maximizing shareholder value the key difference.

That the Japanese company view of the shareholder differs from that in the United States is one of the key findings from a recent set of case studies: "I find that Japanese managers do not feel, and are not in any practical sense accountable to shareholders. Instead it seems that a complex system of responsibilities, reciprocal obligations, and trust ... is important for guaranteeing the accountability of company directors and employees." However, "In spite of the fact that managers did not appear to behave in a way consistent with feeling *accountable to* share-holders, they did appear to feel a strong *responsibility* to all share-holders."[8] In other words, there is a real responsibility to provide the supplier of capital a reasonable return on that capital. The shareholder then has no further claim.

Rather clearly, US approaches to corporate governance, effective or not, are inappropriate for application to Japanese companies. The basis for governance differs; therefore the methods of governance must differ, and do. The Japanese company, as community, builds a strong internal culture. The interests of all members of the community depend on the success of the community as a whole. Members of the community share experiences – and close knowledge of each other – over many years. Compensation is relatively egalitarian and, indeed as in any community, too great aggrandizement of a few is clearly at the cost of many – and is simply not tolerated. Promotions are from within, thus reinforcing the culture of the community – an outsider from another culture is not suitable for a position of leadership, when values are held in common and communication close. Misuse of company funds, in any fashion, is an attack on the community and is controlled by community sanctions.

Information in the community is shared, as are the futures and fortunes of the members, and their families. Investment in member training and education is to be encouraged and valued, since the bene-fits of that investment accrue to the company. There is little risk of their being purchased away by a competitor. Peer-group constraints comprise the enforcement mechanism of Japanese governance. Being promoted to director of a Japanese company is the culmination of the career, being recognized by peers for career achievement. The board serves as trustee, overseeing the interests of the employees of the company and its obligations to suppliers, customers – and shareholders. The Japanese company, as community, is a superb mechanism for ensuring that the highest level of human values is attained, while operating a highly competitive company at the highest levels of technology.

Is the system perfect? Of course it is not. Management of otherwise outstanding Japanese companies have yielded all too often to the blackmail demands of sokaiya, in violation of law. Scandals involving food and drug regulations recur. High-flying expenses by self-indulgent executives are not unknown. And no system can entirely cancel out sheer incompetence. But this level of scandal is familiar enough, in one form or another, in every developed economy – political payoffs, regulatory scandals, expense account games, and the like.

However it is clear that the Japanese management system, with inside directors, promotion from within, career employment, egalitarian compensation, enterprise unions, long-term supplier relations, and the other characteristics of the Japanese company have made for highly competent companies. These companies drove the economy from poverty to wealth in only two generations, and lead the world in many industries. For all the current nonsense about not being competitive, Japan's companies still provide the nation a very large surplus on the trade account – while the United States and the United Kingdom have massive trade deficits. Who is most competitive? And Japan's high level of competitiveness is achieved without the "efficient" apparatus of mass layoffs and firings and their attendant human cost so commonplace in the United States.

Indeed, the very most successful of Japan's companies, even now as the economy goes through a painful restructuring, are the companies that most closely adhere to traditional Japanese business practices. Toyota proudly maintains its long-standing personnel policies. The CEO of Canon, Mr Fujio Mitarai, states,

> Employment practices differ from country to country because cultures are different. If we employ people in countries where we operate, we have to respect their culture. For Japan, it is lifetime employment. I believe that such an employment practice conforms to Japanese culture and is our core competence to help survive global competition.[9]

On another occasion, Mr Mitarai noted: "I do not intend to end the lifetime commitment. Also, the American use of outsider executives, with the top bringing in their friends, has no function in Japan. Generally company outsiders have no capacity to be able to make judgments concerning the internal affairs of the company."[10]

Honda, Takeda Chemical, Fanuc, Fuji Photo Film, Shin-Etsu Chemical – the list of companies that continue to pursue the traditional approach to corporate governance is a long and distinguished one. However, parallel to this list can be prepared another list of companies that have moved in recent years from competitive success to deep trouble. Question: Is this the result of a failure in Japanese corporate governance? And if it is, what is the source of the problem? What changes in the system are needed?

Bear in mind that the strength of the Japanese company, and the system of governance, has derived from the development of a close-knit community, with a common culture. The system has retained its strength in many great companies. Where the system is failing is in the governance of the very large, highly diversified companies that have come into major positions from boom of the 1980s. Remember that with high growth, diversification is easy – everything is growing so success is assured, money is plentiful and cheap. Diversification means more growth – and growth is the target (or so it seemed during the bubble of the 1980s).

This push for diversification by many of Japan's companies involved two terrible dangers. The first is the strategic danger – success comes through carefully concentrating and focusing the resources of the company in those few areas in which there is competitive advantage. Diversification risks achieving growth at the expense of effective market share and control, of becoming a player in many games and the winner in none. The first rule of successful strategy is "Focus. Concentrate." The focused competitor will win.

The second great danger of diversification is a deep-reaching dilution of the corporate culture. This is not simply a matter of size. A very large company, like Honda for example, can be focused – Honda is a motor company, not a diversified conglomerate. It makes a range of products that use motors – but there is a common theme, motors. The hazard is being in many different businesses – and often through a large number of subsidiary companies – each business with its own peculiarities, its own special categories of information and its own culture. The Japanese company at its best exemplified a common culture. The highly diversified company dissipates and scatters its culture.

Japan's leading electronics companies, drunk on the high growth of the 1980s, diversified wildly, giving up leading share in segment after segment, and forming more than 1000 subsidiaries in several cases. Leaving aside the disastrous strategic implications, discussed elsewhere, one critical result was a loss of a common business culture through aggregating a very wide range of different businesses. The result was business failure, and a costly decade of drastic restructuring. The fault was not that of a poorly performing Japanese economy, nor was it a case of a dying electronics industry. An equal number of highly focused companies in the same economy and industry enjoyed consistently high growth and profitability – with tightly focused corporate cultures.

The difference in performance in recent years between diversified and focused electronics company is a devastating commentary on the management of the diversified firms (see Table 7.1). This is not only a phenomenon in electronics and manufacturing – contrast for example the deep troubles of diversified Daiei with the successes of focused Ito-Yokado in mass retailing.

However, a Japanese approach to the management of these troubled diversified companies is now emerging. A key development was the legalization of the holding company, allowing these firms to separate their various businesses into autonomous units, and when appropriate, prepare them to be spun off and taken public. Each homogeneous group of businesses can establish its own culture, under the umbrella of the parent holding company, thus restoring at the operational level the strengths of the focused Japanese company.

The board of directors of the holding company is developing into a smaller group, in the case of Toyota for example 20 or 30, half of the present number, in the case of Matsushita two-thirds of the current 27. Indeed, by now a majority of listed companies have fewer than 10 directors. All of this allows more rapid decision-making and a focus on policies. Thus the board is concerned with policy, with operational

Table 7.1   Focus vs diversification in the electronics industry

Company results	Diversified players[a]	Focused players[b]
Average sales, 2002	5057 billion	310 billion
Average number of subsidiaries	416	41
Annual sales growth, 1997–2002	0.5%	2.7%
Annual net profit, 1997–2002	–0.49%	10.97%
Debt: Equity ratio	1.9:1.0	0.13:1.0

Notes: [a] Hitachi, Toshiba, Mitsubishi Electric, NEC, Fujitsu, Sony, Matsushita, Sanyo, Sharp.
[b] TDK, Hirose Denki, Kyocera, Mabuchi Motor, Murata, Rohm, Keyence, Fanuc, Nidec.
Source: Kaisha Shikiho. Tokyo: Toyo Keizai Shinposha.

supervision placed at the divisional level, with the divisions integrated in product line and often organized as separate companies for operational purposes.

With this shift to centralized policy making and decentralized operational management, the changing governance system of Japan will bring in outside opinion through the device of an Advisory Board. Rather clearly, the traditional Japanese governance method tends to close off outside view and risks becoming narrow in outlook. Beginning with the success of Teijin with an outside Advisory Board, more and more Japanese companies are finding that this provides most of the advantages of outside directorships with few if any of the disadvantages.

The Advisory Board can be staffed with true outsiders, not cronies of the CEO, but experts in various fields, who bring their expertise to bear on the issues facing the company. The Advisors do not however preempt Directorships that otherwise would be the reward of long-serving employees. They do not presume that a visit of a day ever few months provides a basis to know the company well enough to make key decisions regarding personnel compensation, operations, or strategy. It is an elegant solution to the problem of introducing outsiders without doing damage to the corporate culture.

Although recent legislation allows "US style corporate governance," a majority of Japanese firms have decided not to adopt the US system. As of now, only a dozen firms have brought in the cadre of outside directors necessary to staff the US system. And as seen, despite all the claims for it, the US system has terrible faults, in any case not suitable for the Japanese organization. Instead we are seeing, as we must, the development of a truly Japanese governance system with holding company structures to deal with product and geographic diversity and a strong Advisory Board to provide advice and criticism to company management.

Family, Inc.

All of this discussion has dealt with the large, publicly traded corporation and with the differences between Japanese and US governance. Yet a great many of the most successful US companies are in fact governed much as Japanese companies, with strong family-like structures and an emphasis on long-term continuity. Berkshire Hathaway is, as noted above, family-dominated, with the man who really founded it as an investment company, Warren Buffett, in full control with his family. The company is a great success, and Buffett an enormously rich man. Family, Inc. can do well.

> Business Week has found that a surprisingly large share of Corporate America – 177 companies, or a third of the S&P 500 – have founders or families still on the scene.... We defined family companies as those in which the founders or their families maintain a presence in senior management, on the board as significant shareholders. For our group of family companies, the annual return to shareholders averaged 15.6 percent, compared with 11.2 percent for non-family companies. The family outfits trumped the others on annual revenue growth, 23.4 percent to 10.8 percent, and income growth, 21.1 percent to 12.6 percent.

These companies' boards are made up of family members and close friends, with a strong sense of company history and a willingness and ability to take a long-term perspective.

> With tight-knit family leaders at the top, decision-making can be easier and faster, allowing family companies to pounce on opportunities others might miss. Their often paternalistic corporate cultures may lead to lower turnover and development of management talent. And unlike outside CEOs, family chief executives know that their families are in it for the long haul, making them more likely to invest in the business.[11]

Most discussion of corporate governance assumes outside management, gun-for-hire executives, in impersonal, bureaucratic settings. These US family firms are much like Japan's companies, paternalistic, investing in staff, taking the long view, run by persons who know each other well and for long periods of time. Corporate governance discussion takes no account of these family companies which play so large and successful a role in the US economy.

In Japan's economy, the family company has a similar but larger role. By the US definition, Toyota, Takeda Chemical, Hoya Glass, Fanuc, and Canon are all family companies – and are among Japan's most successful. A study by the Fuji Research Institute of the 30 companies that have had best share price performance since 1989 (when most share prices were collapsing) finds that of the 30 top performers, 8 of the top 10 and 17 of the top 30 are family companies, using the same definition as in the US studies. Executive Director Toshiki Kurashina of Fuji Research argues that the high success rate of family companies is due to their ability to take fast decisions, command high employee loyalty and take a long-term view of business. He notes that "family company" has negative implications, quite incorrectly; that the term in fact reflects success.[12]

In our meeting with Chairman Takeo Kato of Fuji Electric he also and quite independently made the point that Japan's most successful companies are often run by founding individuals who can take quick decisions and are willing to assume considerable risks. And he notes too that a good many of these companies are in the Kansai region – Rohm, Keyence, Murata, Omron, and Nidec for example. Independent, away from the political centers, highly focused, these companies are Japanese family companies at their most effective, as are Canon and Toyota.

These Family, Inc., companies put the governance issue in a rather different light. It suggests that governance systems become an issue when the company is in fact at the full mercy of the impersonal marketplace, in the jungle. They also indicate that the basic Japanese approach to the corporation as a social organization, working as a community works in mutual self-interest, and with controls against malfeasance the controls of a tightly integrated social unit, provide the most effective system of corporate government. Here again the conclusion must be that Japan's companies should focus on developing their own governance methods, shaped by Japan's own customs and values in order to achieve real and lasting effectiveness in governance.

Notes

1. Joseph E. Stiglitz, *The Roaring Nineties*, New York: W.W. Norton, 2003, pp. 116, 122–123.
2. Arie de Geus, *The Living Company*, Boston: Harvard Business School Press, 1997, pp. 101–102.
3. Michel Albert, *Capitalism vs. Capitalism*, London: Whurr Publishers, Ltd, 1993, p. 18.
4. Jonathan Charkham, *Keeping Good Company. A Study of Corporate Governance in Five Countries*, Oxford: Clarendon Press, 1994, p. 74.
5. Ronald Dore, *Stock Market Capitalism: Welfare Capitalism. Japan and Germany versus the Anglo-Saxons*, Oxford: Oxford University Press, 2000, p. 79.
6. Robert A.G. Monks and Nell Minow, *Corporate Governance*, 2nd edition, Oxford: Blackwell Publishing, 2001, p. 1.
7. "Capital Markets and Investing. An Interview with Peter Drucker", *Forbes Global Business and Finance*, 7 September 1998, p. 68.
8. Simon Learmount, *Corporate Governance. What Can be Learned from Japan?* Oxford: Oxford University Press, 2002, pp. 3, 145.
9. Mitarai Fujio. *Nikkei Weekly*, 19 March 2002.
10. *Aera*, 3 March 2003, p. 86.
11. *Business Week*, 10 November 2002. From Dow Jones Reuters Business Interactive LLC, 2004.
12. Kurashina Toshiki, *Fuamiri Kigyo no Keieigaku*, Tokyo: Toyo Keizai Shinposha, 2003.

8
The Mysterious Foreign Investors

Given the very great distances in geography and social systems as well as in history, between Japan and the industrial nations of the West, it would seem natural that the level of foreign investment in Japan would be rather low. In point of fact, however, substantial foreign investment has a long history in industrial Japan and, with three decades of free access, is at a significant level with revenues of foreign companies in Japan around 15 percent of GDP accounted for by the more than 3000 foreign capital companies in Japan.

Unfortunately, foolish and mistaken notions regarding the Japanese economy are all too common, at home and abroad. It seems likely that more nonsense is written about the issue of foreign direct investment in Japan than about any other single subject about Japan. An all-too-common misstatement about foreign investment is a Harvard Business School Press report of some years ago: "...Foreign investors have played no important role in generating Japan's national income. Throughout the 1960s and 1970s, foreign direct investment contributed just one-tenth of one percent to the gross capital formation of Japan – the lowest figure among all industrialized countries."[1]

In a recent and typical polemic, not surprisingly from the self-serving American Chamber of Commerce in Japan, the usual clichés are offered up regarding the current situation.

According to IMF statistics in the year 2000, Japan's FDI stock stood at just 1.1 percent of GDP, lagging far behind the United Kingdom (32.4 percent), the United States (27.9 percent), and Germany (22.4 percent), among others.... Japan's lonely single-digit cumulative FDI figure reflects postwar domestic policies that were designed to meet specific national industrial structure goals.[2]

Later in the same recently published document, "Japan's policies and practices have inhibited inward FDI for more than a hundred years. As a percentage of GDP, the country's inward FDI stock is currently one-eleventh that of the United States and a twenty-eighth that of the UK."[3]

These views are reinforced by ill-informed and ignorant reporting on Japan in the Western press. For example, in the *Financial Times* of 24 March 2004, "...Japan remains extraordinarily closed to foreign investment." Again, in the *FT*, a headline in 21 August 2003 – "Hidebound Japan keeps investors at arm's length." Ironically, the photo illustrating this misbegotten story shows a Louis Vuitton shop window. Vuitton does well over a billion dollars in annual sales in Japan with a pre-tax return of 25 percent, a most attractive arm's length.

Part of the problem as we will see is the use of FDI as a percent of GDP to measure foreign presence, rather than measuring foreign companies revenues against total economic activity. The size of sheer capital investment says little or nothing of the ability of foreign companies to operate in a given environment. Part of the problem is from persistent underestimates of the total of FDI, taking no account of the input of foreign technology to obtain share of joint venture capitalization (rather than cash,) part from a failure to adjust for exchange rate differences as the yen moved from 360 to US$1.00 toward 100 to US$1.00, and in part from the failure to include reinvestment of earnings by highly profitable foreign-owned companies. FDI as percent of GDP is understated and in any event is a poor measure of the actual presence and power of foreign-owned companies.

The negative view of the situation by the foreign investment community is even repeated in the rhetoric of the government of Japan, itself a major source of errors regarding foreign investment levels. An early, careful, and critical analysis of the actual situation was provided in 1996 by David Weinstein, who noted "One of the biggest problems in studying the level of FDI in Japan is that most of the Japanese data are highly flawed and the US data only give a very imperfect picture of the structure of foreign firms in Japan."[4] After reviewing in some detail the various causes of errors in estimating FDI, Weinstein concludes, "...a reexamination of the data suggests that levels of FDI are not nearly as out of line with international levels as is widely believed." This analysis leads to the conclusion that "the actual level of sales by foreign affiliates or FDI is probably somewhere between 4 and 12 times larger than the reported levels."

A recent study for a major Japanese government agency also raises questions about the accuracy of the usual information on FDI.[5] Major differences between the reports of the Management and Coordination Agency, MITI and Toyo Keizai are noted. Unfortunately no final resolution of the problem is provided, or even attempted, in this study.

Needless to say, cautionary notes regarding underestimates of foreign company positions in Japan have gone unnoticed, or ignored, by those bent on making a political case against Japanese policy, by press reporters who in most cases are simply ignorant of Japanese facts, and by foreign businesses who like to plead for sympathy and support as they deposit their Japan earnings in foreign banks. There is no rational explanation however for the failure of the Japanese government to provide accurate data. What possible purpose is served by continuing to accept the view that foreign direct investment is at a low level? Is this due simply to lack of analysis, or to some odd desire to concur in views held abroad?

Some notion of the actual size of foreign investment can be pieced together from various sources. A final measure is not available, but the most superficial review makes nonsense of the 1.1 percent cliché that is in nearly universal usage. A first notion of the large presence of foreign investors in Japan comes from the detailed reports of Toyo Keizai, presented annually. Toyo Keizai defines as "foreign capital related companies" all listed companies in which foreign direct investment accounts for 20 percent or more of total equity, and non-listed companies in which foreign direct investment totals 49 percent or more of total equity.

In the most recent report, there are 3383 such cases of FDI in Japanese companies. In three-quarters of the total cases, the foreign equity share is 51 percent or more, reaching 100 percent in more than 60 percent of all investment cases. It is important to note that the total of more than 3000 takes no account of foreign companies in Japan that work through branch offices rather than corporate structures. Many of these are substantial – for example Boeing, British Petroleum, Weyerhaeuser, and professional firms like McKinsey & Co., PriceWaterhouseCooper, and White and Case. So the Toyo Keizai listing is itself an incomplete reflection of the overall foreign direct investment position.

A measure of size has been developed for this study, analyzing the top 50 foreign companies in Japan (excluding finance and insurance). The average foreign equity holding in these 50 companies is 69 percent, representing full management control. Forty eight of these foreign-owned companies have annual sales of more than $1 billion. Total sales of the "nifty fifty" are $317 billion, generally results as of year-end 2001. This is 7.2 percent of Japan's 2000 GDP, a number that immediately invalidates most of the conventional discussion of foreign investment in Japan. Assume that Pareto's law applies and these 50 might be as much as 80 percent of the total foreign position outside finance and insurance. Following the Pareto rule, another 20 percent needs be added to reach an estimate of the total. That would bring foreign share of revenues in Japan to 9 or 10 percent – not including banking, brokerage, investment banking, consumer finance, and life and casualty insurance.

These are not all new or even recent entrants. GE founded the predecessor to Toshiba around the end of the 19th century, when Western Electric founded what is now NEC. IBM began in Japan in 1937, Nestle in 1933, General Motors in 1927, Bayer in 1941, and Siemens co-founded Fuji Electric with the Furukawa interests in the 1920s. Even Coca-Cola as a company in Japan dates from 1957. There has been no time in modern peacetime Japanese history when foreign companies were barred from entry into the Japanese economy. They may have found entry difficult and may on occasion have done badly – such are the vagaries of business fortune – but they have not been kept out.

This data-based estimate that foreign manufacturing firms account for some 10 percent of the economy leaves out of consideration the area of real change in foreign direct investment – the financial sector. While not closed to foreign operators in the past, it was tightly regulated. Some foreign insurance companies, notably the several subsidiaries of AIG and the remarkable American Family Insurance Company, have been in the market for several decades, as have such foreign banks as Deutsche Bank, Credit Suisse, and Citigroup, with Banker's Trust, Chase Manhattan, and others in Japan with subsidiaries until the demise of their parents. However, since the mid-1990s or so, increased bankruptcies made insurance companies and bank acquisitions possible and the Hashimoto "Big Bang" began a thorough-going deregulation. As a result, changes in foreign investment position in the financial sectors have been remarkable.

In 1980, there were four foreign life insurers in Japan, out of a total of 26 companies. A decade later, by 1990, there were 10 foreign firms, out of a total of 34. Now there are 18 foreign firms out of a total of 41. The foreign firms' collective share of the domestic market, only 2.5 percent in 1990 is now a full 17.3 percent. Will all of the foreign firms do well? Certainly not. GE acquired the failing Toho Seimei, renamed it after the family saint, Edison – and later gave up and sold the remnants to AIG. Fixing failed Japanese companies offers substantial hazards, as Merrill Lynch discovered after losing hundreds of millions of dollars from proudly acquiring the retail operations of failed Yamaichi Securities. Not all the many foreign-acquired bankruptcies have been or will be repaired.

In insurance as in manufacturing, the most successful foreign firms have been those that built their own businesses, kept full control of the businesses and their know-how, and patiently invested for success. AFLAC, founded in Japan in 1973 and reviewed as a case history later in this chapter, has the largest number of insurance contracts of any company in Japan, including giant Nippon Life, and reported over ¥110 billion in profits in 2002. The AFLAC case and the general inroads into the life insurance business by foreign firms have been spectacular.

The securities business and investment banking are also sectors of foreign success in fairly recent years. Morgan Stanley, Nikko Salomon, Goldman Sachs, and Merrill Lynch are ranked, in order, 4th, 5th, 6th, and 7th in operating revenue among securities firms in Japan in 2002, with Goldman Sachs reporting profits on revenues of 54 percent. Merrill Lynch reported zero profits for the year. Not everyone is doing well. Still, the foreign share of revenue among Japan's top ten securities firms was 19.9 percent, with only 9.7 percent share of employees. In M&A advisory work, five of the top ten firms in Japan are foreign firms, with Goldman Sachs in 3rd place in the business with a 17 percent market share followed by Lehman Bros, J.P. Morgan, Morgan Stanley, and Citigroup.[6] M&A advisory is a field in which few Japanese firms have useful or extensive experience; foreign success is not surprising. Overall, for the major foreign securities firms, growth since the mid-1990s or so has been very rapid, a compound 10 percent annual growth rate in a deflationary economy.

Another major and recent factor in foreign investment is the appearance of large private equity funds from abroad, attracted by the drastic declines in real estate and other asset values and by the opportunities for purchase of businesses as Japanese firms have restructured and separated out non-core businesses. Perhaps the best known is Ripplewood, with some ¥240 billion in fund size. Leading a consortium, Ripplewood acquired a controlling position in the failed Long Term Credit Bank, a government sponsored institution. The Japanese government spent $38 billion writing off the banks' bad debt, while Ripplewood's consortium put in new management and $1 billion. The investment group realized a profit of more than ¥100 billion when the bank, re-named Shinsei, went out on an IPO. Not surprisingly, criticism of the government's handling of that bank problem is substantial; so generous an arrangement will certainly not recur even if needed.

Another foreign investor, the Lone Star Group, with a ¥1000 billion fund is largest of the foreign equity funds and has been very active indeed. Lone Star bought the failing bank, Tokyo Sowa. Now renamed Tokyo Star it seems to be doing well with new management and with new approaches to the customer. Lone Star is also reported to have bought 35 golf courses, casualties of Japan's deflation, although how one might profit from owning 35 Japanese golf courses is not obvious. Carlyle, Cerberus, Colony Capital, Warburg Pincus, W.L. Ross & Co, and other private equity funds operating in Japan have picked up Japanese hotels, golf courses, and other pieces of real estate and such small manufacturing firms as might be available.

An end to Japan's deflation and a continuation of Japan's economic growth along with an appreciating currency could well make even some of these miserable purchases a financial success. In any case, along with the propensity of some of these funds – Cerberus, Colony, and the like – to engage in vulture activities in and around Japan's bankruptcy courts, the equity funds are a new and possibly significant addition to the foreign direct investment scene. However, deal flows are sparse and managers of funds for potential investment search desperately for buys, all too few in numbers and size. Despite this, foreign investment of all kinds increased in the first half of 2004 by 2.5 times the first half of 2003. Direct investment is at a high and fast-growing level.

The retailing business is of some special interest regarding the position of foreign firms. Japan's is the world's second largest retail market, and retailing in Japan has some remarkable features. There are about 1.4 million retail stores in Japan, half with only one or two employees, and more than half owned by individuals. These are classic "mom-and-pop" shops. And they suit the Japanese consumer well who shops often, expects and gets personal services and expects and gets totally reliable products. The Japanese consumer has been trained to be very particular and demanding, and is.

The retailing debate now is about new directions and the potential in Japan for giant retail outlets. Carrefour came into Japan about four years ago with a hypermarket in Chiba's Makuhari and ambitious plans. The original plans have been scaled back. Carrefour had a total of seven Japan outlets, now up for sale and retreat. Costco came in at about the same time, with an ambitious program, and has four outlets to date, featuring direct sales from producers and wholesale prices to both the trade and to consumers. Costco is reported to be doing fairly well. Wal-Mart, the world's largest retailer, bought into Japan's failing Seiyu chain of supermarkets, taking a 37 percent share of equity and supported by

Sumitomo Trading which holds 10 percent of equity. Wal-Mart is to decide by 2007 whether or not to acquire a fully controlling 66.7 percent of Seiyu's equity. Presumably Wal-Mart will go for hypermarkets and very low prices in Japan as it has elsewhere. The Seiyu road may be a difficult one however. Seiyu announced in end-2003 a second year of losses, and a third year of losses in 2004 of ¥4 billion. Wal-Mart faces a tough decision, and the Carrefour experience is not encouraging. Still another hypermarket operator, Germany's Metro, has entered Japan with an outlet in Fukuoka, Marubeni Trading a 20 percent shareholding partner.

While these foreign hypermarket firms are starting up, Aeon, one of Japan's three largest supermarket operators, has made it clear that it looks on Wal-Mart, Metro, Tesco, and the others as its real competitors of the future, and has set out to build similar large-scale shops at various of its malls in Japan in an effort to get ahead of the intruders. However, Aeon rival Ito-Yokado has stated that it feels the hypermarket has no place in Japan and that it intends not to play the game, influenced no doubt by its ownership of the highly successful convenience chain, Seven-Eleven, with more than 10,000 outlets.

The head of international for Tesco, UK retail leader and new entrant to the Japanese market, is quoted in the *Financial Times*: "In America you have big cars, you can drive several miles in five minutes, you can buy in bulk and store it in your double-garage. Chalk and cheese compared to Japan. In Japan we learned that some housewives shop on bikes and shop daily, visiting six or seven shops looking for deals. You've got to understand these things."[7]

Tesco has been a leader in very large supermarkets. However, Tesco came into Japan after much study by acquiring C-Two, a rather small Tokyo area discount operation, who have what Tesco calls a "discount convenience format." It is the case that retailing in Japan has come to be largely controlled by convenience store chains, with Seven-Eleven's 10,000 outlets managed through a computer system matched in the world only by Wal-Mart in power and sophistication. Seven-Eleven has a curious Japan history. It was originally a US company that licensed to Ito-Yokado the name, format, and approach of the US chain. Eventually, to prevent damage to the brand, Ito-Yokado bought out worldwide its former licensor – and went on to ever-greater success. The issue: Is the Japanese market, given cost structures and consumer habits, the place for giant hypermarkets and terrific price competition or is it the place for tightly managed, omnipresent convenience stores? Or can the two extremes co-exist and both do well?

Whatever the outcome of this intriguing game, the fact is that some retailers have entered Japan and failed – Boots from the United Kingdom is a recent example, Sephora another and e-Bay still another. However, foreign retailers with unique identities are doing very well indeed. Toys "R" Us has annual sales of ¥180 billion, and is steadily profitable in Japan, unlike its US experience. The luxury specialty outlets are in their way even more spectacular, Louis Vuitton being the prototype. Vuitton has Japan sales of ¥124 billion, with a reported profit of ¥32 billion, or a pre-tax profit of more than 25 percent. Hermes is second in total reported profit, sales not reported. This group of successful foreign retailers includes Nike, GAP, Brooks Bros, Chanel, Gucci, LeviStrauss, Ferragamo, Bulgari, and Estee Lauder. All are 100 percent foreign owned, all have sales of more than ¥12 billion yen annually and all are nicely profitable, with Japan sales larger than those in any other market for most of these firms.

A rather amusing footnote to the success of foreign luxury goods retailers in the Japanese market is the report that

> an average of 56 percent of the floor space at the (department) stores' cosmetic departments was dedicated to foreign products, with the percentage going as high as 80 percent in some outlets. At the Sakae store in Nagoya, owned by Mitsukoshi Ltd., the five best-selling cosmetics brands were all foreign ones.... For department store operators, shops selling foreign cosmetics are important because they give added cachet to their stores and help attract more customers. As a result, they offer foreign firms benefits not accorded domestic cosmetics makers, with one department store picking up the 20 million yen tab for opening a new shop, an executive at a foreign cosmetics producer said.[8]

Barriers to foreign companies?

Japan a closed market and a closed economy? With a lack of foreign investment and a need to encourage more? Multiple nonsense. The real mystery is how the myth that foreign investment in Japan is tiny in amount and extent gets perpetuated, in utter disregard for the highly visible evidence of major foreign positions.

Discussion of foreign investment into Japan is shadowed by history and is often naïve and simply uninformed. The focus tends to be on Japanese government policies and on Japanese business practices, as in the extraordinary American Chamber statement that "Japan's policies and practices have inhibited inward FDI for more than a hundred years."

Inward investment has of course been affected by government policy and domestic business practices. However, it has been affected no less by the ignorance of and indifference toward Japan of the potential foreign investors. A brief review of policy patterns may help explicate the real causes of investment problems.

We might start with the immediate post-World War II period. Individual company decisions determined investment policy. The major oil companies – Mobil, Exxon, Caltex, and Shell – all re-established their prewar operations at the earliest possible occasion and developed their Japan position with considerable success. Similarly, IBM, NCR, and Nestle, long in Japan in the prewar period, rebuilt and became major players. Government policies and local practices of course shaped these companies' decisions, but in no way stood in the way of growth and success.

Other companies with substantial prewar operations took different approaches. Ford and General Motors did not renew their operations, despite holding substantial Japan assets, Ford's Yokohama facilities for example. Otis Elevator and Carrier in air conditioning had prewar virtual monopolies in the Japan market. They renewed their businesses, but with local partners, and allowed their shares to decline precipitously by taking out profits rather than investing in the very fast growing market. IT&T sold out its one-third equity position in NEC, a classic example of short-sighted greed. GE chose not to maintain its large shareholding in Toshiba, passing up recapitalizations rather than investing as it might have done.

The crucial differences in investment behavior of these companies with prewar positions were company strategic choices, not government regulations. Certainly many industries, notably petroleum, were under tight government regulations during the 1950s and 1960s, with Japan then a siege economy. But these regulations did not focus on foreign investors nor yet did they preclude foreign successes – nor did they account for the differences in investment decisions between companies.

It is rather often forgotten in discussions of government restrictions that through the entire period from the Peace Treaty in 1951 to the mid-1960s, the period in which modern Japanese industry took shape, entry into Japan by foreign direct investors was not restricted. Japanese companies could be established by foreign investors in nearly all industries with no limit on the equity ownership by the foreign parties. The investor was to invest hard currencies from abroad, at a time when the yen was not convertible. The investor was gambling then on Japan's economic success providing in good time an opportunity to repatriate earnings and, if needed, capital as well.

This was the so-called "yen company" route to investment. The fact that virtually no foreign companies took advantage of this open investment opportunity provides one measure of the ignorance of Japan, and indifference toward Japan, of most foreign managements. Coca Cola set up its yen company in 1957 after long experience supplying US forces in Japan and took advantage of the inability to repatriate profits to mount a massive advertising and marketing campaign. Japan at one point in the mid-1970s provided a third of Coca Cola's worldwide profits, the result of building so powerful a market position early on. The chairman of Pepsi Cola was for a long time a leading complainer about Japanese government restrictions. Like most failed investors, he chose not to dwell on his company's own mistakes, preferring to blame the government for his failed competitive position. Winners do not complain, nor testify at US government committee hearings. Losers blame the Japanese government, not their own weaknesses and errors.

Other companies like AMP and General Foods also took advantage of the yen company route – but they were few. Most would-be foreign investors insisted on rights to repatriate earnings and capital. The yen was in short supply in a capital-scarce economy. Japan's payments balance was in chronic crisis through the 1950s and 1960s. Not surprisingly then the government insisted on the right to review proposed investments and determine their value to the economy, under the powers of the laws governing access to foreign exchange. As part of this policy, the government regulations required that manufacturing investments be done jointly with a Japanese company, with the foreign equity participation no more than 50 percent. It was these restrictions that earned MITI its reputation as a fierce gatekeeper and allowed critics to argue that Japan was closed to foreign investments – disregarding the availability of the yen company route and ignoring the exigencies that required exchange controls.

The basic issue is corporate strategy and corporate choice. Most potential investors were not prepared to invest in Japan without government guarantees regarding repatriation of funds. They chose not to gamble in yen convertibility. They chose instead to go through the regulatory apparatus – or stay out of the market. In evaluating the weight of government regulations, it needs be noted that as regulations were eased in the 1967–73 period, and subsequently largely abolished by 1980, there were no significant increases in foreign direct investment into Japan.

Certainly regulations played a part in the amount and pattern of foreign investment, at least until the 1980s. But along with this went a widespread indifference to Japan as a market and as an investment site.

Japan was seen as geographically remote, culturally distant and complex, and not important either as a market or as source of competition. It was this that caused the strategically disastrous sale of technology to Japan's companies, and it was this indifference that was at least as great a cause of low direct investment as was government policy.

Lack of interest or concern regarding Japan's economy led directly to a strategic disaster, the mass, low priced sale of the world's best technology. And it is this that has, perhaps more than any other single factor, limited foreign investment into Japan. The potential competitive advantage of the foreign entry would be technology – not capital and not management skills or labor. Technology was the lever to open the door to successful investment. But it was given away.

Remember that Japan came out of World War II with a massive shortfall of technology in nearly every industry. Domestic R&D had been, for a decade or more, military-focused and controlled. Isolated from much of the developed world, the lack of technology was acute and an absolute barrier to growth. Japan had a make-or-buy decision and the choice was to buy technologies from abroad, with close reviews of the terms of the purchases to ensure real value at a reasonable price – unsupervised, Japan's companies might have paid anything to get key technologies, and unsupervised, purchases might allow monopolies. Buy, but with care, was the policy.

Over the next decades a massive purchase of world technology took place. By 1985, some 45,000 contracts had been entered into, at a cumulative cost that was a fraction of the then annual US R&D expenditure. Annual purchases have in fact somewhat increased since, to a total by 1998 of more than 85,000 contracts. (Interestingly, the larger share of contracts in recent years has been for software technology rather than hardware.) For most Western companies, the revenue from technology sale was seen as a windfall. The R&D cost had been written off. A stranger comes in and offers a down payment and continuing royalty – the perfect answer for an executive striving to meet his quarterly revenue targets. It is a no risk, pure profit transaction.

This sale of technology not only took away the key to Japan's investment door, but also – because the contracts were limited in duration and had no provision for reciprocal technology exchange – made it possible for Japanese buyers to improve on the technology and become major world competitors. And they did.

The entry of Texas Instruments into Japan in the 1960s demonstrated vividly the power of technology when used strategically. TI held a vital semiconductor patent, basic to all semiconductor production. Japan's industry desperately needed patent access in order to prevent the US market being closed to imports for patent violation. MITI insisted that TI come in with a Japanese joint venture partner, while allowing patent licensing. TI insisted on full ownership of a production company in Japan as a condition for making patent licenses available, and TI used a Texan then in the White House to help press the point. And finally in a complex arrangement with Sony serving as a passive partner for three years, TI got precisely what it wanted. Technology, intelligently used, is a powerful entry instrument but one that most companies simply sold off.

In an earlier period, the joint venture was the chosen entry vehicle, with equity roughly equally divided between the Japanese and Western partner. (Often the equity of the Western firm was in payment of technology inputs, still another reason why FDI numbers are inaccurate.) Joint ventures suited naïve foreign investors – capital costs were halved, facilities and staffing were available, distribution could be arranged, positive cash flow was in early sight. Greenfield efforts offer none of this.

Yet few of the great many joint ventures have survived. One side or the other agrees to sell out. GE and Hewlett Packard both took control of ventures with Yokogawa. Xerox has sold down its interest in the highly successful Fuji Xerox (always run in any case by Fuji Film since its founding in the 1960s). Sumitomo 3M is a success, and has always been run by 3M; NEC has recently sold its 25 percent interest to 3M, which now holds 75 percent of total equity. McGraw-Hill sold out to Nihon Keizai and lost ownership share of the highly successful business magazine, Nikkei Business. Honeywell sold out of Yamatake Honeywell. Kimberley Clark and Scott Paper each retreated from what had been joint ventures in consumer paper products. (Note: there is foreign direct disinvestment as well as direct investment.)

Joint ventures are hard to manage. Toshiba once argued that they are doomed to lose market share because by the time the dual management of a joint venture reaches a decision, competitors have already moved ahead. Partner interest, warm and close during the early honeymoon period, grows cool with increasing disagreement over venture objectives. For example, Sanyo Kokusaku, Scott Paper's partner, felt that profit over 5 percent of sales was taking undue advantage of customers. Scott felt that profit of 5 percent was entirely inadequate. End of joint venture. The successful joint ventures – there are a few – are managed by one party or the other, not jointly. There needs to be only one cook in the corporate kitchen. And the numbers of joint ventures are few and declining. The joint venture is seldom a vehicle for moving to high success.

Patterns of foreign direct investment changed greatly from the early 1980s. Japan's economic importance, complete deregulation of investment rules, the lessons learned from the reckless sale of technology – all these came together to these conclusions: We must be in Japan. We can and must control our business there. We must keep control of our technology. With this, the number and scale of successful foreign companies in Japan increased steadily, virtually all with 100 percent ownership of operations, including such companies as Samsung, Intel, Microsoft, Sun Microsystems, Apple, Dell, Oracle, and SAP. All are 100 percent owned, all are based on recent technologies, and all are among the very largest and fastest growing of foreign companies in Japan. No local partners (although many local suppliers and distributors), no acquisitions, ample profits. An interesting exception on the profit side is Samsung of South Korea, a company whose founder and present top executive had long experience in Japan. Samsung is one of the ten largest foreign non-finance operations with sales in Japan of more than $6 billion, but with a reported profit of only $12 million!! Creative accounting?

The foreign entry to Japan had for long suffered from a real disadvantage in recruiting staff. The foreign company was seen as an unreliable employer, even assuming that Japanese could aspire to top positions in a foreign company. Companies like Kodak and Reader's Digest had by ruthless discharging of employees in what became highly publicized cases damaged the interests of all foreign firms. The young Japanese starting a career had good reason to view the potential foreign employer with some suspicion. This is now changing but slowly. As one indicator, a survey of graduating students found that of the top 100 companies seen as most desirable employers, only 7 foreign companies made the list – IBM Japan, P&G Far East, Accenture, PwC Consulting, Nestle, and Astra Zeneca. The foreign companies still have further work to do in building their repute.[9]

A comparison of foreign equity shares and types of businesses in 1991 and in 2002 makes clear the important changes in the approach of the foreign direct investors when positioning in the Japanese economy (Table 8.1).

Two clear trends over the decade are apparent, and indeed are continuations of earlier trends: one, a sharp decline in the number of 50–50 ventures and increase in wholly owned companies, with foreign majority interest in three-quarters of the 3200 companies studied; two, a sharp increase in foreign capital-related companies dealing in finance, IT and software, and non-manufacturing in general. Japan is no longer the place to focus manufacturing except in very specialized or unique products.

Table 8.1   Foreign capital-related companies (total of 3244)

Foreign equity share of "foreign capital related companies"			Type of business		
Equity share	2002 (%)	1991 (%)	Type	2002 (%)	1991 (%)
100 %	61.4	47.8	Manufacturing	24.5	30.6
51–99	15.4	17.0	Distribution	25.9	44.7
50	9.3	21.3	Finance	8.9	4.6
Less than 50	13.9	13.9	IT and software	12.1	4.8
			Services	5.8	8.4
			Other non-mfg	22.8	6.9
Total	100	100		100	100

Source: Toyo Keizai Gaishi-kei Kigyo Soran, 2003.

Any discussion of foreign direct investment in Japan must lead finally to a discussion of mergers and acquisitions – M&A. The conventional view is that entry to a highly developed market with complex and expensive distribution channels and strong local competition is best done through acquisition of a local company which provides facilities, staffing, distribution, and immediate cash flow. Greenfield entry presumably is higher risk, with front-end high expenses and a long wait for a payback on the investment. In this view, a major barrier to foreign investment in Japan is the low incidence of M&A activity, and without M&A entry is more difficult and costly.

This view disregards the fact that all studies of the effects of acquisitions conclude that in most cases acquisition reduces the values of the companies involved – although they reward handsomely the investment banks, consultants, and others whose fees are paid at time of purchase. Moreover, it is apparent that while all acquisitions have a high risk of causing losses of value, acquisitions across cultures are especially hazardous. It is said that before the Daimler acquisition of Chrysler, an internal Daimler study showed that three-quarters of cross-border acquisitions failed. This did not deter Daimler, and its Mitsubishi acquisition looks like proving again that cross-border acquisitions generally fail. Note Bridgestone–Firestone and Matsushita–Universal along with General Motors–Isuzu and Ford–Mazda as painful examples of how cross-border acquisitions pose dangerous problems. Toyota, Honda, and others in the United States, and IBM, Samsung, and AFLAC in Japan show how well companies can do without local acquisitions.

In any event, M&A in Japan is a complex topic. First, in Japan especially M needs be viewed separately from A. Most reports on M&A activity are by parties whose business interest is in advising on M&A deals. Their reports combine M with A, giving an impression of much more activity than is in fact the case. And very often they class as A quite small share purchases that cannot reasonably be considered acquisitions. The reported numbers must be viewed with considerable skepticism.

Mergers of Japanese companies are frequent, most often simple combinations of two or more subsidiaries of a single parent company – for example, combining several sales subsidiaries into one. And with holding companies now legal, mergers under the umbrella of a holding company have become more numerous. Some are of real importance, for example Kawasaki Steel and NKK into a very large steel combination, JEF. A recent case is that of Minolta and Konica combining their operations. These kinds of mergers allow combining operations over time without the threat to employees and the company structure that acquisition would imply. Japan's high-growth economy led to an over-supply of competitors in a great many industries, as growth allowed the less efficient to survive. As demand growth slowed, the marginal competitors are under threat. And world competition demands scale in many industries. Thus since the mid-1990s or so, Japan's fourteen petroleum operators went to four, seven cement producers became three, ten paper and pulp companies became four. And so on.

In contrast, acquisition – the sale of a business – remains in Japan the last resort of a failing company, or the chosen option of a company that sees it has no future. The company is a social organization, not a mere aggregation of financial assets, and social organizations are not to be easily bought or sold. Only impending disaster for its people leads Japanese management to consider sale. Thus successful companies with promising futures are not for sale, nor yet even successful parts of companies. Most of the reported numbers indicating active acquisition activity report on Japanese companies raising their equity stakes in affiliates, or acquiring majority control of affiliates to strengthen their core businesses. The avoidance of acquisition is not at all aimed at preventing purchases by foreign companies; these strictures apply at least as much to Japanese companies.

This is not to say that there are no acquisitions in Japan. There of course are, and they are not simply recent. The writer was very much involved in an early one, the purchase by General Motors of slightly over a one-third interest in Isuzu. Isuzu was in deep trouble, with Nissan threatening to take it over. The foreign acquirer was more attractive to

Isuzu's management (as is often the case) because with Nissan, Isuzu's staff would be second-class citizens for the rest of their careers, while the foreign acquirer needed them all in place. GM has been up and down with Isuzu, in 2002 holding 48 percent of Isuzu's equity – and managing to record a loss of $1.2 billion. Put politely and briefly, GM's adventures in Japan have not been a success. Ford, holding a one-third interest in the former Toyo Kogyo, now Mazda, since 1979, has not done much better, changing presidents annually for the past several years as the company struggles.

The Renault adventure with Nissan is seen now as an exception to these painful rules. Share ownership is now 44 percent of Nissan Jidosha, with record profits in 2002 and 2003 of nearly $5 billion compared to losses of nearly $7 billion in 1999. This change has made something of a hero in Japan of Carlos Ghosn, the Nissan CEO from Renault. He did very much what Lee Iacocca did in the early 1980s as he took over a failing Chrysler – and indeed what every savvy CEO does when turning around a disaster. First, write off all the mistakes made by others. Bury the bad ones. Total cost, $7 billion (the 1999 loss). Second, sell all assets that are not core and that have any marketability. All this becomes immediate income. Third, slash the scope of the company – Nissan built 26 platforms, and had massive over-capacity. Fourth, squeeze suppliers unmercifully. Results – immediate profits, and apparent success. Long term? Chrysler lasted another 15 years. It will be interesting to see how long Nissan lasts. Supplier problems already surface, as the cuts in steel prices that made Ghosn famous have resulted in steel shortage and production cuts – suppliers will get their own back. With Toyota and Honda as competitors, Nissan's time will no doubt be shorter. In the meantime, it is a fine story.

Mitsubishi Motors was bought into by Daimler-Chrysler in much the same manner as Renault with Nissan – a 37 percent shareholding and management control. Sales are down and losses very much up – ¥215 billion. Management is being changed yet again, and the Mitsubishi group companies are contributing to the effort at repair. This looks already much like the GM and Ford cases after only a few years, with Daimler in full retreat.

Vodaphone will be another interesting test case as it acquired Nippon Telecom, somewhat shopworn from manhandling by British Telecom and AT&T earlier. The scale of the company is very large, $15 billion in 2002, but with a $600 million loss. The issue here too is competition. Neither Docomo nor KDDI are likely to give up market share or profits to a relatively weak outsider. It is curious to note how often company problems are seen as internal when in fact the real problems are highly competent and larger scale competitors. Cable and Wireless has announced retreat through sale to a Japanese company of their marginal position in Japan. Vodaphone next?

Still, acquisitions in Japan can work, and sometimes do. Again, the writer was very much involved in a rather early one, the acquisition in the mid-1980s of Banyu, then about 12th or 13th in sales amongst Japan's pharmaceutical companies, by Merck, then America's largest and most successful drug company. Merck had a joint venture with Banyu – but others did too. The critical variables to this takeover were the recognition by Banyu's management that the company could not produce new products – in an industry where success is a function of new products, and Merck's splendid record of product development. At the same time, Banyu boasted a strong sales force, which Merck needed for success in Japan.

It should be noted here that the success of the negotiations did not depend on price, but instead on a clear and formal understanding regarding Merck's willingness to adhere to Japanese personnel practices, signed by the chairmen of both companies and made public to the Banyu personnel. The fit was fine – each had what the other needed, while recognizing the sensitivity of the personnel issue. And the acquisition, now complete, has been a success. Note too that Merck in its annual report paid respects to the Japanese Ministry of Finance for assistance in the merger arrangements – so much for government hostility to foreign investment.

There have recently been other cases of acquisition in the pharmaceutical industry by foreign interests – the takeover of SSP Company by Boehringer Ingelheim and the acquisition of Chugai, 10th in sales in the industry, by Roche. No doubt the special demands of product patents in this industry are a factor in acquisition. In any case, foreign companies account for about 25 percent of total pharmaceutical sales in Japan, probably the highest penetration by foreigners of any Japanese industry. And this high penetration in what is almost certainly the most regulated of all industries still.

Acquisitions in Japan by foreign companies are not new. Most have not done well, but a few have succeeded. The pressures of sustained deflation and the needs to restructure in the 1990s and after have opened more possibilities for acquisition. But they remain cases of acquiring troubled companies – and like Merrill Lynch, Daimler, General Motors, and Ford, it does not follow that somehow foreign management can accomplish what Japanese management has not been able to do. The stars in the foreign direct investment firmament are the IBMs, Nestles, Coca Colas, Intels, the Samsungs, and the like who have built their own companies based on their own technologies and skills, and have produced winners.

To conclude all this on a positive note, the following case study of the entry of AFLAC into Japan illustrates a number of key points – not least, the importance of patience, of taking time to get affairs properly arranged, of building relationships in a tightly integrated community, of staffing carefully, of taking time in all this and then realizing great success in what was then an exceptionally tightly regulated industry. The following case study is based on the insightful research of Brian Riordan, who generously made it available for this review.

American Family Life Assurance Co., provides the best single example of how doggedly pursuing an opportunity in Japan can pay massive dividends. Founded in 1955 in Columbus, Georgia, AFLAC derives 70 percent of its operating earnings from its business in Japan, with more than $9 billion in revenues. A small, rural, family company, its shares are now traded on the New York Stock Exchange. It is the largest foreign insurer in Japan and claims one in four Japanese as a customer. It has more policy holders even than Nippon Life, the giant of Japan's very large insurance industry, although AFLAC's average policy value is a good deal less that that of Nippon Life.

The company got started in Japan in 1974 when it persuaded the Ministry of Finance to award it one of the licenses newly available to foreign insurers. For better or worse, the license limited AFLAC in the type of policies it could offer – no mainstream life insurance policies were allowed. With no infrastructure in Japan, and no distribution channel, AFLAC initially approached every major Japanese life insurer about a joint venture but was rejected by all. With no partners, and a license that severely limited the type of products it could sell, AFLAC tried to find a product to sell that would not require substantial capital to launch.

Founder and then President J.B. Amos quickly identified a virgin niche in which his company had some US experience, cancer care insurance. Most health insurance policies cover cancer treatment broadly, but leave many costs uncovered, notably lost wages. AFLAC had a cheap product, less than $200 per year, that covered extended hospital stays and lost wages. The company had been in the cancer insurance market in the United States for 13 years and held a two-thirds market share there. For Amos, Japan was an obvious market because cancer rates were higher than in the United States and Japan struck him as the most health conscious society on earth.

To do the early preparatory work and to help finalize license arrangements, Amos recruited Yoshiki Ohtake in 1972, a 30-year-old top salesman at American-owned insurer AIU in Tokyo. Ohtake, now Chairman of AFLAC Japan, had studied in California in the 1960s, spoke English fluently, and had helped AIU establish Alico Japan, a life insurance operation. Thus he had some experience in prying licenses out of the Ministry of Finance as AFLAC began its negotiations with the Ministry that led to its license in 1974.

Unable to access an established distribution channel through local partner, and faced with the hugely expensive and time-consuming task of building its own channels, AFLAC needed to make a bold move to get its business off the ground. Willing to change the rules of the game to reach success, AFLAC hit on a brilliant way to access new customers. Instead of having sales ladies selling door-to-door, the usual Japanese method for insurance sales, AFLAC constructed an entirely new channel, inside corporations. Rather than hiring its own sales ladies, AFLAC approached Japan's corporations and asked to establish one-person "agencies" within the personnel department of each company.

Just when the 1973–74 oil crisis was hitting hard on company profits in Japan, AFLAC offered companies a powerful incentive to join in their new scheme – a 40 percent commission on each insurance policy sale. To companies badly in need of profits, this was a real opportunity. Setting up agencies inside corporations did not impose new costs and thus was easy to approve. The agency would be responsible for explaining the product, processing sales and collecting premiums, which could be deducted from salary payments. If the corporation had 100,000 employees, the AFLAC proposal could potentially bring in a net earning of $8 million each year.

Management of AFLAC had a real surprise. The new cancer insurance was a runaway success from the very beginning. Having been told that cancer was a taboo topic for most Japanese, and that no one would in any case be comfortable buying insurance except from ladies visiting homes, AFLAC managers projected sales of perhaps 30,000 policies during the first year of operations. In the event, more than 300,000 policies were sold in the first nine months.

Local insurers cast an envious eye on AFLAC's extraordinary success, but AFLAC had the only license to sell its type of cancer insurance, and competitors could not go directly after the segment. Clearly, good relations with the Ministry of Finance were a key factor in continued success. Rather than complaining publicly about Japan's bureaucracy, AFLAC quietly and assiduously cultivated ties with the Ministry staff. One wonders if having come from the Georgia of America's old South, the AFLAC team had a particular advantage in understanding the usefulness of using a soft touch. Through this kind of approach and with dogged persistence, AFLAC managed a real triumph in being able to hire as its first President Makoto Watabe, the ex-chief of casualty insurance with the Ministry.

Now, 30 years after selling its first policy, there are ten or more competitors trying to take over AFLAC's cancer niche, but AFLAC still holds a more than 80 percent market share. It is likely to hold that position for a long time, given that 95 percent of all public companies in Japan offer AFLAC's product to their staffs. And meantime, AFLAC extends its product line into traditional life insurance, building on its broad and powerful customer base.

* * *

AFLAC is a winner, but only one of the many foreign company winners in the Japanese economy. Fifty-two foreign-owned manufacturing companies have annual revenue in Japan of over $1 billion annually. The foreign share of the insurance industry nears 20 percent. Foreign-owned companies are major players, even leaders, in a range of businesses including investment banking, contract personnel staffing, and mobile phone systems. The regulations covering foreign investment fully meet OECD standards. The economy is open, the government stable, the currency strong, the market huge.

The mystery is why the foreign press, foreign governments, and oddest of all even the Japanese government persist in describing foreign investment in Japan as very small in amount and very difficult in execution. Surely perpetuating this massive myth is of no help to anyone concerned, least of all to potential foreign investors who are intimidated by all the negative reports on Japan as investment site. It is in the interest of all to grasp and state the real conditions of foreign investment in Japan accurately. Foreign successes are a great many, of great size and fine profitability.

Notes

1. Dennis J. Encarnation "Cross-Investment: A Second Front of Economic Rivalry", in Thomas K. McGraw (ed.), *America Versus Japan*, Cambridge, MA: Harvard Business School Press, 1986.
2. *Foreign Direct Investment Policy in Japan: From Goals to Reality*, American Chamber of Commerce in Japan, 2003, p. 2.

3. Ibid., p. 6.
4. David E. Weinstein, "Foreign Direct Investment and Keiretsu: Rethinking U.S. and Japanese Policy", NBER Working Paper Series, Working Paper 5612, Cambridge, MA: National Bureau of Economic Research, June 1996, pp. 2ff.
5. Ito Keiko and Fukao Kyoji, *Tainichi Chokusetsu Toshi*, RIETI Discussion Paper Series 03-J-004, February 2003. See Table 2.
6. *Kojima Ikuo. Gaishikei Kigyo no Nihon Koryaku Chizu*, Tokyo: Nihon Jitsugyo Shuppan Sha, 2003, p. 171. This volume has a good deal of useful information on foreign companies in Japan.
7. *Financial Times*, 16 February 2004, p. 18.
8. *Nihon Keizai Shimbun*, evening edition, 8 December 2003.
9. *Nihon Keizai Shimbun*, 1 March 2002.

9
The Changing World Map of the Kaisha

The kaisha in the 21st century are dealing with a greatly changed domestic society and domestic economic structure but, more important still, are deeply involved in a world system that is changing dramatically. The center of the world map for the kaisha is moving rapidly from North America to East and Southeast Asia, from the North Atlantic to the Western Pacific, truly a sea change. The momentum of economic forces drives the nation and its kaisha toward ever-deeper East Asian involvement and identity, led by business leaders but with dangerously little vision or support from the country's myopic and US-obsessed officials and political leaders.

For East Asia to continue its rapid development into the dynamic center of world manufacturing and technology, institutional change in the region must take place. Region trade arrangements, not simply bilateral free-trade agreements, must be agreed on, with goods flowing freely throughout the area. This will be in effect an enlargement of ASEAN to take in the entire East Asian region. ASEAN plus three – the ASEAN nations plus China, Japan, and Korea – is already a forum for policy discussion, and potential basis for real regional union. This enlarged ASEAN needs to become equivalent to the European Union and to NAFTA in trade affairs. Beyond trade matters, currency arrangements for the region leading to a common currency in the not-distant future is required, beginning now with currency swap agreements between the countries of the region.

"Under the emerging regional financial architecture, a financial arrangement has become well established under the Chiang Mai Initiative (CMI). . . . Agreed by countries of the ASEAN+3 Group . . . 16 bilateral swap arrangements amounting to $44 billion have been concluded."[1] This is a first step in addressing the issue of a common currency. What is needed is explicit agreement to move to an Asian currency and an Asian central bank, necessary to realize full East Asian potential and to deal with Europe and North America effectively. Political leaders outside Japan are taking strong positions. President Macapagal of the Philippines has proposed a common currency as the region's next goal. And Thaksin Shinawatra, the Prime Minister of Thailand, called for establishment of an Asia bond fund (*Nikkei Net Interactive*, 8 June 2003). Prime Minister Abdullah of Malaysia has stated recently, "It's not too early to start pondering deeply about the virtues and problems of having a single Asian currency. We must move on the establishment of an Asian monetary institution" (*Nikkei Net Interactive*, 3 June 2004).

In all this effort to establish a trade and monetary union across East Asia, the government of Japan must play a central role. Yet the only clear and firm public position taken in Japan has been by Japan's business community whose head, Hiroshi Okuda, chairman of Toyota Motors and Nippon Keidanren, has repeatedly called for Japanese government leadership in forming an East Asian free trade area beginning with full opening of the Japanese market itself in Japan's own self interest. Opinion polls in Japan, China, and Korea report that well over two-thirds of business leaders in all three countries believe that regional free trade is crucial to economic growth (*Nikkei Net Interactive*, 24 March 2004).

The role of government in the restructuring of the economy since the mid-1990s or so has been largely negative, and Japan is the better for it. Government did not plan or direct industrial and corporate redesign. Apart from helping deal with the banking crises, government's role in the economy has been to greatly diminish by deregulation and transfer of functions to the private sector the powers that government had held over the local marketplace. However, reshaping East Asia into a trade and currency union requires government leadership; corporations can only be supportive in these transnational arrangements. Japan's economic future depends in large measure on achieving an East Asian trade and financial entity – once attempted by Japan in a disastrous military venture, this time to be accomplished by close cooperative work with all the other nations in the region. All will benefit; all must agree on methods; all must take part. Japan can be at the center of all this effort, and in any case its government must put the effort at the very top of its agenda, now.

The 21st century is Asia's

East and Southeast Asia are where the action is – and will be. The nations of East and Southeast Asia make up a full third of the population of the world. These nations' economies comprise over a fifth of the total world economy. The region's trade is already well above a quarter of world trade and is fast increasing. East and Southeast Asia's share of the world economy and of trade will increase much further as high growth rates continue throughout the region. Much of the region was battered by the financial crisis of the 1997–98 period, but rather quickly recovered and resumed economic growth of 4–6 percent per year, growing again fully two to three times as rapidly as the rest of the world. Now well over half of the world's foreign currency reserves are held by East Asian nations. The increasing scale of the region's economy makes Asia's rise to real economic power the central economic event of the 21st century. The 19th century centered on Western Europe; the 20th century centered on the United States; the 21st century is Asia's.

With China very much the current and over-stated hot topic, the importance of Southeast Asia can easily be overlooked. The nations of the southeast – Indonesia, Thailand, the Philippines, Malaysia, and Singapore in particular – grouped together in ASEAN have a combined population nearly half that of China, 525 millions, with per capita output substantially greater than China's. ASEAN is an effective economic group with a considerable integration in trade within the group as tariffs fall off sharply. Vietnam is achieving rapid growth and will be a significant factor in the region, with Myanmar not yet a player but one with considerable potential. And to the North of course Korea is a major economic power already. It is these disparate nations that make up this complex region; Asia is a geographic but not cultural nor ethnic nor economic entity – yet.

Japan's position in the region is a complicated one. Japan's economy alone makes up more than 60 percent of the total economy of the region. Japan's economy is four times larger and its per capita GDP more than 35 times that of mainland China – even accepting Chinese numbers that are no doubt inflated. The obvious candidate for policy leadership in economic matters, both Japanese diffidence and regional discomfort with Japan have meant that Japan plays only a modest role – but a Communist China is not yet able to fit into the leadership uniform. Some of this shortfall in leadership role on Japan's part owes not to economics but rather to history and to culture – and to the use of history as a negotiating weapon.

The cultural issue was put dramatically by Huntington:

As a society and civilization unique to itself, Japan faces difficulties developing its economic ties with East Asia... However strong the trade and investment links Japan may forge with other East Asian countries, its cultural differences from those countries, and particularly from their largely Chinese economic elites, preclude it from creating a Japanese-led regional economic grouping comparable to NAFTA or the European Union. At the same time its cultural differences with the West exacerbate misunderstanding and antagonism in its economic relations with the United States and Europe. If, as seems to be the case, economic integration depends on cultural commonality, Japan as a culturally lone country could have an economically lonely future.[2]

As will be seen in discussion of attitudes below, Huntington much exaggerates both the extent of Japan's differences and its "isolation," and exaggerates too the importance of the "cultural issue." In any case a Japanese-led regional grouping is not at issue. No one nation leads now nor led the development of the European Union – where antagonisms and misunderstandings do in fact persist and rather often surface without ending the regional movements. (Much the same might be said of the federal system of state governments in the United States.)

Memories of World War II are allowed still to inhibit Japan's international policies and make taking a larger role in East Asia difficult, while Japan's culture, social structure, and wealth set it apart in many ways from other Asian societies. However, economics is the powerful driving force. Japan's role in East and Southeast Asia is a growing and critical one; wartime memories dim with passing years; cultural and social differences can be bridged. After a century of murderous wars, France and Germany moved to close collaboration economically and politically. In similar fashion, given competent and responsible political leaders, Japan's differences with much of East Asia will lessen, and Japan can and indeed must play a more active leadership role in Asia Affairs as the century progresses.

From a US focus to an Asian one

For several decades after war's end, the external world of the kaisha focused almost entirely on the United States. Trade was mainly with the United States, technology was drawn primarily from US companies, and investment into and from Japan centered on the United States. Many business and political leaders studied and trained in the United States. All of this business involvement was much reinforced by the policies of the Japanese government in international affairs which were tied closely to those of the United States.

The world has changed. Half of Japan's import and export trade now is with East and Southeast Asia. With the renewed high growth of the ASEAN economies and the Chinese economy, it is trade with East Asia that is central for Japan, with the trade share to and from the United States down and declining as share for some years. China is a main driver of recent change, with exports to China from Japan in 2003 up by a third over year before and still rising, while imports from China to Japan exceeded imports from the United States, with Japan–China trade about in balance. The US accounts directly for only 15 percent of Japan's imports and a quarter of its exports, with the US share dropping steadily.

Investment into the United States remains largest in total amount, driven not only by large-scale manufacturing investments – auto production a leading example – but also by heavy investments in finance and distribution. Investments into the countries of East Asia are smaller in amount generally, as would be expected given the smaller scale of the economies. The numbers however have become very considerable.

A Ministry of Economics, Trade and Industry survey in early 2002 found that one in seven of Japanese manufacturers had moved some part of their production out of Japan to a foreign site. Of all these plants, 80 percent are in Asian locations, 40 percent in China, 36 percent in Southeast Asia, and 4 percent in Taiwan. This focus on Asia can only intensify given Asian economic growth rates. Of special interest, nearly half of all foreign manufacturing output is intended for sale in the country of manufacture, with only a third for export to Japan, the remaining fifth for export to third country markets. This is not a hollowing out, but rather the development of regional marketing strategies. It provides needed capital and technology to developing countries and forces a shift of Japanese domestic resources to higher value-added sectors of manufacture and services.

Of the total overseas entities of all types of Japanese companies, some 20,000, over half are in East and Southeast Asia, with around 3500 in ASEAN, similarly some 3500 in the NIES, with the number in China now about 3000. Japanese corporate entities in China increased by nearly ten times in the 12 years from 1990 through 2002, dramatic evidence of the intense interest in production and marketing in China on the part of Japanese managers. Only about 20 percent of all Japanese foreign operations are in the United States with a similar proportion in Europe, and these tend to be focused in finance and distribution, with East Asia the site for most manufacturing ventures.[3] The data are various however. Another estimate is that there are "some 14,000 Japanese firms having established operations in China."[4] Leave it at that – Japan's companies with operations in China are very many, and increasing rapidly, as they are in ASEAN and the NIES.

While many of these Asian operations are still rather small in scale, not all are limited in size by any means. On the contrary, many kaisha have major commitments already in place. For example, Honda produces 6.4 million motorcycles per year at 10 locations in eight Asian countries. Thailand is auto production center for Southeast Asia with Toyota the major player. Nippon Steel is joint venturing steel production in the Shanghai region. Matsushita Electric has 45 manufacturing facilities in mainland China alone, with sales of over $3 billion and plans to go soon to $9 billion. And so it goes for a great many of Japan's leading kaisha.

China as competitor

The economic forces drawing Japan and China together are very strong. Fundamentally, the two countries have complementary needs. China needs very much the flow of capital and technology from Japan that has been taking place over through the 1990s and into the early 21st century. Japan needs very much the access to the low cost, reasonably effective labor supply of mainland China as well as access to China's rapidly growing market.

It is often suggested that China is a competitive threat to Japan. This issue can be very much overstated. At China's stage of economic development early in the 21st century, its trade is in most direct competition with the economies of Southeast Asia – Thailand, Indonesia, and the Philippines especially. In contrast, Japan's main Asian trade competitor is South Korea, and to a lesser degree Taiwan and Singapore, Asia's most sophisticated economies. C.W. Kwan of RIETI, the METI-sponsored research group, argues that "Japan competes less than 10 percent with China," noting the high import contents of Chinese products among other factors.[5] The issue is further complicated by the fact that a good deal of the exports into Japan from China are produced in Japanese-owned factories in China, now the source of much of the lower value-added, labor intensive work produced by Japanese companies. China's labor rates are one-thirtieth to one-fiftieth those of Japan. This is price, not cost – but for labor intensive, low-skilled work, price and cost are similar.

Japan's manufacturing strength is no longer in simple manufacture and assembly of products, unless the processes can be very highly automated.

Real strength is in sophisticated parts and components, especially for electronic goods, with companies like Rohm, Keyence, Murata, Mabuchi Motors, and Hirose specialized producers of components with high value added and with high world market shares. These have been for some years now Japan's "excellent companies." It is these sorts of products along with machine tools and other production equipment that China must import, with Japan the obvious and dominant supplier. Will China in time replicate these goods in its own plants? Probably. That is another, and compelling, reason why Japan must focus on R&D, moving forward to still more sophisticated and unique goods in Japan.

In sum, competition between the two economies is now limited and the relationship will be economically complementary for a considerable period. Each economy has in some abundance what the other economy is most in need of. In the longer run, China's continuing growth – assuming that is in fact the future pattern – will force the kaisha to develop new products, dropping lower end businesses, thereby continuing Japan's own economic growth. Or else the kaisha fail in the R&D task, and China does in fact displace Japanese output and diminishes the Japanese economy. Some of this will happen in any case as the mature Japanese economy focuses more on services and finance, moving away from straight manufacture, making product imports from China appropriate.

Problems in China: The issues of piracy and a legal apparatus

Management issues in China for the kaisha include all the usual – price competition, finding and retaining good staff, distribution. China offers a rather special problem however – flagrant and virtually unlimited piracy of brands, products, and technology. This is sometimes called "copying," and it is argued that all developing countries, the United States and Japan in their turn, engaged in it. Inevitable, it would seem.

However, using copyrighted materials or patented technology is not simple copying. Rather, it is simple thievery. In postwar Japan, business and government realized the absolute necessity of obtaining foreign technology, and mounted a massive effort at identifying and bringing this technology into Japan – with great success as the imported technology was improved on and turned against the sellers. Still, business and government in Japan realized that to obtain all this technology there had to be total confidence that it would be obtained by legitimate purchase, with full penalties administered by Japanese courts in cases of piracy or breach of technology contract. There was full confidence abroad in this system.

And full prices were paid by the kaisha. A spectacular case was the purchase of patent license by then Toyo Rayon, now Toray, for nylon technology from DuPont. Toyo Rayon had developed its own nylon technology before and during the war. But for full development of the business, a DuPont patent license was necessary. As noted earlier, the CEO of Toyo Rayon at the time, Shigeki Tashiro, paid a price for patent access that was equal to the entire capital of Toyo Rayon in 1952 – and received only a patent license with no further technology support. The deal was possible only with DuPont appreciation of the Japanese legal system, in full knowledge that the contract would be honored by Toyo Rayon and if necessary enforced by Japan's courts.

This kind of confidence in the legal system as the defender of patents and copyrights is notably absent in the Chinese case. Purchase of technology and trademarks by contract is not necessary in the Chinese system where the legal system is weak and fragmented and where patented and copyrighted materials can in fact be truly "copied" with little or no fear of reprisal from the legitimate holders through the courts. In autos, Toyota, Honda, and Nissan have all had designs and trademarks stolen – and have been unable to obtain recourse in China's courts. A Japanese government booklet contains hundreds of photos of Japanese originals and Chinese copies.

This is not preventing investment. But it is limiting it, clearly to China's disadvantage. It seems likely that over time China will have in place a legal system with full authority throughout the country, where fairness is the rule and patents and copyrights will be upheld. But this is not yet the case, and will not be for some time a real handicap for Japan's companies in China.

A miracle? forever?

The piracy issue is of current importance, but will be resolved at some point. An issue of far greater significance is that of the extent and duration of China's economic growth. The world has ample evidence, from Japan's case earlier, from the case of Southeast Asia more recently, and from America's dot com adventure that miracles are not forever. All bubbles burst. The China case will be no exception.

A prior issue however is that of the real extent of Chinese economic growth. There have long been questions about the accuracy of government reporting, by no means confined to economic matters as the SARS incident reminded all. The government announced long since that to prevent increased unemployment a growth rate of at least 7 percent per annum was required. And by some miracle, growth has been at the rate of 8–9 percent year after year – and continued at an even higher rate in 2003 and 2004.

Questions arise from the fact that this is a centralized, Communist government. All governments lie all too often, but Communist governments have on the whole set the pace for systematic lying. If the center orders that the growth be more than 7 percent, then be assured that all sensible provincial leaders will report growth of more than 8 percent to ensure continued high positions. It does seem quite likely that the main coastal centers of China – leaving out Dalian and the rust-belt of the Northeast – have in fact been growing very rapidly for some years, and that growth no doubt continues.

This is however far from all of China. It is in fact a fraction of that immense land with its immense population. We learn of power shortages and water shortages, and of grave damage to agricultural land through erosion. We hear of 100 million unemployed, with a rush off the country-side to the cities. More substantially, repeated studies have shown that for some years, electric power consumption in China as a whole increased hardly at all, while total growth was reported at 8 percent or more. When a central Communist government declares a growth target of 8 percent, oddly enough all local entities report growth of rather more than that.

A news story on one phase of economic reporting from China makes the point of exaggerated government statistics in rather amusing fashion.

"For years, marine scientists have reported that too much fish has been caught from the world's oceans and called for drastic measures to curb widespread over-fishing. Yet the reported global yield of marine fisheries continued to rise through the 1990s, particularly because of large increases reported by China.

"Now a detailed analysis of fishery statistics has found evidence of substantial over-reporting during the last decade, mainly by China. Apparently, under the Communist system of matching result with plan, the same bureaucrats were responsible for not only counting the catch but also meeting targets to increase it – so they simply exaggerated the count to match their allotted goals.

"As a result, instead of rising by an average of 330,000 tons per year since 1988, as recorded in United Nations data, the world's catch has actually declined by an average of 360,000 tons per year, according to a study in the current issue of the journal Nature."[6]

While China has grown economically it certainly has not grown as fast as its government would have us believe. This fact casts some light on the question of competitiveness. Lesser growth means slower moves to higher value-added outputs – except by foreign firms who may or may not choose to continue production in China. Lesser growth means a more limited consumer market – and a more limited industrial market as well, so investment caution is advised China's economic power is being over-estimated, and Japan's government and corporations need to keep that fact clearly in mind when forming policy. It means as one example that in the Asian equation the economies of Southeast Asia need be given much greater weight in business and government strategy formulations than is rather often assigned to them now.

Whatever the growth, policy planning for East Asia must assume a drop, probably sudden and perhaps drastic, in China's real growth rate. The banking system is massively over-extended. Over-capacity is reported for a whole series of key industries. Capital pours in from abroad in expectation of an abrupt increase in the exchange rate – making runaway inflation a real possibility. Much information – on unemployment for example – is simply not available. But all experience tells us that high growth does not indefinitely continue. Growth has cycles, and miracles have ends. Japan's era of high growth was in fact a series of growth cycles with some nasty low points in such years as 1965 and 1974. The East Asian miracle went from miracle to disaster almost overnight in 1997 with the collapse of the baht the beginning of a regional crisis, followed by recovery again. No one would be foolish enough to predict the timing of the crisis in China – but it will happen, and the economic and political consequences will be massive.

China deconstructs?

A recurring question regarding China and its future role in East Asia concerns the stability of the present political system in the mainland. For a good deal of China's history, there has been no effective central government, not least over the last half of the 19th and first half of the 20th century. The nation is vast in geography. The central peoples of China are the Han, but there are entire parts of the nation's geography in which the Han are few, and other peoples and tribes are dominant. There is still wide variation in language from one part of China to another. The diet of the north is quite different from that of the south of the nation. In short, this is a nation of exceptional complexity and a rather low level of homogeneity. The contrast with Japan could hardly be greater – and the complexity raises real question of how the nation can best be held together as a unit.

This complexity is now added to by the great differences in output and income levels as growth in the economy has focused on the great cities of the Pacific Coast. There can be no doubt that the differences in unemployment, in housing facilities, in all manner of living standards are greatly different from one part of China to another. Add this to ethnic differences and language differences, and the vast spread of geography, and one would assume that the government of China would be comprised of a regional system, a federation of semi-independent political units, not unlike the federal system produced early in US history, the German state system, and the pattern developing now in the European Union.

A change in governance that would accommodate deep regional differences is much complicated by the fact that China remains the rare case of a country whose ruling elite is made up of Communist Party members who continue to profess allegiance to Communism and its system. But the Communist system essentially requires central control, with the party in control of all aspects of government. It is difficult to imagine a Communist government presiding over a federation of semi-autonomous states.

Consider now a sudden economic crisis that would challenge the competence of the present government and stress China's systems of governance to an extreme. It is the combination of deep and important differences within the whole of China, along with the real possibilities of an economic trauma, that raise the possibility of a China that might "deconstruct" and move to a decentralized, even fragmented government or governments.

All of this is not at all meant as a critique of China for the sake of critique. Rather, the effort here is to make clear that the corporations of Japan, and the government of Japan, must keep China in perspective. Notably, a proper balance must be struck between relations with China on the one hand, and relations with the Koreas and with the nations of South-east Asia on the other. In the excitement of the current preoccupations with China, it is all too easy to lose sight of the necessity to take a long view of how East Asia will develop and pursue policies accordingly. China is a part, but by no means the center of the East Asian future.

Japan part of East Asia?

A framework for East Asian unification is slowly developing, as noted earlier. The first meeting of ASEAN plus three was in 1999, a forum for region-wide discussions and negotiations. China and ASEAN signed an initial agreement looking toward a free-trade agreement in 2002; completion of arrangements is expected by 2010. Japan ended its long commitment to multi-lateral trade agreements with a FTA with Singapore. A series of bilateral FTA negotiations are underway throughout the region, but real progress depends on a regional arrangement – and here the Japanese government is lagging behind events, negotiating now with Malaysia, Thailand, and the Philippines, but with the appallingly late schedule for a free trade pact with all of ASEAN by 2012!!! Others in the region will not wait as Japan dawdles. Japan risks being left behind in Asia's development, and could even be left out, unless political vision and leadership come into play.

In the currency area, various bilateral currency swap agreements have been entered into, as noted. An Asian Monetary Fund, proposed by Japan in 1997, was vetoed by the United States in support of that country's own narrow interests. The MOF seems now to be deferring again to US interests and not re-addressing the possibility of an Asia Monetary Fund.

The United States sees an Asian Monetary Fund as undercutting the IMF which is a US instrumentality – and which performed badly for Asia's economies in the 1997–98 crisis period. The US interest in blocking Asian unity is clear enough. However, Japan's long-term interests are opposite those of the United States, and Japan's interests must be pursued, even at risk of US antagonism.

There are many ways in which Japan is separate from Asia. All the more reason then, one would think, that Japan should make special efforts to take part in and indeed to lead the movements toward Asian regional unification and governance. It is in Japan's economic interest certainly, and in its political/strategic interest as well. The leaders of Japan's kaisha seem generally to appreciate this necessity. One would hope they will bring sufficient pressure on the political leaders of Japan to in fact ensure that Japan works to become part of East Asia – not simply in isolated alliance with the United States.

Do attitudes and feelings matter?

Discussions of Japan in East Asia all too often center on attitudes toward Japan. Much is made of lasting memories of wartime experiences, even though that war ended 60 years ago – rather more than two genera-tions, and populations in Asia tend in any case to be rather youthful. Some of the problem is rooted in the use by Asian governments in public negotiations with the government of Japan of real or fancied wartime damage, ensuring that negative attitudes toward Japan remain fresh, and in total disregard of Japan's repeated apologies and reparations payments. China finds this negotiating ploy of special value, both in hoping to arouse Japanese guilt feelings and in asserting a right to special favors to balance past injustice. Since independent public opinion polls in China are not much used by that dictatorial government, real attitudes in China remain unknown, with only occasional dramatic incidents (government calculated?) as indicators of attitudes.

For Southeast Asian nations, public opinion is a matter for public surveys. The Ministry of Foreign Affairs does a survey periodically of attitudes toward Japan across Southeast Asia, and Table 9.1 shows the results comparing 1978 with 2002. These surveys are of course subject to the usual sampling errors, but are probably reasonably accurate as measures of opinions over time. Overall, attitudes toward Japan appear to be quite positive. There are wartime memories, but in each country active resentment seems a distinctly minority feeling. Relations with Japan on a national level are seen as positive now and in the future in all these countries.

Relative to the other countries, the Philippines and Singapore seem to be less positive toward Japan, with Singapore looking more to China and the Philippines to the United States – natural enough given the histories of these two countries. But even in the case of these two nations, there is little evidence that public attitudes are a problem in relating to Japan.

Still another survey by the Ministry of Foreign Affairs in 2003 found Asian attitudes as given in Table 9.2.

There is a wealth of data on Japanese attitudes but perhaps the material in Table 9.3 will suffice as a rough indicator of feelings about nations. The United States is by a great margin the most favored nation by the Japanese public by this and other measures, with the other nations of the developed West also considering very positively. Distance is greatest from Russia, and from the Middle East, Russia in other surveys close to North Korea in being disliked, China generally not faring well at about a balance of like–dislike, with Southeast Asia distant and rather unknown.

These Japanese data provide little comfort for advocates of close relations with the East Asia region. Even though there is little negative in Japanese attitudes toward East Asians, the tendency is rather more toward indifference or sheer lack of interest. Here again active programs and government efforts to increase awareness and knowledge are

Table 9.1   Asian attitudes toward Japan, 1978 and 2002 (replies in %)

Q. Which country do you know best?

	Japan		United States		China	
	1978	2002	1978	2002	1978	2002
Indonesia	46	64	30	16	–	8
Malaysia	16	26	11	30	21	13
Philippines	24	25	53	62	2	2
Singapore	15	10	9	18	21	35
Thailand	24	29	22	43	14	16

Q. What do you think of the relationship between Japan and your country?

	Friendly		Not friendly		Don't know	
	1978	2002	1978	2002	1978	2002
Indonesia	97	92	1	2	2	6
Malaysia	90	93	2	2	8	5
Philippines	93	90	4	7	5	4
Singapore	87	96	2	1	11	4
Thailand	91	89	2	2	7	10

Q. What do you expect of the relationship with Japan in the future?

	Continue current relationship		May become worse		Don't know	
	1978	2002	1978	2002	1978	2002
Indonesia	74	77	23	13	3	10
Malaysia	83	91	12	7	5	1
Philippines	73	68	23	29	4	3
Singapore	82	87	7	11	11	2
Thailand	73	73	16	16	11	12

Source: ASEAN shokoku ni okeru tainichi yoron chosa, Ministry of Foreign Affairs.

needed. Japan's is a highly literate population; it can be reached readily if one tries.

Attitudes toward Japan in the nations of Southeast Asia are in general positive as are Taiwan attitudes toward Japan. However, in the northeast

Table 9.2 Asian attitudes toward Japan, the United States, and China (replies in %)

Q. Which country do you like best?

	Japan	United States	China	Others
Koreans	7	72	21	0
Thais	38	40	21	2
Malaysians	44	30	21	5
Indonesians	44	43	12	2
Indians	43	47	3	6

Source: ASEAN Tainichi Yoron Chosa, Ministry of Foreign Affairs.

Table 9.3 Attitudes of the Japanese public regarding countries/regions (replies in %)

Country/region	Feel close to	Not feel close to	Do not know
USA	76	20	4
EU	59	32	9
Australia, New Zealand	59	31	10
South Korea	54	41	5
China	46	49	5
Southeast Asia	38	50	12
Southwest Asia	18	69	13
Russia	15	78	7
Middle East	12	73	15

Source: Yoron Chosa, April 2003, Naikakufu Daijin Kanbo Seifu Kohshitsu Hen.

of Asia there are real attitude problems. Korea–Japan attitudes are of mutual distaste on the whole, although younger people are much more positive than older people. In one survey, when asked if they like, dislike, or are neutral toward Japan, absolutely no Koreans aged 70 or over expressed liking, with two-thirds opting for dislike. For Koreans in their 20s, dislike dropped to a third, with a quarter of the age group expressing liking. Time is on the side of better relations. Key attitude questions for Japan in East Asia then is the continuing but lessening negative Korean–Japan feelings and the unknown Chinese factor. Conclusion: If attitudes are a significant factor, there are problems in the Northeast, with few if any in the rest of the region. And again, if France and Germany can reach close economic and political accord despite their histories, surely Northeast Asia can as well.

South Asia?

What of the rest of Asia? If China is the giant of the east, India is no less giant of the south of Asia. Despite its huge population and recent substantial economic growth, India is simply not on the radar screen of Japanese companies. India's potential has been much highlighted in the United States as it became a center for the outsourcing of IT functions and a political issue around off-shore job transfers. Indians have played major parts in the success of Silicone Valley companies. Indian students are a good part of the population of US graduate schools. There has however been no equivalent visibility in Japan for Indians, nor yet equivalent reason for Japanese interest in India.

The data on Japan–India trade are rather shocking. India is market for only half of one percent of Japan's exports, and 0.6 percent of imports. The small total exports are almost entirely machinery, and the imports are almost all shrimp, diamonds, and iron ore. Not only is India trade very small as share of trade, but the totals of both imports and exports, far from growing, have in fact over recent years diminished somewhat.

Investment into India from Japan is similarly insignificant, well under one percent of total foreign investment, with no signs of increase. There is a total of 190 Japanese corporate entities in India, increasing by perhaps a dozen annually, less than one percent of total numbers of foreign operations. None of the nations of South Asia show up on lists of trading partners of Japan or of investment sites. Bangladesh, Sri Lanka, and Pakistan seem not to have a place on the Japanese map.

Various explanations are on offer for the fact that India is not a significant business site for Japanese companies. There is a general agreement that, for most Japanese, India is simply not part of Asia. As Japanese cross the Irrawaddy River, they leave Asia and enter another world, it is argued. Another cause is held to be the rather frequent changes in Indian foreign investment rules and regulations; Japanese firms do not mind barriers but they do mind inconsistencies and frequent rule changes, it is said. Still another factor is India's social complexity, with great regional differences and elaborate systems of status and religious differences complicating personnel management greatly.

A curious fact about foreign investment in India is that much the largest source of FDI into India has been Mauritius, that small island in the Indian Ocean, with a population of about one million persons.

A tax treaty between Mauritius and India made Mauritius the avenue for investment flow, a total of $7.5 billion in the decade of the 1990s, more than twice the flow from the United States. Investment into India appears to have its complicated aspects.

No doubt continued Indian economic success will attract Japanese attention. But no doubt too India will not be seen to be a part of East Asia, nor yet in the center of Japanese business and government concerns. For better or worse, it is marginal in the Japanese scheme of things.

Japan's difficult balancing act

Japan is subject to countervailing pressures. East Asia is where Japan's trade and investment is greatest. It is the direction in which the economic forces at work drive Japan's companies – and must increasingly drive Japan's international linkages. As the leaders of China declare for an open trading East Asia, certainly political leadership in Japan, pressed by the business community, must take initiatives to ensure Japan's full membership and indeed leadership in the process of East Asian unification.

With this however are Japan's strategic concerns. There is the very real threat of nuclear capability in North Korea. Japan has failed to put in position an effective missile defense system, and is dependent on the United States to provide the equipment – and to provide a protective nuclear umbrella. With this is the uncertainty around the status of Taiwan and the continuing possibility of Chinese military action there – along with China's periodic claims to territories considered by the Japanese to be theirs.

The issues and prospects were well-stated recently by Immanuel Wallenstein.

> Geopolitically, what we may expect is the emergence of both Europe and East Asia on the world scene acting independently of the U.S. . . . Working together, Japan, Korea and China could be the principal motor of the world economy. (However) if East Asia is to play the economic role that is possible for it, it must resolve political problems. Neither China nor Japan will be able to fulfill its economic potential without the other. And I would add even China and Japan together cannot do it without Korea. This means that a major intra-Asian political negotiation must occur, of the kind that occurred in Western Europe over the last half century.[7]

And it is useful to be reminded that the European Union emerged nearly 50 years after the Treaty of Rome began the union process. Perhaps East Asia can move more rapidly.

Japan can and should be proud of the fact that it exports no arms to any country, and has no interest in changing governments of other peoples. It can and should be proud of its constitutional prohibition on military action abroad. But there is a price, and that price is the requirement to maintain at least for now an alliance with the United States as presumed protection against military attack. The Japanese government has a long history of alliance with the dominant military power, beginning with the Anglo-Japanese treaty of the Meiji government. As the dominant military power in the early 21st century, alliance with the United States is a continuation of an established pattern. But the United States needs Japan as well, as base, as source of funds and in general as an ally in world affairs. Japan has more room to negotiate with the United States than it takes current advantage of.

While there is a need for a balance between the economic force of the East and the military force of the United States, Japan runs the risk of being America's pet poodle in Asia much as Blair has positioned Britain in Europe – and the negative political consequences. For a time a balance can be struck although it risks failing to take the Asian initiatives that are desirable on Japan's part. The real question of the 21st century for Japan is whether that balance can be maintained as Asia continues to increase strength, as China moves toward Great Power status, and as the United States acts increasingly unilaterally in world affairs. Certainly Japan's position will, over the coming decades, shift markedly toward Asia, with steadily increasing distance from the West. For this to happen in the national interest requires a degree of vision, leadership, and competence on the part of Japan's political leaders that is sadly lacking now. We must hope for change, for full collaboration with the East Asian nations in trade and finance, and for a careful building over two or three decades of the East Asian system on which Japan's future well-being depends.

Notes

1. "Asia's New Financial Architecture Needs Support" by Haruhiko Kuroda and Masahiro Kawai, *Financial Times*, 17 June 2004.
2. Samuel P. Huntington, *The Clash of Civilizations and the Remaking of World Order*, New York: Touchstone, 1997, pp. 134–135.
3. *Toyo Keizai Shinpo Sha, Kaigai Shinshutsu Kigyo Soran, 2003.*
4. *Nikkei Net Interactive*, 17 November 2003.

5. C.H. Kwan, *Overcoming Japan's China Syndrome*, Tokyo: RIETI, 2002, p. 6.
6. Erik Eckholm, "FISH: China Reports Whopper of a Tale", New York Times News Service, *Herald Tribune*, 1–2 December 2001, p. 1.
7. Immanuel Wallenstein, "East Asia Emerges as Rival to U.S. Amid Changing Geopolitical Role", *The Nikkei Weekly*, 23 August 2004.

Index